John McLoughlin's Business Correspondence, 1847–48

John McLoughlin's
Business Correspondence,
1847–48

Edited by
WILLIAM R. SAMPSON

*Published in cooperation with
the Washington State Historical Society*

UNIVERSITY OF WASHINGTON PRESS
SEATTLE AND LONDON

Library of Congress Cataloging in Publication Data

McLoughlin, John, 1784–1857.
 John McLoughlin's business correspondence, 1847–48.

 Bibliography: p.
 1. McLoughlin, John, 1784–1857. 2. Oregon —
History — To 1859 — Sources. 3. Hudson's Bay Company.
I. Sampson, William R., 1932– ed. II. Washington
State Historical Society. III. Title.
F880.M1684   1973   979.5'03'0924 [B]   73-8747
ISBN 0–295–95299–7

For Vernon Carstensen
And in memory of Mary B. Carstensen

JOHN McLoughlin has long held an honored place as "the Father of Oregon," and his role as chief factor in the Columbia Department of the Hudson's Bay Company has been appraised many times. His career following his retirement from the Company in 1846 is less well known, however, partly because there is less interest in him as a private business-man than as the "White-Headed Eagle" who dominated the Oregon scene from 1824 until 1846. Another factor in the usual, hasty treatments of McLoughlin's life in Oregon City after 1846 has been the lack of adequate materials to document his business activities. In 1962, however, the United States National Park Service acquired the McLoughlin letter book, which is here published for the first time. These letters provide new insights into the wide range of his interests and affairs in Oregon City, and they show his continuing relations, both economic and per-sonal, with the Hudson's Bay Company and its officers. The letters also provide the reader and student with an increased understanding of the problems and frustrations that a frontier community had in struggling to diversify and expand its economy.

The editor of such a work as this soon finds himself indebted to many individuals and institutions for aid and encouragement. But no one can be adequately prepared for the amount of help that is so generously given. Officials of the United States National Park Service have kindly consented to the publication of the letter book, and the three letters in Appendix A are used through the courtesy of the McLoughlin Memorial

Association in Oregon City, Oregon, which supplied photostats of letters in their possession. Frank A. Hjort, the late Harold O. Edwards, and Eliot Davis, superintendents of Fort Vancouver National Historic Site in Vancouver, Washington, between 1962 and 1972, and the late Mrs. Gertrude Brumbaugh of the McLoughlin Memorial Association generously supplied materials and answered my queries. Thomas Vaughan and Robert Fessenden of the Oregon Historical Society; David C. Duniway of the Oregon State Archives; Alice M. Johnson, formerly archivist of the Hudson's Bay Company; Allan R. Ottley of the California State Library; Cecil L. Chase of the Bancroft Library; Stephen T. Riley of the Massachusetts Historical Society; Haydée Noya of the Henry E. Huntington Library and Art Gallery; Margaret Titcomb of the Bernice P. Bishop Museum in Honolulu; Agnes C. Conrad of the Public Archives of Hawaii; W. Neil Franklin of the United States National Archives and Records Service; and the Office of the County Clerk, Clackamas County, Oregon, replied to lengthy inquiries and provided otherwise unobtainable information from their collections.

I owe especial thanks to the patient and resourceful staffs of the libraries of the State Historical Society of Wisconsin and the Provincial Archives of British Columbia. At the latter, Provincial Archivist Willard E. Ireland showed unflagging courtesy and interest in smoothing my way. Former Assistant Archivist Inez Mitchell, Assistant Archivist David Mason, Dorothy Blakey Smith, Frances Gundry, and Wendy Teece were patient and tireless in locating materials and answering my many requests. The Bancroft Library at the University of California, Berkeley, very kindly loaned microfilms of several items from the invaluable Oregon Manuscripts collected by Hubert Howe Bancroft. Bruce Peel, librarian to the University of Alberta, and the staff of the Cameron Library were most helpful in permitting me to use the then uncatalogued Robert Woods and Alfred Powers Collections of printed materials.

John A. Hussey of the United States National Park Service, San Francisco; David Lavender of the Thatcher School, Ojai, California; Professor J. M. S. Careless of the University of Toronto; and the late Father William L. Davis, S.J., of Gonzaga University in Spokane, Washington, all read the manuscript and gave me the benefit of their learning and critical judgment.

Robert Hitchman, chairman of the publications committee of the Washington State Historical Society in Tacoma, Washington, has spent countless hours arranging for the publication of this volume and has been a source of great encouragement. Professor Henry Kreisel, vice-president (academic) at the University of Alberta, made possible a generous grant from the President's Humanities Research Fund, and Marilyn Waesche of Seattle, Washington, was responsible for the commendable final typescript.

Several institutions have been most generous in giving permission for the inclusion of illustrative materials in their possession. The United States National Park Service, Fort Vancouver National Historic Site, Vancouver, Washington; the American Antiquarian Society in Worcester, Massachusetts; the Oregon Historical Society in Portland, Oregon; and the Nelda C. and H. J. Lutcher Stark Foundation of Orange, Texas, all provided copies of valuable materials from their collections.

I have tried the patience and exhausted the eyes of several proofreaders who gave unstintingly of their time in the hope that my errors might be minimized. To Donald C. Green, Mrs. Jo Tice Bloom, Temple G. J. Maynard, and Freeman Patterson I owe a great deal. That their efforts were not wasted may in some measure show my gratitude to them.

Mr. and Mrs. Howard J. Burnham of Vancouver, Washington, first persuaded me to undertake an edition of these letters during many pleasant hours in their cheery home overlooking the Columbia River and the hills bordering the Willamette Valley. Lastly, I wish to thank Professor Vernon Carstensen of the University of Washington, who persevered in guiding this book from its inception at the University of Wisconsin to publication. He deserves more than he receives.

WILLIAM R. SAMPSON

Edmonton, Alberta
February 1973

Contents

Illustrations

Introduction

JOHN MCLOUGHLIN: THE EARLY YEARS, 1784–1824

John McLoughlin was born near the village of Rivière-du-Loup on the south bank of the St. Lawrence River, about one hundred twenty miles below Quebec. His grandfather, John McLoughlin, had come to the area from Ireland, where he had been born about 1714, and had acquired a small farm in the seigneury of Rivière-du-Loup. There his first son, John the second, succeeded him. About 1778, John the second married Angélique, the daughter of Malcolm Fraser and his French-Canadian wife, Marie Allaire. The third child, and first son, of John and Angélique McLoughlin was born in the Rivière-du-Loup farmhouse on 19 October 1784, and on 5 December he was taken to the parish church at nearby Kamouraska and baptized Jean Baptiste; but he grew up signing his name simply John McLoughlin, and it is by this name that all others have known him.

From his father's side of the family, John McLoughlin was heir to the Catholic traditions of the Irish peasantry, while from the Fraser background of his mother he was influenced by a strongly Protestant and aristocratic heritage. Malcolm Fraser was descended from the Frasers of Lowat who had supported the Stuart cause at Culloden in 1746. He himself had had a distinguished military career in the British army; and for his services at the Battle of Quebec in 1759, he had been rewarded with the seigneury of Mount Murray, which stretched for eighteen miles east of the Malbaie River along the north bank of the St. Lawrence

[xv]

River. Angélique Fraser forsook the religion of her father when she married the "cultivateur" John McLoughlin; and although her father provided well for his other children in his will, he made no mention of Angélique, nor did he give any reason for not including her in his bequests. Nevertheless, although opposed to the conversion of his daughter to the faith of her husband, he gave the young McLoughlins a farm fronting on the St. Lawrence at Rivière-du-Loup; and the two families must have been further reconciled when young John's older sister, Marie Louise, went to live with her grandfather Fraser in 1786.[1]

The influence of his mother's family seems to have been dominant in young John McLoughlin's life. As early as 1792, John and Angélique McLoughlin were living in Quebec City so that they could obtain adequate schooling for their children. A man of McLoughlin's class could hardly have afforded such a move without some financial aid,[2] and a letter written to Malcolm Fraser from Quebec City by John McLoughlin in July 1796 indicates that such assistance probably came from his father-in-law; but the price was high, for the doughty Scotsman was able to insist that the McLoughlin brood be raised as Protestants.

> With Regard to the first paragraph, I thought that I answered you several times heretofore on that subject. I Refer to Mr. Jones that has them under his Charge I believe and I am sure that he will let you know what Directions I Ever give him whether any or not with Regard to Religion.
>
> I feel it Rather hard that you should Compell a parent to bring his Children up in a Religion that he wass not brought up himself and Consider that it is a weakness to Aquiese. However, If it is your Request I find myself Obliged to Agree With what you Request.[3]

Young John did not return to his baptismal faith until 1842, many years after he had left Quebec for Oregon; and his reaffirmation of faith was made in a predominantly Protestant community which resented his Catholicism.

Not only was the impressionable boy guided by the Fraser religious beliefs but his later career as doctor and fur trader was no doubt inspired

1. Burt Brown Barker, *The McLoughlin Empire and Its Rulers*, pp. 23–31, 55–57.

2. Ibid., pp. 26, 29.

3. John McLoughlin, cultivateur, to Malcolm Fraser, 27 July 1796, ibid., p. 143.

by his mother's brothers, Alexander and Simon Fraser. Alexander was a fur trader who entered the service of the North West Company prior to 1789 and became a wintering partner about 1799.[4] Simon studied medicine at the University of Edinburgh, served as a physician with the Black Watch until he was wounded in Egypt in 1801, and then settled in Terrebonne near Montreal.[5]

During the autumn of 1798, John McLoughlin apprenticed himself as a student in medicine, surgery, and pharmacy in the household of Dr. James Fisher, a prominent Quebec physician whose influence secured the earliest medical legislation in Lower Canada. After four and a half years of study McLoughlin petitioned the lieutenant-governor of the Province of Lower Canada for an examination so that he could obtain a license to practice. His license "to Practice in Surgery and Pharmacy or as an Apothecary" was granted in May 1803, when McLoughlin was nineteen years old.[6]

McLoughlin's petition to the lieutenant-governor was written from Terrebonne, where he was evidently staying with his uncle, Dr. Simon Fraser. Although Simon proposed that his nephew should go to the West Indies, Simon McTavish, the dominant figure in the North West Company, encouraged the young doctor to enter the fur trade. From bitter letters written some years later, it appears that McLoughlin was offered £ 100 per annum if he would serve as a surgeon. However, McTavish urged McLoughlin to go on the common wages of the company, in which case he would have to serve an apprenticeship of only five years, while for those who lacked such specialized training the term of apprenticeship was for seven years.[7]

Accordingly, in the summer of 1803, McLoughlin entered the North West Company as an apprentice at a salary of £ 20 a year.[8] He was sent to the company's major post at Kaministiquia (renamed Fort William

4. William Stewart Wallace, ed., *Documents Relating to the North West Company*, p. 443.

5. Ibid., pp. 72–73; John McLoughlin, *The Letters of John McLoughlin from Fort Vancouver to the Governor and Committee, First Series, 1825–38*, ed. E. E. Rich, p. xxx.

6. Barker, *The McLoughlin Empire*, pp. 268–70. The petition, Fisher's affidavit, and the permit to practice medicine are reproduced as plates 10, 11, and 12.

7. McLoughlin to Simon Fraser, 2 August 1810, ibid., p. 155.

8. McLoughlin to S. Fraser, 13 July 1808, ibid., p. 149.

in 1805) on Lake Superior where he spent the summers assisting Dr. Henry Munro, the post physician, in ministering to the partners and traders who gathered for the annual meeting of the company. During the summer months Fort William was the scene of noisy, and sometimes roisterous, activity as traders and wintering partners arrived from the western posts with the winter's fur catch, and voyageurs, the *"mangeurs du lard"* or pork eaters, arrived from the east bringing supplies for the long winter ahead. During these months the young doctor was kept occupied treating the sick; but with the coming of cold weather the great fort was all but deserted, and McLoughlin was sent to various posts nearby. It was during these periods that he gained experience in trading and handling the natives.[9]

When his term of apprenticeship was up in 1808, McLoughlin thought seriously of "going down" (returning east), for he had understood that if he was required to practice medicine during his apprenticeship he would be paid £ 100, and this sum had not been forthcoming. In a letter written at Fort William on 1 July 1808 he informed his uncle Simon that he would retire from the fur trade unless the company paid him £ 200 a year with the promise of a share in the profits at the end of two or three years, for, as he explained:

> I sincerely prefer living on potatoes and milk than in this country on any Other terms, what makes me of this Opinion is that the Country is geting ruin'd more and more every year — so that in time it will be little better than exhaust'd and that even the length of time to come in could be better employ'd and more agreably spent in any other place than this at the same time that when a man has been for any time in this Country he is entirely unfit for any other while the shares are so small that even after a Person has been ten or 12 Years he cannot boast of Any great riches. . . .[10]

Later in the month, McLoughlin met with William McGillivray, who had succeeded McTavish as chief agent for the North West Company in 1804, and rejected an offer of £ 150 a year. He was determined to settle in Detroit, but feared that such a course might jeopardize the medical education of his younger brother David, whom he was largely supporting while the latter studied medicine at the University of Edin-

9. McLoughlin, *Letters, First Series*, pp. xxxii–xxxiii.
10. Barker, *The McLoughlin Empire*, p. 148.

burgh.[11] McGillivray reconsidered and offered McLoughlin £ 200, which was the salary paid to McLoughlin's superior, Dr. Henry Munro.[12] His new engagement was evidently for a period of three years, for in August 1810 McLoughlin told Simon Fraser that he was about to depart for his winter quarters and that this would perhaps be the last winter he would spend in the fur country.[13] However, he again reconsidered, for in March 1812 he informed Simon that he was engaged for another three years, at the end of which time he was to be made a wintering partner with a share in the profits of the concern for Outfit 1814.

During the winter of 1811/12 he was stationed at Vermilion Lake (west of Lake Superior in modern Minnesota), and while there he received an offer to go to the Columbia where the North West Company planned to drive out its competitor, the Astor-owned Pacific Fur Company.[14] In view of his later career in the Oregon country, it is interesting to note that he turned down this first offer to serve in the west. He had recently married, *"au façon du Nord"* (without benefit of clergy), Marguerite Wadin McKay, the daughter of a Swiss Protestant fur trader and an Indian mother, and the widow of Alexander McKay, who had died in the explosion of Astor's ship *Tonquin* at Clayoquot Sound, Vancouver Island, in 1811. The first of their four children, John, Jr., was born in the "west" on 18 August 1812, and the responsibility for a growing family no doubt determined McLoughlin's decision to remain in the Lake Superior region.[15]

McLoughlin spent his first year as a wintering partner at Lac la Pluie near Lake Superior, but by 1815 he was stationed at Fort William, and it was from that place that he and other Nor'Westers set out to disperse Lord Selkirk's Red River Colony in 1816. The Scottish philanthropist's colony of impoverished crofters was located at the junction of the Assiniboine and Red rivers (today's Winnipeg) on lands granted by the Hudson's Bay Company, of which Selkirk was a major

11. McLoughlin to S. Fraser, 13 July 1808, ibid., p. 149.
12. McLoughlin to S. Fraser, 16 July 1808, ibid., p. 150.
13. McLoughlin to S. Fraser, 2 August 1810, ibid., p. 154.
14. McLoughlin to S. Fraser, 22 March 1812, ibid., p. 159.
15. Ibid., p. 38; McLoughlin, *Letters, First Series*, p. cxix. This was not the first liaison for McLoughlin, for in 1809 his eldest son Joseph had been born to a Chippewa woman from the Red River country. Barker, *The McLoughlin Empire*, p. 329.

shareholder. Although it was primarily agricultural, the settlement posed a threat to the trade of the North West Company because it straddled the long cross-country supply lines from Fort William. In 1815 the Nor'Westers had attacked and dispersed the colonists; but they had since returned to their farms, and a second attack was planned for the summer of 1816. Fortunately for McLoughlin, the Fort William contingent was "judiciously late" in arriving,[16] and the Seven Oaks Massacre of 19 June 1816 was carried out without its support.

McLoughlin had privately expressed his opposition to the violence against the colonists, but his position in the concern had forced him to participate. On hearing the report of the massacre, in which Governor Robert Semple and a score of colonists were killed, McLoughlin immediately returned to Fort William, where he found William McGillivray. Selkirk, who was en route to Red River with a party of new settlers and a corps of one hundred uniformed and armed mercenaries from the de Wattville and de Meuron regiments, received news of the massacre at Sault Sainte Marie. He changed his destination, and by 12 August he had landed and formed a camp near Fort William. The following morning, using his authority as magistrate in the Indian Territories, he issued a warrant for the arrest of McGillivray. McGillivray, accompanied by John McLoughlin and Kenneth McKenzie, went before Selkirk to arrange bail; but all three were arrested and on 19 August were sent to Upper Canada for trial. Selkirk settled down to occupy Fort William for the winter and confiscated its vast and valuable stocks of furs and provisions for the use of his men.

The Nor'Westers sent to Upper Canada found that the attorney-general was absent, and after obtaining a writ of habeas corpus, they were freed on bail at Montreal on 10 September. Not until March 1818 were the disputants brought to trial at York in Upper Canada. There were twenty-nine charges against the Hudson's Bay Company and Lord Selkirk, while the latter had raked up one hundred fifty charges against the Nor'Westers. McLoughlin and five others, including his kinsman Simon Fraser the explorer, were charged with being accessories after the fact in the murder of Robert Semple. McLoughlin's trial began on 30 October and concluded the following day when the jury returned a verdict of "not guilty" after being out three-quarters of an hour. In the end, only one charge was

16. McLoughlin, *Letters, First Series*, p. xxxviii; Chester Martin, *Lord Selkirk's Work in Canada*, p. 113.

sustained: a former member of Selkirk's guard who had deserted to the North West Company was sentenced to be hanged for the murder of a one-time Hudson's Bay Company employee.

During his enforced stay in Montreal, evidently his first visit there since 1803, McLoughlin was elected to membership in the exclusive and convivial Beaver Club, whose members were prominent agents or wintering partners of the North West Company and had met the rigors of at least one winter in the Indian country or *pays d'en haut*.[17]

McLoughlin, his name cleared, returned to the Fort William depot where he had been placed in charge as successor to Kenneth McKenzie, who had drowned when one of the seriously overloaded canoes bearing the North West Company prisoners had capsized in rough weather on Lake Superior.[18] Despite the attempts of the North West Company to resume normal operations, the years between the end of the Selkirk trials and 1821 were marked by a rapid decline in the fortunes of the concern. Since 1815, when the first attack on the Red River Colony was planned, several of the wintering partners of the company, McLoughlin among them, had been disturbed by the lawlessness that accompanied the intense competition with the Hudson's Bay Company for the furs of the rich country drained by the Athabasca River. Further, the superior resources of the Hudson's Bay Company and its more direct supply routes from Hudson Bay had checked the profits of the North West Company at a time when its own resources were strained to meet the financial demands occasioned by the costly trials and the destruction of the supplies stored at Fort William. After 1814 the North West Company moved toward bankruptcy. The company's profits were distributed among the wintering partners in the field and the agents in Montreal at the end of each annual venture, and there was no reserve fund to meet the unexpected and heavy drain of the prolonged conflicts with the Selkirk forces.[19]

Dissatisfaction and uneasiness concerning the affairs of the North West Company, although not widespread, were evident among a few of the partners as early as 1819. That year Colin Robertson, a discharged

17. Marjorie Wilkins Campbell, *The North West Company*, pp. 225–39; McLoughlin, *Letters, First Series*, pp. xxxvii–xl; Clifford P. Wilson, "The Beaver Club," p. 64. McLoughlin was elected to membership on 21 January 1817.

18. McLoughlin, *Letters, First Series*, pp. xxxix–xl.

19. Ibid., pp. xl–xli; Wallace, ed., *Documents Relating to the North West Company*, p. 28.

Nor'Wester who had gone to work for the Hudson's Bay Company, was held prisoner at the North West Company's Fort Chipewyan in the Athabasca country, and in a coded letter to George Moffatt, a leading Montreal merchant who was friendly to the Hudson's Bay Company, he remarked that

> I have discovered strong symptoms of dissatisfaction among the wintering partners. . . .
>
> . . . The majority of the wintering partners were not on the best terms with the agents, whom they considered the authors of all their misfortunes. Their [the agents'] wild speculations have reduced them to poverty, nor do they know the extent of their losses, arising from the law suits, and to add to their misfortunes, is this second attempt on Athabasca, the only source of anything like profits. . . .
>
> . . . But were we to attempt to separate the wintering partners from the agents, and select from amongst them men of character, I fear notwithstanding the mighty spirit of dissatisfaction they profess, that it would be a more arduous task than at first sight appears. There are none possessing firmness of character amongst them with the exception of Leith, McLaughline and McDonald and perhaps the two Keiths. A good dinner, a few fair promises would waltz the remainder about, to any tune the McGillivray's chose to strike up.[20]

The split was widened when the partners and the representatives of the agents gathered at Fort William for the annual meeting in July. The agreement with McTavish, McGillivrays & Company was due to expire in 1822, and McLoughlin took advantage of the fact to support a proposal to investigate the possibility that "the fruits of their [the wintering partners'] labors might be rendered more secure. . . ."[21] No decision was made that summer, but McLoughlin determined to investigate an alternate arrangement. He and Angus Bethune, a North West Company partner who was related to McLoughlin by marriage, approached George Moffatt who put them in touch with Samuel Gale, a prominent Montreal barrister and journalist. Gale supported the cause of the Hudson's Bay Company in ending the strife that was ruining

20. Colin Robertson, *Colin Robertson's Correspondence Book, September 1817 to September 1822*, ed E. E. Rich, pp. 81–82. The McGillivrays were the principal owners of McTavish, McGillivrays & Co., the Montreal agents of the North West Co.

21. McLoughlin, *Letters*, *First Series*, p. xlii, quoting Samuel Gale to Lady Selkirk, 10 September 1819, in *Selkirk Correspondence*, 6500.

the fur trade, and in September 1819 he reported to Lady Selkirk that he had received an inquiry "on the part of a wintering partner now in the Indian Country [McLoughlin]; by a Gentleman of this place whose name I promised not to mention [George Moffatt] . . . whether the Wintering partners if they should persevere in their refusal to renew their agreement with McTavish, McGillivrays & Company could obtain from the Hudson's Bay Company their outfits or supplies of goods & sanction to trade on condition of sending their returns of furs to the Hudson's Bay Company." The weight of the inquiry was made clear in Gale's comment that the wintering partner requesting the information "possesses influence to withdraw almost every useful member of the North West Association who are all dissatisfied & alarmed at being unable to get what is due to them from the Montreal houses."[22]

The disaffected partners could not have realized the importance of their letter to the governor and committee of the Hudson's Bay Company. The letter arrived in England in late December 1819 just at the time when Lord Selkirk was considering the sale of his controlling interest in the company. The prospective purchaser was Edward Ellice of the firm of Inglis, Ellice and Company which was the London supply house for McTavish, McGillivrays and Company. The British government was concerned by the long period of strife in the fur country and had, through the colonial secretary, Lord Bathurst, appealed to Ellice in the hope that he might be able to bring about a union of the contenders and end the disturbances on the frontier. The receipt of Gale's letter revealed to the Hudson's Bay Company that although its own solvency was strained by the struggle, the North West Company's position was even more precarious. The committee therefore decided to open negotiations with the dissident partners and to reject Ellice's offer.[23]

Little is known of the secret negotiations between the Hudson's Bay Company and McLoughlin, but the final decision to withdraw from the agreement with McTavish, McGillivrays and Company was not made until the annual meeting of the North West Company partners and agents at Fort William in July 1820. Although the problem of Selkirk's influence in the policies of the Hudson's Bay Company was removed

22. Robertson, *Correspondence Book*, pp. xiv, civ; McLoughlin, *Letters, First Series*, p. xlii, quoting Gale to Lady Selkirk, 10 September 1819, in *Selkirk Correspondence*, 6500–6501.

23. Wallace, ed., *Documents Relating to the North West Company*, p. 29.

with his death in April 1820, McLoughlin and his followers stood firm in their decision to leave the North West Company. Even McGillivray made it clear that an end to the strife was essential and that to this end Edward Ellice was negotiating with the Hudson's Bay Company. The precarious financial position of the North West Company was made clear to all, and although McGillivray was able to sign up the partners who were related to him and a few others, eighteen of them gave McLoughlin their powers of attorney and sent him to Montreal to negotiate a new agreement with the Montreal agency houses so that they might continue their trade free from collisions with the Hudson's Bay Company.

McGillivray's only triumph at this stormy meeting was to remove McLoughlin from his position at Fort William. McLoughlin, accompanied by Angus Bethune, was in Montreal by September 1820; but the Montreal agencies rejected his proposals, and in November he and Bethune sailed from New York on the *Albion* to pursue the negotiations with the Hudson's Bay Company in London. Their task was complicated by the arrival of William and Simon McGillivray who, with Edward Ellice, opened negotiations with the Hudson's Bay Company on their own account. The division within the North West Company worked against the interests of McLoughlin's group. On the one hand, the objective of the Hudson's Bay Company was to eliminate competition, and if the Montreal supply houses were not included in the agreement, they could recruit more traders and resume their operations. On the other hand, an agreement with the supply houses would leave the independent traders without agents, and they would thus be unable to resume large-scale operations.[24]

McLoughlin and Bethune thus served as a lever which the governor and committee could use to force the surrender of the McGillivrays, for the financial condition of the latter was too precarious to attempt a resumption of independent operations. Agreement was at length reached between the Hudson's Bay Company and the McGillivray interests in March 1821. The agreement, or indenture, signed on 26 March provided that the united fur trade was to be conducted by the Hudson's Bay Company for a period of twenty-one years beginning on 1 June 1821. Although the capital stock was to be equally subscribed, the North West

24. McLoughlin, *Letters, First Series*, pp. xliii–xlvi.

Company was obliged to deduct £ 5,000 from its share which was to be added to that of the Hudson's Bay Company as compensation for all "matters in difference" between the two concerns. The profits accruing to the firm were to be divided into one hundred shares — twenty for the governor and committee of the Hudson's Bay Company, twenty for the McGillivrays and Ellice, forty for the chief factors and chief traders who conducted the actual trade in North America; and of the remaining twenty shares, five went to the Selkirk heirs, five to Simon McGillivray and Edward Ellice as compensation for the loss of their London agency, and ten were kept in reserve. However, twenty shares accruing to the North West Company were to be retained by the Hudson's Bay Company for defraying the deficiency in the North West Company's share of the capital.

All operations of the two companies were to be united, and the business was to be conducted in the name of the Hudson's Bay Company from its headquarters in London. The financial precariousness of the North West Company was indicated by an article making the North West Company alone responsible for all of its debts and claims. A board of five members for "consulting and advising as to the management of the Trade" was constituted, composed of the governor or deputy governor of the Hudson's Bay Company, two members of the Company's committee, and Simon McGillivray and Edward Ellice to represent the North West Company.[25]

In 1824 these arrangements were altered through the issuance of a block of stock to the McGillivrays and Ellice in return for their surrender of all present, reversionary, and contingent interests in the Company. The former Nor'Westers thus became ordinary stockholders in the Hudson's Bay Company, and the joint board of management was dissolved. Only three years after the union of 1821, the Hudson's Bay Company had twisted coalition into absorption, and unity of management was achieved.[26] But the Hudson's Bay Company, although retaining its old supply and finance structure, was radically reorganized; the new firm assimilated the whole of the field practices of the North West Company,

25. "Agreement for carrying on the Fur Trade by the Hudson's Bay Company exclusively under the terms within mentioned," 26 March 1821, Robertson, *Correspondence Book*, pp. 302–27.

26. E. E. Rich, *The History of the Hudson's Bay Company, 1670–1870*, 2:436–37.

the most distinctive feature of which was partnership for field officers who would share in either the profits or losses from the trade.[27]

By the "Deed Poll" which had accompanied the agreement of 26 March 1821, the forty shares of the profits of the new concern which were allocated to the chief factors and chief traders were further divided into eighty-five subshares. The twenty-five chief factors were each to receive the profits from two of these subshares, and each of the twenty-eight chief traders was to receive the profits from one of them. The remaining seven subshares were to be used to provide an income for the retired servants of both companies: four being allocated to the servants of the Hudson's Bay Company and three to the servants of the North West Company. At the end of seven years these seven subshares were to be added to the ten full shares already held in reserve for retired personnel.

The chief factors were to superintend the trade, while the chief traders were to conduct the business in their respective departments. The lands held under the Company's charter were divided into a northern and a southern department, each with a governor and council composed of the chief factors of the department to regulate the trade and its personnel. Of the twenty-five chief factors, fifteen were former Nor'Westers, while seventeen of the twenty-eight chief traders had formerly served the Canadian firm. This led William McGillivray to boast that the North West Company had emerged with 55 percent of the stock in the new company, but such was hardly the case; even though the field structure of the firm was altered to incorporate the efficiency that came from field partners who had a direct interest in the profits, the controlling management remained with the London committee of the Hudson's Bay Company. Although the union was termed a coalition, the North West Company ceased to have an identity. The arrangements of 1821 and 1824 shielded the Hudson's Bay Company from the litigation over the debts of the North West Company which continued until 1851 and led to the bankruptcy of the principal Montreal partners of the old concern.[28]

Although he was probably disappointed by the terms of the coalition, there is no indication that McLoughlin was greatly dissatisfied at the time. In fact, considering the financial condition of the North West

27. George Simpson, *Fur Trade and Empire: George Simpson's Journal*, ed. Frederick Merk, p. xiii.

28. "Deed Poll," 26 March 1821, Robertson, *Correspondence Book*, pp. 327–44; Rich, *History of the Hudson's Bay Company*, 2:398.

Company and their own revolt against the domination of the McGillivrays, McLoughlin and the other dissident partners emerged in a stronger position than might have been expected. Both McLoughlin and Bethune were made chief factors by the Deed Poll of 1821, and although McLoughlin's debts incurred during the last profitless years of the North West Company were troublesome, the new arrangements assured him of an income. On 31 March 1821, McLoughlin and Bethune sailed from Liverpool in company with Nicholas Garry, a member of the committee of the Hudson's Bay Company who had the responsibility for putting the terms of the agreement into effect in North America. Their Ship, the American packet *Amity*, docked in New York on 10 May, and McLoughlin and Bethune left two days later for Montreal. McLoughlin, whose health had been a source of concern prior to his departure from Canada in November 1820, became "extremely ill"; and he was unable to attend either the last assemblage of the North West Company wintering partners and agents at Fort William in July or the first council of the reorganized Hudson's Bay Company which convened at Norway House at the upper end of Lake Winnipeg in August. His colleagues in opposition to the North West Company were thus deprived of his leadership and conciliatory influence, and Simon McGillivray was able to impose the changes agreed to in London without opposition.

McLoughlin spent the winter of 1821/22 in France with his brother David, but returned to Montreal, via London, in May and hurried on to York Factory on Hudson Bay where he delivered the spring packets from the governor and committee. On 8 July 1822, George Simpson, the newly appointed governor of the Northern Department, convened the council, and McLoughlin was appointed chief factor for his old district at Lac la Pluie, where he served for the next two years.[29]

On 5 December 1821, Parliament granted the newly reorganized Hudson's Bay Company a twenty-one-year license for exclusive trade in the Pacific Northwest. This license excluded only other British concerns and individuals from the trade of the Oregon country, for by the terms of the Convention of 1818, the Northwest Coast was to be "free and open" to the citizens of both the United States and Great Britain for a period of ten years. In 1827 this joint occupation was extended indefinitely, and in 1839 the trading license was renewed for an additional twenty-one

29. McLoughlin, *Letters, First Series*, pp. xlviii–li.

years. The North West Company had been operating along the Columbia River since the purchase of John Jacob Astor's Fort Astoria, which they renamed Fort George, in October 1813; and the Hudson's Bay Company had appointed two chief factors to that region in 1821. However, poor management, an excessive reliance on imported foodstuffs and manufactured goods, increasing American competition, and the great distances from market and supply centers combined to make the trade of the Columbia, potentially rich as it was, unprofitable.[30] The time had come either to reorganize the department or abandon it; and George Simpson, whose Northern Department included the Columbia District, was not one to give up without a fight.

The fourth annual council of the Northern Department convened at York Factory on 10 July 1824 "for the purpose of establishing such Rules and Regulations as may be considered expedient for conducting the business of the said Department and in order to investigate the result of the Trade of last year and determine the Outfits and arrangements of the current year. . . ."[31] Governor Simpson and thirteen chief factors were present, and John McLoughlin had come from Lac la Pluie for what was to be his last meeting with the council until 1839.[32] Shortly after the council began its sessions, McLoughlin found that he was being transferred to the Company's Columbia District.[33] Governor Simpson has left no record of his reason for transferring McLoughlin from the relatively unimportant post at Lac la Pluie to the general superintendency of the Columbia, but it seems probable that rumors of American intentions to establish themselves on that important waterway may have influenced the governor, for McLoughlin had just spent two years successfully meeting determined American opposition in his frontier district.[34] Certainly, there is no indication that Simpson was attempting to isolate McLoughlin. In spite of McLoughlin's bitter feelings toward the North West Company during his early years in the fur trade, and his abortive attempt to lead a revolt of the partners against the Montreal agents

30. Simpson, *Fur Trade and Empire*, pp. xxii–xxv; Rich, *History of the Hudson's Bay Company*, 2:404–5, 650.

31. R. Harvey Fleming, ed., *Minutes of Council Northern Department of Rupert Land, 1821–31*, p. 69.

32. Edmund H. Oliver, ed., *The Canadian North-West*, 2:774.

33. Fleming, ed., *Minutes of Council Northern Department*, pp. 69–71.

34. McLoughlin, *Letters, First Series*, pp. li–lii.

in 1819–20, Simpson seems not to have taken these signs of rebellious independence into consideration, nor could he have foreseen that these same traits were eventually to cause an irreparable breach in their relations which would cause the Company to force McLoughlin into retirement.

JOHN MCLOUGHLIN ON THE COLUMBIA, 1824–46

Chief Factor John McLoughlin left York Factory for his new assignment on the Columbia on 27 July 1824, three weeks before Simpson embarked on a tour of inspection of the Company's western territories; but to the latter's amusement and satisfaction, the two met at the Athabasca River in late September. Simpson's record of the meeting provides an interesting picture of a disgruntled and disheveled McLoughlin.

> On the 26th at 7 O'Clock A.M. came up with the Dr before his people had left their Encampment altho we had by that early hour come from his Breakfasting place of the preceding Day; himself and people were heartily tired of the Voyage and his Surprise and vexation at being overtaken in Riviere la Biche notwithstanding his having a 20 Days start of us from York is not to be described; he was such a figure as I should not like to meet in a dark Night in one of the bye lanes in the neighbourhood of London, dressed in Clothes that had once been fashionable, but now covered with a thousand patches of different Colors, his beard would do honor to the chin of a Grizzly Bear, his face and hands evidently Shewing that he had not lost much time at his Toilette, loaded with Arms and his own herculean dimensions forming a tout ensemble that would convey a good idea of the high way men of former Days. . . . Slackened our speed in order to give the Dr an opportunity of keeping up with us.[35]

Simpson and McLoughlin arrived at Fort George on 8 November, and by the time Simpson left on his return trip in March 1825, the administration of the Columbia District had been completely reorganized. The district encompassed the watershed of the Columbia River, and although its northern limits were not precisely defined, the boundary was generally considered to be the height of land dividing the waters of the Columbia from those of the Fraser River. To the south, the boundary was the forty-second parallel, the northern limit of California, although to the east the Company's brigades often trapped below that line in Nevada and Utah. On the east and west the limits were quite

35. Simpson, *Fur Trade and Empire*, p. 23.

definitely set at the summit of the Rocky Mountains and the Pacific Ocean. To the north of the Columbia District was the District of New Caledonia. The two were combined in 1826 to form the Columbia Department under Chief Factor McLoughlin, although New Caledonia retained much of its autonomy.[36]

The potential value of trade along the Columbia River and the Northwest Coast was apparent to Simpson, but he found the affairs of the district in a chaotic state: "Everything appears to me on the Columbia on too extended a scale *except the Trade*. . . . I feel that a very Severe reflection is cast on those who have had the management of the Business, . . . and that sound judgment has not been exercised but that mismanagement and extravagance has been the order of the day."[37] Simpson planned to rehabilitate the region by substituting home-grown for imported foodstuffs, by establishing a coastal trade with Company-owned ships which would put down all American seaborne competition, by engaging in vigorous opposition to American traders in the interior, particularly in the Snake River country, and by moving the headquarters to the mouth of the Fraser River.[38]

Before a site could be chosen on the Fraser, it was necessary to remove the chief post on the Columbia from Fort George. The governor and committee in London were concerned about the inevitable boundary settlement in the Oregon country, and they realized that the Company had little hope of securing any of the territory south of the Columbia River. On 22 July 1824, they instructed the chief factor, J. D. Cameron, to select a new site on the north bank of the river.[39] Before Cameron could select a suitable site, Simpson and McLoughlin had arrived on the Columbia, and in November McLoughlin and Chief Factor Alexander Kennedy selected the site for the new depot. Since an area suitable for agriculture was a prime consideration in the location of the new post, McLoughlin and Kennedy finally determined on the broad tablelands on the north bank of the Columbia above the mouth of the Willamette.[40] Construction was begun almost immediately, and by March 1825 the

36. John A. Hussey, *The History of Fort Vancouver and Its Physical Structure*, pp. 31–32, 56; McLoughlin, *Letters, First Series*, p. xii.

37. Simpson, *Fur Trade and Empire*, p. 65.

38. McLoughlin, *Letters, First Series*, pp. xxvi–xxviii.

39. Simpson, *Fur Trade and Empire*, pp. 241–42.

40. Hussey, *History of Fort Vancouver*, pp. 38–40.

new post was far enough advanced for Governor Simpson to break a bottle of rum on the flagstaff and name the establishment Fort Vancouver. This he did at dawn on 19 March; by nine o'clock he was on his way up the Columbia, bound for Canada.[41] Simpson was accompanied by Chief Factor Kennedy, and McLoughlin became the sole chief factor in the Columbia District.

Once in command of the Columbia District, McLoughlin worked energetically to develop agriculture, trade, and industry so that the Company's operations there might prove profitable. Grains and vegetables were planted at Fort Vancouver in 1825, and soon thereafter apples and other fruits were planted. By 1828, herds of cattle and hogs were increasing, and McLoughlin could foresee the day when basic foodstuffs would no longer have to be imported. McLoughlin erected a gristmill at Fort Vancouver, and about 1828 he erected a sawmill on a small creek five miles to the east of the fort. He imported salt and began packing salmon which he traded, along with the lumber, in the Sandwich Islands and California. And, in an effort to extend the coastal trade, he established a shipyard at Fort Vancouver where two small vessels were built in 1827–28.

But the greatest progress was made in the interior where Peter Skene Ogden had charge of the Snake River brigades from 1824 to 1830. Through intensive trapping and sharply competitive practices in the east the Company sought to protect northern and western Oregon from American trapping parties. As a result, the Snake country almost became a "fur desert," and Ogden ranged as far afield as the Gulf of California to obtain profitable fur returns. The superior organization, capital, familiarity with the terrain, and rapport with the Indians possessed by the Hudson's Bay Company made the fur trade in the Snake country unprofitable to the numerically superior but loosely organized American trappers. On the other hand, Ogden's returns of some two thousand beaver a year during the 1820s showed a profit which averaged £ 2,500 during his first three years in the Snake country.[42] By 1828, when Governor Simpson returned to Fort Vancouver, McLoughlin's administration of the Columbia Department had produced many of the results anticipated in 1824. Simpson was generous in his praise of McLoughlin's accomplish-

41. Simpson, *Fur Trade and Empire*, p. 124.
42. Hussey, *History of Fort Vancouver*, pp. 58–62, 63–65; John S. Galbraith, *The Hudson's Bay Company as an Imperial Factor, 1821–1869*, pp. 91–98 *passim.*

ments, and on 15 March 1829 he addressed McLoughlin as follows: "Your whole administration is marked by its close adherence to the spirit of the Govr & Committees wishes and intentions, and is conspicious [*sic*] for a talent in planning and for an activity & perseverance in execution which reflect the highest credit on your judgement and habits of business, I do no more than my duty to you to the concern at large and to myself."[43]

The first serious threat to the dominance of the Hudson's Bay Company came in the spring of 1829 when the Boston brigs *Owhyhee* and *Convoy* entered the river to trade. The loss of the London supply ship *William and Ann* with its cargo of trade goods hampered McLoughlin's ability to compete with the Americans, and the two ships were able to carry away 2,900 land pelts, principally otter and beaver, when they departed in July 1830. McLoughlin had been forced to pay five times the normal price for furs (about 30s. 6d., or $7.62, for a large beaver skin), and it was not until 1832 that the prices charged for trade goods returned to their former level.[44] The second American threat to McLoughlin's district came in 1832 when Nathaniel J. Wyeth arrived at Fort Vancouver preparatory to entering the fur and salmon trade. Wyeth's supply ship was wrecked in the Society Islands, however, and the Boston ice merchant was forced to abandon temporarily his venture on the Columbia.[45]

Before the next onslaught came, McLoughlin received expressions of confidence in his management from both the Company and from Governor Simpson. On the tenth anniversary of McLoughlin's appointment to the Columbia Department, Simpson piloted through the council of the Northern Department a resolution voting the chief factor a gratuity of £500 and an additional allowance of £150 per annum for the years 1830, 1831, 1832, and 1833 in consideration of his professional services as the post doctor during the serious epidemics which almost decimated the Indians of the lower Columbia.[46]

The events of the year 1834, however, proved to be the beginning of a long series of disagreements with the Company which was to result in McLoughlin's retirement from his post in 1846. In mid-September,

---

43. Simpson, *Fur Trade and Empire*, p. 308. See also George Simpson, *Part of Dispatch from George Simpson, Esqr.*, ed. E. E. Rich, p. xxxvii.

44. McLoughlin, *Letters, First Series*, pp. lxxvii–lxxxi; Galbraith, *The Hudson's Bay Company*, pp. 98–99.

45. McLoughlin, *Letters, First Series*, p. xcvi.

46. Ibid., p. cii.

Tintype or daguerreotype of John McLoughlin taken possibly by D. H. Hendee, who arrived in Oregon in June 1853, or by Joseph Buchtel, who arrived in September of that year. Courtesy of the National Park Service, Fort Vancouver National Historic Site

American Settlement, Wallamatta River, Called Oregon City. Watercolor sketch made in 1846 by Lt. Henry J. Warre. Courtesy of the American Antiquarian Society

Oregon City and Falls, 1846. Pencil sketch by Lt. Henry J. Warre showing McLoughlin's house and mills. Courtesy of the American Antiquarian Society

Nathaniel Wyeth appeared unexpectedly at Fort Vancouver to resume his efforts at establishing a profitable trade on the Columbia. McLoughlin felt that strenuous opposition to Wyeth was unnecessary, for he was certain that the second venture would be no more successful than the first. Wyeth began the construction of Fort William on Sauvie Island at the mouth of the Willamette and persuaded McLoughlin to enter into a modest trading agreement whereby Wyeth could buy his supplies from the Company. McLoughlin felt that he could control Wyeth's competition by coming to terms with him, but the Company refused to accept any agreement whatsoever and insisted on vigorous opposition. Wyeth did not succeed according to his expectations, for during the first year his fur catch in the Fort Hall area amounted to only 600 beaver skins, and his salmon fishery produced only half a cargo (300 barrels) of salt fish. In 1836 he abandoned his venture and returned to Boston, and in the autumn of the following year McLoughlin purchased Fort Hall for five hundred dollars. Although Wyeth retained his claim to Fort William, the Company used the area for pasturing cattle.[47] In spite of the Company's official opposition, Wyeth appreciated the kindness shown him by McLoughlin, and the two continued to correspond for many years.

McLoughlin had long disagreed with the London committee, who were acting on the advice of Simpson, on the most efficient method of conducting trade along the Northwest Coast. McLoughlin believed that the coastal trade could best be conducted from fixed posts, for he felt that the use of vessels alone was a needless extravagance. The Company, on the other hand, held the opposite view, and by 1836 was employing seven vessels on the coast, four of which were ships of 200 tons or more. McLoughlin differed with the Company not only on the methods of trade but also on the degree to which he should oppose American traders along the coast. The committee reminded McLoughlin that he was to meet competition, especially that offered by the Americans, with uncompromising vigor until all opposition was driven from the coast. McLoughlin felt that such a course was needlessly expensive, for all that was necessary was sufficient opposition to rule out the possibility of a profitable voyage. This difference of opinion was aggravated in March of 1836 when the new steamboat *Beaver* arrived at Fort Vancouver to

47. Ibid., pp. ciii, cvii–cxiii; Hussey, *History of Fort Vancouver*, pp. 74–75.

have her engines installed. McLoughlin considered the cost of the vessel improvident and he doubted that she would serve efficiently. McLoughlin's doubts were soon proved, for the little vessel could go only a little over two hundred miles between fuel stops, and it took six axmen two days to cut enough wood to run the ship for one day.[48]

In January 1837 McLoughlin was instructed to go to England to discuss the affairs of the Columbia Department personally with the governor and committee. James Douglas was appointed to superintend Fort Vancouver, the lower Columbia trading posts, and the coasting trade in his absence. McLoughlin, whose health would not permit a long voyage to England via Cape Horn, departed from Fort Vancouver with the overland express on 22 March 1838, and probably sailed from New York late in August aboard the *Great Western*.[49] While McLoughlin was in England, the Company came to an agreement with the Russian-American Company which provided that in return for a ten-year lease on a 350-mile strip of the Alaskan coast, the Hudson's Bay Company was to provide the Russians with agricultural products. This arrangement was a further attempt on the part of the Company to destroy American commerce in the North Pacific, for the Sitka supply trade was a principal source of profit for American vessels on the coast. To provide the necessary agricultural supplies, the Company established a subsidiary, the Puget's Sound Agricultural Company, to manage the Company's farms. There is evidence that the governor and committee were not entirely satisfied with the independent manner in which McLoughlin had been running the Columbia Department, but at the conclusion of the agreements concerning the Russians and the Puget's Sound Agricultural Company in February 1839, they reappointed McLoughlin to the principal superintendence of the Columbia and granted him a salary of £500 a year in addition to the profits from his chief factorship.[50]

48. McLoughlin, *Letters, First Series*, pp. cxiv–cxv; and Duncan Finlayson to McLoughlin, 29 September 1836, ibid., p. 328.

49. Ibid., pp. cxxvi–cxxviii.

50. Ibid., p. cxvi; and John McLoughlin, *The Letters of John McLoughlin from Fort Vancouver to the Governor and Committee, Second Series, 1839–44*, ed. E. E. Rich, pp. xi–xii. In reference to McLoughlin's trip to London in 1838, George B. Roberts, a Company clerk, wrote: "*On dit* that Sir Geo: had prepared the Gov & Committee to give the Dr a whiging & that when he came into their presence the Drs fine manly appearance & bearing was such that they had no heart for the fight. . . ." George B. Roberts, "The Round Hand of George B. Roberts," ed. Thomas Vaughan and Priscilla Knuth, p. 183.

McLoughlin resumed his post at Fort Vancouver in October 1839 and during the following year he sent James Douglas to implement the new agreement with the Russian-American Company. Douglas accepted the transfer of the Russian post at Stikine to the Hudson's Bay Company and built an additional post still farther north at Taku. The Company then had five posts along the coast — Fort Langley on the Fraser, Fort Simpson on the Nass River (moved to the present site of Port Simpson at the northern end of the Tsimpsean Peninsula in 1834), and Fort McLoughlin at Milbank Sound had all been built between 1827 and 1833 — and Douglas recommended that one additional post be constructed to serve the Queen Charlotte Islands and northern Vancouver Island.

McLoughlin had long contended that fixed posts were less expensive and formed a more permanent contact with the natives than did shipping, and his prejudice against the steamer *Beaver* increased as her repair bills mounted. Decisions on the posts and the *Beaver* were deferred pending the arrival of Sir George Simpson, who was making his first tour of inspection to the Northwest Coast since 1829. Simpson arrived at Fort Vancouver on 25 August 1841, but remained only a few days before departing for the northern posts in the *Beaver*, which had been patched up for the occasion. On his return to Fort Vancouver in October, Simpson informed McLoughlin that all of the northern posts except Fort Simpson were to be abandoned and that the *Beaver* would be used to carry on the greater part of the trade at a saving of £ 4,000 a year. At the same time, Simpson proposed that a new depot be established at the southern end of Vancouver Island, where it would not be subject to attack and plunder by the growing American community south of the Columbia. McLoughlin protested these measures vigorously, but Simpson remained adamant. The dispute was still unresolved when Simpson left for California and Honolulu on the last day of November, and McLoughlin arranged to meet him in Honolulu for a conference in late February of the following year. After a series of bitter exchanges in Honolulu, many of them by correspondence, Simpson ordered McLoughlin to abandon Taku and Fort McLoughlin within a year's time and to build a new depot on Vancouver Island. Simpson and McLoughlin parted in March never to meet again. The rift over trading policy proved to be permanent, and subsequent events strained their relations to the breaking point.[51]

51. McLoughlin, *Letters, Second Series*, pp. xii–xxii; Hussey, *History of Fort Vancouver*, p. 84; Sir George Simpson, *Narrative of a Journey Round the World during the Years 1841 and 1842*, 1:236, 253.

Almost immediately, another event occurred which caused a more grievous quarrel between the two strong-willed men and forced the governor and committee to intercede. On 25 April 1842 Simpson arrived at Stikine en route to Sitka and Siberia and found the post flags at half mast. He soon learned that John McLoughlin, Jr., who was in charge of the post, had been murdered during the night of 20 April by his own men. Simpson, after a cursory examination into the affair, accepted the story that young McLoughlin had treated the post employees with cruelty and had led an intemperate life. Simpson turned the murderer over to the authorities at Sitka and was disposed to let the matter drop there.

But McLoughlin was not inclined to accept the governor's actions, and conducted his own investigation of the affair. Finding that the young McLoughlin had used little of his liquor supply, that his supposed cruelty consisted of confining the men to their barracks at night and not allowing them to receive Indian women, and that the murder had been premeditated, the embittered father proceeded to blame the murder on Simpson, for the governor had recently transferred young McLoughlin's assistant to Fort Simpson, leaving the former alone at Stikine to cope with his unruly employees. McLoughlin, who had the sympathy of the governor and committee in London, pressed his personal charges against Simpson too far and made excessive demands that the Company bring to trial all of the men at Stikine. For the next four years, McLoughlin wrote at length on the subject of the murder and the cursory treatment of the case by Simpson. His preoccupation with the matter and his efforts to protect his land claim at the falls of the Willamette River caused McLoughlin to neglect more important aspects of the Company's operations on the Columbia; and his personal attacks on Simpson grew more bitter as time passed. Eventually the governor and committee were forced to make new arrangements for the management of the Columbia Department.[52]

Doctor McLoughlin's troubles in the 1840s were not confined to his disputes with the Company committee over trading policy and the murder of his son, and there remains for consideration a brief survey of his land claim at Willamette Falls and his relations with the American

52. For a full discussion of the complicated events connected with the murder, see McLoughlin, *Letters, Second Series*, pp. xxii–xlviii. See also Simpson, *Narrative of a Journey*, 2:181–82.

settlers south of the Columbia. As early as 1828, McLoughlin had selected a site on the east side of the Willamette Falls for a sawmill, and a canal was blasted in 1832. However, Indians in the area were troublesome and, as the small sawmill east of Fort Vancouver was still able to supply current requirements, nothing more was done at the Falls until 1838, when McLoughlin had some timber squared and hauled to the site. There he erected a small building to serve as a house and store to replace one which had been constructed in 1829 but destroyed by the Indians.

In July 1840, Jason Lee, the superintendent of the Methodist Mission who had arrived with Wyeth in 1834, applied to McLoughlin for the use of some of the squared timber to build a mission at the Falls. McLoughlin consented and even permitted Lee to place the building on the Company's land claim. Lee, in an evil moment for McLoughlin, assigned Rev. Alvin F. Waller to the Willamette Falls mission. Waller, who had arrived with the "Great Reinforcement" of Methodists aboard the *Lausanne* in June 1840, began a continuing effort to whittle down or extinguish the claim which McLoughlin held for the Company. In 1841 Felix Hathaway, a mission employee, built a house on the island (later called Abernethy Island) in the Willamette just off the mainland which McLoughlin considered to be part of his claim; to safeguard his interests, McLoughlin built a house there as well. Later that year, the Island Milling Company, composed mostly of mission personnel, was formed; and George Abernethy, the mission steward who had established a mission store at the Falls earlier in the year, was appointed to manage the new concern's affairs.

When Governor Simpson visited the area in 1841–42, he directed that the Company's officers should recover the site and take possession of the water privileges on behalf of the Company. He also ordered that milling machinery should be installed to compete with the American interlopers. In spite of protests by McLoughlin, the Island Milling Company built a mill on the island in 1842. In December, McLoughlin employed J. M. Hudspeth, a recent immigrant, to survey and lay out the town of Oregon City at the site of the falls, and Lansford Hastings was hired to serve as McLoughlin's agent in protecting the interests of the Company. McLoughlin paid fifty dollars for the land Waller had cleared for the mission, but the minister refused to acknowledge McLoughlin's prior claim to the land. Waller apparently took it for granted that the Company was the claimant and that in a region where the jurisdiction of the United States would ultimately be established, the rights of the foreign corporation could safely be ignored. In the spring of 1843, McLoughlin asked the Company's officers for an official ruling on the land claim. He declared that there were three alternatives open to him: hold the claim in the Company's name, hold the claim for the Company in his own name, or hold it in his own name on his own account. The reply was vague, and McLoughlin, who had constructed a sawmill and begun a gristmill opposite the island, took the claim in his own name.

On 5 July 1843, the newly organized Provisional Government of Oregon, which was dominated by the Methodists, passed a Law of Land Claims which excluded McLoughlin from the Oregon City site. After making provision for individual claims of 640 acres, the law prohibited individuals from claiming water privileges on city or townsites. However, such claims made by any mission previous to the passage of the act were exempt from this provision provided that the claim was not more than six miles square. The obstacles placed before McLoughlin continued to grow, for in December, John Ricord, an attorney acting for Waller, wrote a proclamation "to the people of Oregon" stating that McLoughlin had made no formal claim to the land until two and a half years after Waller had moved to the Falls, that McLoughlin had never resided on the land he claimed, and that the Hudson's Bay Company, not McLoughlin, was the claimant in fact. This statement forced McLoughlin to deny in writing that the claim belonged to the Company. McLoughlin hired Jesse Applegate, an immigrant of 1843, to survey his land claim and draw a plat of Oregon City, as the settlement had come to be called, and Applegate's survey was filed with the territorial recorder on 16 December 1843 in accordance with the provisions of the land law of 1843.

McLoughlin's prospects for a satisfactory settlement of the issue brightened during 1844. In April the disbanding of the Methodist Mission enabled McLoughlin to come to terms with the troublesome Mr. Waller, who had applied to the U.S. Supreme Court for a ruling in November 1843. By means of arbitration, in which James Douglas, Elijah White, and William Gilpin represented McLoughlin, an agreement was reached whereby McLoughlin consented to give Waller five acres and five hundred dollars, and the Methodist Mission was confirmed in the possession of fourteen lots. In June 1844 a new land law was passed which repealed the article of the 1843 law that had reserved water privileges in townsites. On 15 July, Rev. George Gary, who was in Oregon to close the affairs of the Methodist Mission, offered to sell the mission property back to McLoughlin. He excluded the two lots on which the church was located as well as the warehouse and George Abernethy's house. At a cost of $6,000 ($2,200 for lots and $3,800 for improvements), McLoughlin was finally able to secure undisputed ownership of these properties.

A new crisis developed, however, when Simpson decided that the Company should not accept McLoughlin's bills because there was little likelihood that the Company's rights at the Falls would be recognized by the American government. McLoughlin concluded that the only way to protect the considerable amount he had invested at Oregon City was to show proof that the property was bought and paid for. Therefore, on 20 March 1845 he wrote a private letter to Simpson in which he enclosed two personal drafts totaling £4,173 11s. 6d. in payment for the claim and Company improvements at the Falls during Outfits 1843 and 1844.[53] Because of conflicting evidence within McLoughlin's letter his real intention in forwarding these drafts is not clear. It appears, however, that he wanted the drafts to be on deposit as proof of his personal ownership in the event that the Company could not hold the claim. Simpson, on the other hand, chose to interpret McLoughlin's letter as an indication that the doctor wished to buy the mills and other Company property outright. Accordingly, he accepted McLoughlin's offer and hastily submitted the drafts to London where they were charged to McLoughlin's account on 20 August.[54]

The rapid settlement of the Willamette Valley by Americans during the early 1840s caused further disruption in the affairs of the Columbia

53. The draft for Outfit 1843 (1 June 1842–31 May 1843) was for £685 12s. 2d., which represented the Company's expenses during the year in which McLoughlin began construction of the mills at Oregon City. The draft for Outfit 1844 (1 June 1843–31 May 1844) was for £3487 19s. 4d. Simpson to McLoughlin, Red River Settlement, 14 June 1845, in John McLoughlin, *The Letters of John McLoughlin from Fort Vancouver to the Governor and Committee, Third Series, 1844–46*, ed. E. E. Rich, p. xlix.

54. This summary of the complicated land claim issue is based on the following accounts and sources: Frederick V. Holman, *Dr. John McLoughlin*, pp. 101–20; McLoughlin, *Letters, Third Series*, pp. xl–li, 195–219; *Oregon Spectator*, 6 January 1848.

Department. By the end of 1844 about three thousand Americans were settled in the Oregon country, and with the population increase came renewed agitation for the extension of American law to the Columbia. Oregon City soon became the trading center of the Willamette Valley, and three American trading stores were opened there between 1841 and 1843. In the early days of the immigration, Fort Vancouver was the only source of supply, and even with the coming of the first American merchants, superior capital resources and well-developed markets in Hawaii, Alaska, and California enabled the Company to dominate the economy. The stock of goods in American stores was limited in variety and quantity, and the lack of shipping facilities impeded the development of independent markets for Oregon's wheat, lumber, and salmon.[55]

In the early years of the immigration many of the settlers had arrived with little or no money and a scanty stock of provisions. McLoughlin had clothed or fed them, and in many instances he had loaned them seed and implements with which to begin farming. However, with the large immigration totaling some 875 persons in 1843, he could no longer do this. Instead, he began giving credit, and by the spring of 1844, he had made advances totaling £ 6,606 (about $32,000) to between three and four hundred settlers. Provisions were evidently provided on twelve months' credit without interest charges, and seed wheat was loaned at a charge of six bushels on the hundred until crops were raised. Simpson objected strenuously to this policy; but McLoughlin explained that he was not acting purely from humanitarian motives, for if supplies had not been made available, they would have been appropriated by force.[56]

Although the annual profits from sales and trade at Fort Vancouver for the seven years ending in 1846 averaged over £ 30,000, there was a marked decline in the fur returns as the intensive trapping of the Company's brigades took its toll. McLoughlin's disputes with Simpson over the coastal trade and the murder of John McLoughlin, Jr., had become increasingly disturbing to the governor and committee, and his

55. Arthur L. Throckmorton, *Oregon Argonauts*, p. 30.
56. *Niles National Register*, 4 October 1845, p. 65; Joseph Watt, "Recollections of Dr. John McLoughlin," pp. 24–25; Nathaniel Ford to Dr. John J. Lowry of Fayette, Missouri, dated Oregon, 6 April 1845 (first published in the Fayette *Missouri Democrat* and reprinted in the *Jefferson* [Missouri] *Inquirer*, 25 September 1845) in James Clyman, *James Clyman, Frontiersman, 1792–1881*, ed. Charles L. Camp, p. 271; McLoughlin, *Letters, Third Series*, p. 296.

management was further called into question by Simpson's report of his generous treatment of the American settlers and by the decline in the revenue from the districts west of the Rocky Mountains.[57] In March 1844, Archibald Barclay, a member of the London committee, informed Simpson that McLoughlin would have to be removed from the superintendency of the Columbia Department. In November, when news of the large credit which McLoughlin had extended to the settlers reached London, the committee took action. McLoughlin was told that "the advantages . . . which the Governor and Committee had hoped would be derived from placing the Columbia Department under the charge of one person" had "not been realized," that the department would be divided into at least two districts, and that his salary of £ 500 as superintendent of the unsuccessful Puget's Sound Agricultural Company would cease on 31 May 1845.[58]

In June 1845 the council of the Northern Department, meeting at Red River, set up a three-man board of management for the Columbia Department to be composed of James Douglas, Peter Skene Ogden, and McLoughlin. McLoughlin seems to have had no suspicion that he was to be relieved of his command, and this crushing blow was soon followed by the news that his drafts for the Oregon City improvements had been accepted. On 6 January 1846, McLoughlin moved from Fort Vancouver to Oregon City, and on 20 March he notified Simpson that he did not intend to resume active duty with the Company. McLoughlin's resignation could hardly have surprised Simpson, for the governor knew that in accepting the drafts he would force McLoughlin to give his personal attention to the Oregon property and that the proud chief factor would not remain with the Company in a subordinate position. After a year's furlough, McLoughlin was granted a two-year leave of absence, and his formal retirement was dated 1 June 1849. His full share of the profits accruing to his chief factorship continued through Outfit 1850, and for another five years he received a half share of the Company's profits.[59]

Until the end of the Company's financial year on 31 May 1846, business

57. Galbraith, *The Hudson's Bay Company*, p. 249; McLoughlin, *Letters*, *Third Series*, pp. lii, lvi–lvii, 289.

58. Barclay to McLoughlin, 30 November 1844, quoted in McLoughlin, *Letters*, *Third Series*, p. lviii.

59. Ibid., pp. lx–lxi; Thomas Lowe, "Private Journal Kept at Fort Vancouver Columbia River, 1843–1850," p. 32. Chief factors received 2/85s of the profits on each year's outfit.

at the Falls continued as before. The profits for the year amounted to £ 3,854, and these were divided between McLoughlin and the Company in proportion to the capital each had invested. On this basis, McLoughlin received £ 1,053 and the Company, £ 2,801. McLoughlin then took over the mills and sales shop on his own account; but the Company, left with a large inventory of goods, continued its retail business in Oregon City in quarters which were rented from McLoughlin for £ 121 per year.[60] McLoughlin, after twenty years as superintendent of the vast Columbia Department, now found his role reduced to that of a merchant and entrepreneur. He leased his sawmills to Walter Pomeroy and Absalom Hedges for two years at $1,000 per year, but operated the gristmill and the sales shop, which he had opened for the Company in 1844, himself. McLoughlin did not renew the lease when it expired in June 1848, for with the rising demand for lumber in California, he felt he could do better by managing the sawmills personally.[61]

Merchant and Miller, 1846–57

Until the California gold rush, Oregon's economy was based on a modified barter system. The settlers were largely dependent on wheat for export, and finding markets was difficult. The Hudson's Bay Company monopolized the Alaskan market through its contract of 1839 to supply the Russian-American Company, and by 1846 the Company was shipping an estimated twelve to fifteen thousand bushels of wheat to Sitka annually. In California the market was also limited, and only in Hawaii was there any sizable demand for Oregon wheat and lumber. A lack of shipping facilities gave rise to large surpluses of wheat and a shortage of manufactured goods. The dominant position of the Hudson's Bay Company with its superior capital, its established markets, and its regular supply system served to control prices. Wheat, the standard of trade, generally brought $ .60 to $ .625 cents a bushel and was exchanged at established granaries for orders on the merchants. These certificates passed for currency, and

60. McLoughlin, *Letters, Third Series*, pp. lxi, 138n.

61. Ibid., pp. lxi, 159n. See Letter 76, to Messrs. Starkey, Janion & Co. In February 1846 a thousand feet of lumber were destroyed in a fire at McLoughlin's sawmill. This loss may have encouraged him to put the mills into the hands of men who could devote full time to their management. *Oregon Spectator*, 19 February 1846.

in 1845 the Provisional Government made such certificates lawful tender in an effort to alleviate the chronic shortage of specie.[62]

The shortage of manufactured goods served to aggravate the economic ills of Oregon. During the five-year period 1843–48, only five ships arrived in the Columbia with cargoes of goods direct from the United States, and the quantity of goods imported from Hawaii could not be increased so long as Oregon products found a limited market there. While the Hudson's Bay Company carried a complete line of goods which they sold at 133 percent on the prime London cost, the few American merchants usually carried short, poorly assorted stocks of merchandise. The Hudson's Bay Company, which some settlers called "the monster," was often blamed for this situation, and it was generally agreed that the fundamental and aggravating cause of the economic problems was a lack of competition between both the buyers and sellers of merchandise. Oregon needed more merchants and more capital.[63]

When McLoughlin moved to Oregon City in January 1846, the community had a population of about five hundred; in addition to two blacksmith shops (which McLoughlin called "foundaries"), four tailor shops, a hatter shop, two silversmiths, two churches (Methodist and Catholic), and two taverns, there were four retail stores, two sawmills, two flour

62. Throckmorton, *Oregon Argonauts*, pp. 58–59; James Henry Gilbert, *Trade and Currency in Early Oregon*, pp. 46–47; *Oregon Spectator*, 19 February 1846, 4 March 1847.

The legislature of the Provisional Government passed two acts relative to the use of wheat and wheat certificates as currency. The first, passed on 12 December 1845, was "An Act Relative to the Currency, and Subjecting Property to Execution." This act said, in part, "that in addition to gold and silver, treasury drafts, approved orders on solvent merchants, and good merchantable wheat at the market price, delivered at such places as it is customary for merchants to receive wheat at, shall be lawful tender for the payment of taxes and judgments rendered in the courts of Oregon Territory, and for the payment of all debts contracted in Oregon Territory, where no special contracts have been made to the contrary." The second act, also passed on 12 December 1845, was "An Act to Regulate Weights and Measures," which defined the bushel of wheat used in the payment of debts as sixty pounds, thus making the American bushel rather than the Imperial bushel of seventy pounds the standard. Territory of Oregon, *Laws of a General and Local Nature*, pp. 33, 102.

63. Throckmorton, *Oregon Argonauts*, pp. 56–57, 59; Gilbert, *Trade and Currency*, p. 67; McLoughlin, *Letters, Third Series*, p. 157; *Oregon Spectator*, 10 December 1846.

mills, and a tannery.[64] George Abernethy, who had succeeded to the mercantile and manufacturing interests of the Methodist Mission, operated one of the stores and a flour and sawmill on Abernethy Island. The other mills were those owned by McLoughlin, who also operated the former Hudson's Bay Company store in which he sold building materials, groceries, and clothing. John H. Couch, who arrived in 1842 as a representative of J. P. Cushing and Company of Newburyport, Massachusetts, and Francis W. Pettygrove, who arrived in 1843 to establish a store for Benson and Brother of New York, operated the other two stores. The Hudson's Bay Company soon established a new store in quarters rented from McLoughlin.[65]

In 1846, with an estimated population of six thousand, Oregon had about six grist or flour mills and six or eight sawmills. McLoughlin's square-timbered flour mill with three pairs of French buhrstones (or burrstones), which could grind one hundred barrels of flour daily, was evidently the largest and finest in Oregon. The mill, completed early in 1846, had been begun in July 1843 by Walter Pomeroy and Philip Foster, who contracted to erect a building 63 feet long, 43 feet wide, and 27½ feet high for $2200, all but $400 of which was to be payable in goods at Fort Vancouver. In September 1843 they agreed to complete the mill dam for an additional $1,175. Little is known about McLoughlin's sawmills, but in the spring of 1848, when Pomeroy had decided not to renew his lease, McLoughlin planned to operate them himself and estimated that the two sawmills could produce about one million feet of lumber annually. McLoughlin estimated Oregon's population that year at fifteen to twenty thousand, and with increased local demand, new markets in California, and continuing shipments to Hawaii, the number of mills had increased. There were, in 1848, probably eight flour and fifteen sawmills in Oregon. McLoughlin improved and expanded his mills at considerable expense. Estimates made in 1851 valued his flour mill at $15,347 and the granary at $3,185. McLoughlin's original sawmill was valued at $2,300, and a "new" one at $2,000. In addition, a value of $6,020 was placed on the canals, bull wheels, and gates ancillary to the operation of the mills. Following McLoughlin's death in 1857, his son-in-law, Daniel Harvey, assumed the management of the mills,

64. *Oregon Spectator*, 19 February 1846.
65. Throckmorton, *Oregon Argonauts*, p. 55.

but the severe floods on the Willamette in December 1861 carried away McLoughlin's mills as well as those belonging to George Abernethy.[66]

Unfortunately, few details of McLoughlin's business career in Oregon City have come to light. However, from the letters which follow, a picture of his diverse and far-ranging activities begins to emerge. McLoughlin's twenty-one years as chief of the Columbia Department gave him the advantage of influential contacts in London, Montreal, Honolulu, and San Francisco. It is evident that he was able to order a limited quantity of English goods, which were superior to most American merchandise and yet were cheaper, directly from the Hudson's Bay Company in London. Most of his merchandise, however, was imported from the Hawaiian Islands through his agent, George Pelly, who was also the Company's agent there. Although the California market was limited, McLoughlin shipped both lumber and wheat to his San Francisco agent, William A. Leidesdorff. The lack of shipping facilities was a problem for McLoughlin, but in 1846 he purchased a partnership in the firm of F. W. Pettygrove and Company for his son David at a cost of $20,000.[67] Thereafter he shipped some of his produce on the *Toulon*, which the firm controlled. McLoughlin's financial resources enabled him to speculate in sugar, coffee, and other supplies, and he attempted to open markets for Oregon's wheat and lumber in ports as distant as Tahiti and Manila. Although the letters afford no basis for re-examining the economic history of Oregon for the period, they do provide a tantalizing glimpse into the varied trading ventures of an early "merchant adventurer." The letters also shed new light on a little-known period in the life of "the Father of Oregon."

As some of the letters show, McLoughlin's last years were embittered by the problems of his land claim and his opinion of the treatment which he had received from the Hudson's Bay Company. As has been shown, the Company made generous financial arrangements with

66. Hubert Howe Bancroft, *History of Oregon*, 2:730; Clyman, *James Clyman*, pp. 271, 276; Joel Palmer, *Journal of Travels over the Rocky Mountains*, p. 189; Throckmorton, *Oregon Argonauts*, pp. 92, 218; Charlotte H. Odgers, "Philip Foster, Pioneer Entrepreneur," pp. 30–31; "Cost of Improvements Made by Dr. John McLoughlin at Willamette Falls to Jan. 1, 1851," p. 68. See Letter 76, to Messrs. Starkey, Janion & Co.; Letter 81, to Sir William Drummond Stewart; and Letter 100, to Messrs. Albert Pelly & Co.

67. Francis W. Pettygrove, "Oregon in 1843," pp. 21–23.

McLoughlin on his removal to Oregon City. However, McLoughlin did not fare so well in the matter of his land claim. In 1845 McLoughlin consulted with Jesse Applegate and Peter Burnett, then the chief justice for the Provisional Government, about taking an oath of allegiance to the United States. By so doing, McLoughlin sought to protest his rights when American jurisdiction was extended to Oregon. The Provisional Government had no legal standing, however, and Burnett was not authorized to administer such an oath. The United States acquired territorial jurisdiction in Oregon by the treaty of 15 June 1846; but not until 2 March 1849 did Governor Joseph Lane arrive to organize the territory. On 30 May, McLoughlin took an oath of allegiance to the United States and declared his intention to become an American citizen, and on 5 September 1851 his citizenship was granted.

In the meantime, however, it appears that a conspiracy against McLoughlin was formed in Oregon by George Abernethy and Samuel R. Thurston, Oregon's territorial delegate. Thurston, the candidate of the Methodist Mission faction led by Abernethy, was elected delegate in June 1849; and it was well known that McLoughlin, whom Abernethy called "a Catholic and one of the most bigoted kind," had not voted for the Methodist candidate. Once in Washington, Thurston sought the passage of the Oregon Donation Land Bill which granted a half section to single men and a whole section to married men who were citizens or who declared their intention to become citizens by 1 December 1851. The act further provided that no alien could receive a patent until his naturalization had been completed, and it prohibited those claiming rights under the Oregon Treaty (principally the Hudson's Bay Company and, by extension, McLoughlin) from taking claims under the Donation Land Law. By the infamous eleventh section, Thurston had the "Oregon city claim" reserved to the legislative assembly, the proceeds of which were to be used for the establishment and support of a state university. Abernethy Island, which was confirmed to the legal assigns of Abernethy's Willamette Milling and Trading Company, was specifically exempted from this provision. All lots purchased from McLoughlin, who was named in the act, prior to 4 March 1849 were, however, confirmed to the purchaser.[68]

68. John McLoughlin, "Letter of Dr. John McLoughlin to *Oregon Statesman*, June 8, 1852," p. 296; United States, *Statutes at Large*, "Donation Land Act," pp. 496–99.

In May or June 1850, Thurston, in a letter to Congress, asserted that McLoughlin, whom he labeled "the chief fugleman" for the Hudson's Bay Company, had refused to become a citizen and that he had realized over $200,000 from the sale of land at Oregon City. Thurston referred Congress to William P. Bryant, then in Washington to lobby for passage of the bill, for confirmation of the charge that McLoughlin had refused to file his intention of becoming an American citizen. In a questionable move, Abernethy had sold his mills and logs at Oregon City to Bryant, the newly arrived territorial chief justice, on 29 May 1849 for $35,000, and while Abernethy's correspondence gives no indication of his complicity in having Bryant testify against McLoughlin, Bancroft states that Bryant was bribed outright by the law's reservation of Abernethy Island to the legal assigns of Abernethy's milling company. The transfer appears even more questionable in the light of Abernethy's quick repossession of the claim.[69]

Thurston's letter to Congress was published in the *Oregon Spectator* on 12 September 1850 with a reply by McLoughlin in which the doctor stated that he realized only $20,000 from the sale of his Oregon City lots and that he had donated more than three hundred lots to the Methodists, Catholics, Presbyterians, Congregationalists, and Baptists. On 19 September fifty-six persons, mostly those who had bought property from McLoughlin after 4 March 1849, petitioned Congress for confirmation of their lands. Almost as an afterthought, they included statements decrying the unjust treatment of McLoughlin and praising him for his services to the Oregon settlers.

The resolutions reached Congress too late, however, for the Donation Land Law was passed on 27 September. Although other meetings at Salem and in Linn County praised Thurston, Congress was disturbed by the negative reaction of the residents of Oregon City, and Thurston went to great lengths to defend his actions as being responsive to the will of the people. He made the mistake of writing to Nathaniel Wyeth, who, instead of denouncing McLoughlin as expected, warmly praised him. The damage was done, however, and not during his lifetime was McLoughlin to secure his claim. A memorial to restore McLoughlin's claim to him was presented to the territorial legislature three times between 1852–53 and 1855–56, but each time it was tabled indefinitely.

69. Bancroft, *History of Oregon*, 2:122; Throckmorton, *Oregon Argonauts*, pp. 96–97n.

Finally, in 1862, five years after McLoughlin's death, the state legislature passed an act conveying the McLoughlin claim at Oregon City, except Abernethy Island, to McLoughlin's heirs on condition that they pay $1,000 to the University Fund of Oregon.[70]

McLoughlin was never actually dispossessed of his lands and business, and he continued to occupy the large, white house which he had constructed in 1845–46 near the riverbank at the Falls. In April 1851 he was elected mayor of the city he had founded, succeeding William K. Kilborne under a new charter he had opposed.[71] His term was a short one, however, for he resigned in October for unstated reasons, although an advertisement in the *Oregon Spectator* announced that he planned to leave for the United States.[72] McLoughlin's last years were filled with bitterness toward those whom he had served for over thirty years, the Hudson's Bay Company and the American settlers in Oregon. Yet in the case of the Hudson's Bay Company he had largely brought his troubles on himself through his unbending opposition to Governor Simpson's policies,[73] and in the case of the American settlers he was the victim of a few unscrupulous men. He died in Oregon City on 3 September

70. Holman, *Dr. John McLoughlin*, pp. 121–60, remains the most complete account of the land claim issue. See also Bancroft, *History of Oregon*, 2:120–23; Throckmorton, *Oregon Argonauts*, pp. 96–97n; *Oregon Spectator*, 12 September 1850.

71. *Oregon Spectator*, 2 January, 10 April 1851. McLoughlin received forty-four votes, and his opponent, the incumbent William K. Kilborne, received twenty-two votes.

72. Advertisement running from 14 October 1851 to 16 March 1852, ibid., *Oregon City Enterprise*, 12 August 1948, quoting the first Book of City Council Record, Oregon City.

73. No doubt Simpson frequently had cause to reflect on his characterization of McLoughlin written in 1832. McLoughlin was, noted Simpson, "very zealous in the discharge of his public duties and a man of strict honor and integrity but a great stickler for rights & privileges and sets himself up for a righter of wrongs. Very anxious to obtain a lead among his colleagues with whom he has not much influence owing to his ungovernable violent temper and turbulent disposition, and would be a troublesome man to the Comp'y if he had sufficient influence to form and tact to manage a party, in short, would be a Radical in any Country under any Government and under any circumstances; and if he had not pacific people to deal with, would be eternally embroiled in 'affairs of honor' on the merest trifles arising I conceive from the irritability of his temper more than a quarrelsome disposition.— Altogether a disagreeable man to do business with as it is impossible to go with him in all things and

1857. So closed a career that had embraced and largely guided an entire era of Pacific Northwest history, from trapper's wilderness to city's commerce.

THE MCLOUGHLIN LETTER BOOK, 1847–48

John McLoughlin's correspondence for the period from 22 March 1847 to 27 May 1848 was copied into a letter book which passed into the possession of his daughter, Eloisa Harvey. At her death in 1884, the volume and other family documents became the property of her son, James Harvey, and eventually they were given to Mrs. Frank R. Clawson, a niece of Harvey's wife. In 1962 the United States National Park Service purchased the letter book and other items once belonging to John McLoughlin from Mrs. Clawson. These were deposited in the collections at Fort Vancouver National Historic Site, Vancouver, Washington; but the letter book was later transferred on indefinite loan to the Oregon Historical Society in Portland, Oregon. Since few of McLoughlin's letters for the period following his retirement from the Hudson's Bay Company in 1846 are known to be extant, the letter book is a valuable addition to the scant information available on his business activities in Oregon City.

The letter book, which measures eight by twelve and a half inches, contains one hundred one letters, all but ten of them copied into the book in McLoughlin's own handwriting. The book contains sixty leaves of light blue paper faintly lined and is bound in black board covers. The end paper inside the front cover contains the manufacturer's mark as follows: "Burrup & Blight./ Stationers,/ & Ruled Account Book Manufacturers/ on the Patent Principle./ Retail & for Exportation/ 36 Lombard St. corner of Plough Court,/ Late Royal Exchange/ London./ Engraving & Printing." Page one is blank except for the following which is penciled in the upper left-hand corner in McLoughlin's writing:

In 1842	137
43	875
44	1475
45	3000

a difference of opinion almost amounts to a declaration of hostilities, yet a good hearted man and a pleasant companion." Douglas MacKay, *The Honourable Company*, p. 199, quoting George Simpson, "Book of Servants' Characters" (1832).

Although otherwise unidentified, these figures almost certainly refer to the number of American immigrants arriving in Oregon for the years specified, for they match figures on immigration given by McLoughlin in his remarks on the report of Warre and Vavasour which were enclosed in a letter from Peter Skene Ogden and James Douglas to Sir George Simpson, Fort Vancouver, 16 March 1847. The same figures are also found in a document ascribed to McLoughlin which was published by the Oregon Historical Society in 1900.[74]

EDITORIAL PROCEDURE

The original text of the letters has been reproduced as closely as possible with several departures based on common sense. McLoughlin rarely used punctuation, and his sentences run on interminably. Where the meaning was clear, these lengthy sentences have been broken by periods, and capitalization has been added if necessary. Missing periods or question marks have been supplied, and dashes, which McLoughlin often used to indicate a change in thought, are eliminated where periods have been inserted by the editor. No attempt has been made to punctuate within the sentences thus formed, and all internal punctuation remains as McLoughlin or his copyist used it, even to the extent of leaving quotation marks or parentheses unclosed. In abbreviations, raised letters have been brought down, but no period has been supplied unless it was in the manuscript. McLoughlin evidently wrote rapidly and, I might add, carelessly. He often repeated words and frequently added interlineations or deleted errors. In all cases, words needlessly repeated have been omitted and interlineations have been included. In those cases where the copyist deleted words from the manuscript because he had made an error, they have not been included; in those cases where such deletions would alter or supplement the meaning of the sentence, they have been allowed to stand, but are italicized and inclosed in brackets. Unitalicized words in brackets indicate the editor's interpretation of an illegible word or a clarifying insertion.

McLoughlin was an erratic speller at best, but "*sic*" has been used sparingly to indicate only those misspellings which might confuse the reader. In the matter of capitalization, McLoughlin was at his most versa-

74. McLoughlin, *Letters, Third Series*, p. 289; John McLoughlin, "A Narrative of Events in Early Oregon Ascribed to Dr. John McLoughlin," pp. 198–200, 206.

[1]

tile. Many of his lower case and capital letters were formed alike, and his use of capitals was not always consistent. The man has utterly defeated me in some cases, and faulty interpretation may be the result, but I have coped with the confusing situation as best I can. With these exceptions, the text follows the originals as closely as is typographically possible. Except in the cases indicated in the letter heading, all of the letters are in McLoughlin's handwriting. In those letters where McLoughlin did not address his correspondent by name, internal evidence has indicated for whom the letter was intended. In these few instances, the addressee's name has been inclosed in brackets in the letter heading.

THE NOTES

Biographical material on McLoughlin's correspondents and those individuals mentioned in his letters is found in Appendix C, but only for the first use of the name is there a footnote referring the reader to that appendix. Ship movements are noted where the information is of importance, but as this information is compiled in more convenient form in Appendix B, I have tried to avoid unnecessary footnoting for these vessels.

John McLoughlin's Business Correspondence, 1847–48

1. To Peter Skene Ogden and James Douglas[1]

Oregon City 22nd March 1847

P S Ogden ⎫
James Douglass ⎬   Esqr

Gentlemen

This will be handed you by my Son David[2] and I wish you would inform me by him What Quantity of Wheat you can sell me and the price pr Bushel[3] also what quantity of flour and the price pr Barrel[4] to be paid on Delivery in Cash or Bills on Oahu or Canada or the states.

I am
Gentlemen
Yours Respectfully
Jn McLoughlin

There is a Kiln for drying Wheat will you sell it and let me Know the price?

1. For biographical information on Ogden and Douglas, see Appendix C.
2. David McLoughlin. See Appendix C.
3. According to the *Oregon Spectator*, two measures for wheat were in use in Oregon. The Hudson's Bay Co. generally used the Imperial bushel of seventy pounds, while the American bushel weighed sixty to sixty-three pounds. During 1847 and 1848, the Hudson's Bay Co. paid the farmer $ .60 to $ .625 per bushel delivered at Vancouver and sold wheat at Sitka for $1.20 per bushel.

[3]

2. TO PETER SKENE OGDEN AND JAMES DOUGLAS

Oregon City 29th March 1847

P S Ogden ⎫
            Esqr
James Douglas ⎭

Gentlemen

I Received yours of 25 Instant and will take the four hundred Barrels here at Eight and a half Dollars pr Barrel and pay the cash on Delivery.[5]

The stockton is arrived she carries only Between Six and Seven hundred Barrels flour and is Chartered at six hundred Dollars pr month.[6] My

---

At Champoeg, the Company paid $ .80 per bushel, but there merchandise was priced 47 percent higher than at Vancouver. *Oregon Spectator*, 4 March, 15 April 1847.

4. It is possible to compute the weight of a barrel of flour from statements made in the *Oregon Spectator* that five bushels of wheat yielded a barrel of flour. Since one Imperial bushel of wheat yielded forty pounds of flour, a barrel would weigh 200 pounds. During the spring of 1847 the Hudson's Bay Co. price varied from $6.50 to $10.00 per barrel. *Oregon Spectator*, 4 February, 4 March, 15 April 1847.

5. The Hudson's Bay Co. produced flour at a cost of $6.55 per barrel, but the price quoted to McLoughlin was well under the $10.00 per barrel which the Company charged the Willamette settlers. In spite of the high cost of flour in Oregon, good profits could be made by those who were able to ship it to California or Hawaii early in the season before the market was glutted. In April 1847, Morton M. McCarver announced in the columns of the *Oregon Spectator* that flour was selling in small quantities in California for $25.00 to $30.00 per barrel, while even after the arrival of the *Toulon* with Oregon flour in January 1847, flour sold at $15.00, for a profit of $10.00 per barrel. McCarver added that in Hawaii the navy was buying flour at $17.00 per barrel. *Oregon Spectator*, 15 April 1847.

However, the risks taken by merchants such as McLoughlin were great: the cost of freight to the Sandwich Islands (Hawaii) was estimated at $2.00 per barrel; and the arrival of a cargo of flour could drive the price down to $8.00 or even $6.00 from the usual price of $10.00 to $16.00 per barrel. Ibid., 4 February, 18 March 1847.

The cost of flour in Oregon was considerably higher than east of the Mississippi, and only the high freight charges on flour shipped from eastern ports permitted Oregon's flour to compete in the markets of California and Hawaii. In 1847, according to the *Oregon Spectator*, a barrel of flour sold for $7.125 in New York City, and in July 1848 the price of flour was quoted at $5.50 a barrel in New Orleans, $4.50 in St. Louis, and $6.00 in New York. In

[4]

son David took 1/3 for me as an Experiment But I am of opinion Shelly and Norris will not have flour to fill at Eight and a half Dollars pr Barrel.[7] In case Shelly and Norris cannot fill her up and if I have not the cash will you take a Draft on Oahu as I have cash there and in the Event of my Wanting cash here will you take my Bill on Oahu?

I am

Gentlemen

Yours Respectfully

John McLoughlin

PS I Received a letter from California by the Stockton Requesting to know if I could supply from one to three thousand Barrels flour by contract deliverable Between this and first July. They want to know the price pr Barrel so as to take their measure. Accordingly will you please to inform me so as I may give them an answer?

Boston, a major port in the Pacific trade, the price of flour varied from $5.50 to $8.19 per barrel during 1846 and 1848. *The Commercial Review of the South and West (De Bow's Review)*, July 1848, p. 64; *Oregon Spectator*, 30 September 1847; Carroll D. Wright, *Comparative Wages, Prices, and Cost of Living*, p. 107.

6. The *Commodore Stockton*, originally named the *Pallas*, was a schooner of about one hundred tons which first arrived in Oregon in September 1843 carrying goods consigned to John H. Couch and Albert E. Wilson (see Appendix C) by J. P. Cushing & Co. of Newburyport, Massachusetts. During 1847 the *Commodore Stockton*, P. Young, captain, made one trip to the Columbia River. She arrived at the mouth of the Columbia on 25 March and departed from Portland for California on 12 April loaded with 450 barrels of flour and 7,000 feet of lumber. The *Commodore Stockton* was wrecked near Marguerite Bay, Lower California, on 20 January 1848 while en route from San Francisco to Mazatlán, Mexico, and Callao, Peru. *California Star* (San Francisco), 10 June 1848, quoting the *Polynesian* (Honolulu); John McLoughlin, "Documentary: Letter, Doctor John McLoughlin to Sir George Simpson, March 20, 1844," ed. Katharine B. Judson, p. 235; *Oregon Spectator*, 1 April, 15 April, 13 May 1847, 7 September 1848, quoting the *Polynesian*; Avery Sylvester, "Voyages of the *Pallas* and *Chenamus*, 1843–45," p. 259.

7. The San Francisco trading firm of Shelly & Norris operated during 1847 and 1848 from rooms in the City Hotel, built in 1846 by William A. Leidesdorff (see Appendix C). The partners were Pearson B. Shelly and Samuel Norris, a trader at Sutter's New Helvetia and at San Francisco. In October 1847, McLoughlin reported that the firm had purchased Leidesdorff's property for $75,000 (see Letter 55, to George Pelly). The firm seems to have been dissolved when Norris went to the gold mines on the Yuba River in 1848. Bancroft, *History of California*, 4:755, 5:680, 718.

[5]

3. To James Douglas

Oregon City 6th April 1847

Private

James Douglass Esqr

Dear Sir

The Enclosed came from Mr Roberts[8] of the Hudson Bay house will you do me the favor to deliver it according to address.

I Received yours of the 2nd and allow me to observe you and Mr Ogden have taken a very mistaken view in putting as high a price on flour as nine Dollars pr Barrel. It is true flour was high when my son was in California But if he had not chartered a Vessel I would not of optioned [to] send flour at such high freight to California as it must fall and the object ought to be to Establish a Business to secure the Market and the people will not come here to pay Nine Dollars pr Barrel for flour when they can get it for four at Valparaiso and five or Six in New York. The object of my Correspondent is to Endeavour to get the Contract for supplying the U S Navy with flour and Biscuit from this you must see it is an object to get his custom though perhaps a few Barrels may sell Well still you may depend that flour will have to fall Between five and Six deliverable here and that this very Season and this will bring it on a Level with New York and Valparaiso.[9]

I this Moment Received yours 5th [*April*] Instant and you will oblige me by a Copy of those Extracts to which you allude. Whether they will do me justice or not I cannot say. But the treatment I have Received is very different to what I consider myself Entitled to. I Received a letter from Mr Warre[10] But he says nothing of his Report But that

8. Edward Roberts. See Appendix C.

9. See Letter 2, to Peter Skene Ogden and James Douglas n. 5.

10. In 1845, during the height of the Oregon boundary dispute, the then Lieutenant Henry J. Warre (1819–98) of the Fourteenth Regiment and Lieutenant Mervin Vavasour of the Royal Engineers were selected by the commander of the forces in Canada, in consultation with Sir George Simpson, to conduct a confidential military reconnaissance of the area between Sault Sainte Marie and the Pacific Ocean. Traveling as tourists, they were conducted to the Oregon country by Peter Skene Ogden, who found them to be disagreeable companions. Although Ogden knew the true purpose of their trip, McLoughlin was kept in ignorance. Warre and Vavasour arrived at Fort Vancouver on 25 August

he has Been Well Received got a Captaincy and put on the staff I understand from the Way he Writes for his Services — was questioned to know if Masons Run was South or North of 49. But he could not say.

I am Dear Sir

Yours Respectfully

Jn McLoughlin

David is going to California he will call in passing on you. Mrs McL Mrs Rae and Mrs. E[11] compliments to the family not forgetting mine. The Rev Mr B[12] has not acted as he should he ought not to have gone the lengths he did.

JMcL

1845 and remained on the lower Columbia until 25 March 1846, when they began their return trip to Canada accompanied by Francis Ermatinger (see Appendix C). A portion of their lengthy report to the secretary of state for the colonies, dated at Red River Settlement (Winnipeg) on 16 June 1846, was critical of McLoughlin's policies toward the American immigrants on the Columbia.

"In conclusion, we must beg to be allowed to observe, with an unbiased opinion, that whatever may have been the orders, or the motives of the gentlemen in charge of the Hudson's Bay Company's posts on the west of the Rocky Mountains their policy has tended to the introduction of the American settlers into the country.

"We are convinced that without their assistance not 30 American families would now have been in the settlement. . . .

"Through motives of humanity, we are willing to believe, and from the anticipations of obtaining their exports of wheat and flour to the Russian settlements and to the Sandwich Islands, at a cheaper rate, the agents of the Hudson's Bay Company gave every encouragement to their settlement, and goods were forwarded to the Williamette Falls, and retailed to these citizens of the United States at even a more advantageous rate than to the British subjects. . . .

"Their [the Americans'] numbers have increased so rapidly that the British party are now in the minority, and the gentlemen of the Hudson's Bay Company have been obliged to join the organization [the Provisional Government], without any reserve except the mere form of the oath of office. Their lands are invaded — themselves insulted — and they now require the protection of the British Government against the very people to the introduction of whom they have been more than accessory." Joseph Schafer, ed., "Documents Relative to Warre and Vavasour's Military Reconnoissance in Oregon, 1845–6," pp. 81–82.

Governor Simpson sent extracts from the report (including the above-quoted portions) to Peter Skene Ogden, James Douglas, and John Work at Fort Vancouver. In his letter, dated 30 June 1846, he requested them to reply to the accusations of Warre and Vavasour and to obtain McLoughlin's observations

4. To David McLoughlin

Oregon City 10th April 1847

My Dear David

You will proceed without delay to Vancouver and take the Goods for Mr Leidorff[13]— as Regards myself I am in doubt if I ought to send any or not and you may do as you please. You will draw on me for the Goods you get.

You will sell what you have unless you have good Reasons for leaving

---

as well. Although Simpson had hoped that replies could be sent from Vancouver to London in the autumn, his letter evidently did not reach the Columbia until the spring of 1847. On 16 March 1847, Ogden and Douglas forwarded McLoughlin's remarks on the report (unsigned, undated, and in a clerk's writing) to Simpson with the comment that McLoughlin had furnished "so full and complete a refutation of the absurd and unfounded statements made by Messrs. Warre and Vavasour, that we deem it superfluous to make any further remarks on the subject." McLoughlin, *Letters, Third Series*, p. 285.

McLoughlin, who resented the fact that Warre and Vavasour had acted as spies without his knowledge, felt that they should have availed themselves of his offer to give them information. Above all, he resented the fact that they had not given him an opportunity to explain his actions before they submitted their report to London. Feeling his "character assasinated [*sic*] in the dark," McLoughlin wrote a lengthy and vigorous defense of his treatment of the immigrants. "And while acting as I did, I was only fulfilling the duties of humanity, still I was also pursuing the conduct most condusive to the interest of the Hudsons Bay Company's affairs under my charge, and while I did only what the necessity of the case required. But as it was done in a proper manner It was appreciated As if I had not lent Boats to transport them as soon as possible to the Wallamette if the Columbia froze, before they did, and I have known the Columbia freeze in the beginning of December, they would have fallen on our hands at Vancouver, and we would have to feed them, as of course they could not be allowed to starve, and besides the expense, it would cause us a great deal of trouble and inconvenience, misunderstandings would arise between them and us which might lead to great Evils. . . . And as people will not allow their families starve, when provisions are in their reach, if we had not assisted them Vancouver would have been destroyed, the world would have said we were treated in the manner our inhuman conduct deserved, the Character of the Hudsons Bay Company and its Officers, from the Governor to the youngest Officer, would be censured with obloquy, and the Company's business in this department would be ruined for which injury they never could get any indemnity and the troubles that would have arisen might have involved the British and American Nations in War.

[8]

it to be sold by Mr Leidsdorff and turn your cash into U S Bills and get them in triplicate. Two Bills you will send me the other you will send to Oahu to be remitted to my agent the Honble George Moffatt of Montreal to be carried to my credit.[14] You will draw them in your Name, Endorse them and Enclose in a letter Copy of which is subjoined. Of Course if you cannot go to Oahu you will if you can Return here Immediately. But if possible you ought to go to Oahu settle your Accounts with Mr Pelly[15] and the surplus funds I have (taking what you Require for your Business) you will Remit to Mr Moffatt one Bill of Exchange leaving one Copy at Oahu on deposit and Bringing the third here to be forwarded by the Express. You will Keep in Mind Mess Pomeroy and Hedges[16] have a large stock of Lumber and will supply

---

"As the Officer conducting the Hudsons Bay Company's business in this department, it was my duty to use my utmost exertions to manage it to the best advantage consistent with the duties of religion and the usages of business. As a good and faithful Subject it was my duty to do my utmost to maintain peace and order between the British Subjects and American Citizens, and I exerted my utmost endeavours to do so. . . . If difficulties unfortunately arose between British Subjects and American Citizens in this Country the two Nations would be involved in War. And if I have been the means by the measures I adopted, and the conduct I pursued of averting any of these evils I dreaded I will be amply repaid by the approbation of my own conscience and of all good men who will say I have done well. . . ." McLoughlin, *Letters, Third Series*, pp. 296–98.

Warre and Vavasour's report, or at least that portion of it relating to McLoughlin's conduct of the Company's affairs, was evidently the subject of a dispatch from the governor and committee to James Douglas dated 7 October 1846. Douglas mentioned this to McLoughlin in his letter of 5 April 1847, and a week later he sent copies of the extracts to McLoughlin. In his obvious haste to comment on Warre and Vavasour's criticisms in March, McLoughlin had evidently not made a copy of his remarks for himself, and on 30 July 1847 he asked Douglas to send him a copy of his original reply to the report. (See Letter 10, to James Douglas; Letter 20, to Peter Skene Ogden and James Douglas; Letter 29, to James Douglas.)

11. Eloisa McLoughlin Rae and Catherine Sinclair Ermatinger. See Appendix C.

12. Herbert Beaver. See Appendix C.

13. William A. Leidesdorff.

14. For biographical information on Moffatt, see Appendix C.

15. George Pelly. See Appendix C.

16. Walter Pomeroy and Absalom F. Hedges. See Appendix C.

Demands. They have given you their selling prices. Of course you will not make yourself Answerable for the freight on Chartering a Ship for them — let the Vessels come and they may depend on purchasing Lumber.[17]

If a Vessel comes I may have about a hundred Barrels flour for sale which I merely Mention for your information perhaps Mr Leidsdorf might find it worth his While to send for lumber.

Mind if you go to Oahu send me a Letter giving every information of Interest to us.

Keep in mind the price Mess Ogden and Douglass tell you about the flour. You may perhaps find some opportunity of transferring the Bargain at a profit for me.

There is one Wornbough Who is now in California[18] he Went away in my Debt you will try and get it collected for me you can put it in Mr Hastings[19] hands if you think proper. You will mention to Mr. Douglass that Hastings is in California — and perhaps he may write him about his Debt.

As to my funds which you will Realise in California or Oahu you will Remit them to Mr Moffat till further order as you may Deem Best.

Your affectionate parent

Jn McLoughlin

17. On 7 January 1847, the *Oregon Spectator* estimated that four of the six mills in Oregon had produced 1.5 million feet of lumber, the greater part of which was ready for shipment. Although few figures are available on the export of the products of Oregon's farms and forests, the *Spectator* did publish the figures for the exports during April 1847. Lumber exports on the American ships *Toulon, Commodore Stockton*, and *Henry* amounted to 171,000 feet, and the *Henry* also carried 96,000 shingles. In addition to the lumber carried on American vessels, it was estimated that the Hudson's Bay Co.'s bark *Columbia* carried 20,000 feet of lumber on her voyage to Honolulu. *Oregon Spectator*, 13 May 1847. During the spring and summer of 1847, pine lumber sold for $50 per thousand feet in California, while shingles brought $5 per thousand. Ibid., 10 June 1847. At the same time, lumber could be purchased in Oregon for $18 per thousand feet, but the freight charges to California amounted to as much as $20 per thousand. (See Letter 22, to George Pelly.)

18. M. M. Wornbough, who evidently left Oregon for California sometime during the spring of 1846. *Oregon Spectator*, 30 April 1846.

19. Lansford W. Hastings. See Appendix C.

5. TO [WILLIAM A. LEIDESDORFF]

Oregon City 10th April 1847

Private and Confidential

Dear Sir

I have the pleasure to Acknowledge the Receipt of your Kind favour 20th Feby last and Beg to Return you my thanks for your Kindness to my son David. He now Returns to see you again and has less flour than I might have put on Board if I had had more time as having only begun last year I have not got my affairs in order to do the flouring Business on a large Scale on Account of the Unsettled state of the Country and a Kind of Indecision from a Desire of selling out and a Desire to join you in California.[20] But in the mean time the prospect Brightens and I will have to Extend and it seems to me a good Business could be done Between this and California in

20. McLoughlin's intention to leave Oregon was probably already known to Leidesdorff through his close association with Thomas O. Larkin, the United States consul in Monterey. John A. Sutter, writing to Larkin on 2 March 1846, had announced that McLoughlin intended to establish himself in California. McLoughlin seems never to have taken positive steps to move to San Francisco, although in 1849 John Work informed Edward Ermatinger that McLoughlin "might obtain $200,000 for his property and is making money fast. I regret to hear that he lowers himself by keeping a shop and retailing out trifling articles to the Yankees." In October 1851, following his resignation as mayor of Oregon City, McLoughlin announced his intention of leaving for the United States. His extensive investments in Oregon City and the probability that full value could not be realized should he try to liquidate his holdings in land and mills evidently prevented McLoughlin from making any move from Oregon. Thomas Oliver Larkin, *The Larkin Papers*, ed. George P. Hammond, 4:219; advertisement in *Oregon Spectator*, 14 October 1851–16 March 1852; Paul C. Phillips, ed., "Family Letters of Two Oregon Fur Traders, 1828–1856," p. 41.

McLoughlin's depression concerning his business affairs and his growing bitterness toward both the Americans and the Hudson's Bay Co. was a source of concern to his former associates in the spring of 1847. On 15 March 1847 Peter Skene Ogden informed Governor Sir George Simpson of his concern for McLoughlin's mental health. "The old Doctor," said Ogden, "was in a most desponding state and at one time became so melancholy that serious apprehensions were entertained would loose his reason but from this unpleasant state he was in a great measure relieved by leasing his Saw Mills to an American by the name of Pomeroy. . . ." McLoughlin, *Letters, Third Series*, p. 159n.

[11]

lumber and flour as the U S Government will Require a Good Deal of Building and a good Deal of Lumber can be supplied during Summer from April to September Easily from the Columbia and during that time the persons who have my Mills[21] would Undertake to furnish 5 or 6 hundred thousand feet of lumber at [blank] Dollars pr M feet in Cash pr M and perhaps even your small Vessel the stockton might pay you a good freight. By purchasing the Lumber from them you could get lumber of any Dimensions in the Month of May say from the fifteenth to the fifteenth of June the Stockton could come to my Mills or very nigh and if you had clean Wheat the Grinding will cost you a tenth of the Wheat (this is Cheaper than Usual because you come from a Distance and While Grinding she might take a Cargo of Lumber to San Francisco and Return for the flour But you would have to pay for flour Barrels 75 Cents packing and Coopering [blank] Cent pr Barrel which I mention in case it be of use.[22]

I have noticed your Remarks to make a Contract with Government for flour. As I had some I Enquired of Mess Ogden and Douglas my Successors in Managing the Hudson Bay Companys affairs the price of flour (But this was before I Received your letter) and they would only sell me four hundred Barrels half of which I let Crossby[23] have the other half I send pr Stockton.[24] On Receiving your letter and seeing

21. Walter Pomeroy and Absalom Hedges. McLoughlin, as indicated by this letter, managed his flour mills himself, while Pomeroy and Hedges leased his sawmills.

22. The only figures available on the toll for grinding wheat into flour are for the spring of 1846. Joel Palmer reported at that time that the mills above the Falls were grinding for a toll of one-eighth, while the mills at the Falls exchanged thirty-six pounds of flour for an American bushel of wheat or forty pounds of flour for an Imperial bushel. The Hudson's Bay Co. charged eighty cents for the barrel, packing, and cooperage. Palmer, *Journal of Travels*, p. 189; *Oregon Spectator*, 4 March 1847.

23. Nathaniel Crosby, Jr., master of the American bark, *Toulon*. See Appendix C.

24. During April 1847 a total of 1,736 barrels of flour were shipped from Oregon. Nine hundred barrels were shipped by the Hudson's Bay Co., the remainder being sent in two American ships, the *Toulon* and the *Commodore Stockton*. McLoughlin's cargo of 400 barrels, divided equally between the two ships, thus amounted to almost half of the total exports from the five flour mills which operated independently of the Hudson's Bay Co. *Oregon Spectator*, 13 May 1847; Throckmorton, *Oregon Argonauts*, p. 56; Tallmadge B. Wood, "Tallmadge B. Wood to Isaac M. Nash, February 19, 1846," p. 81.

Reproduction of Letter 16, to Captain Thomas Baillie, 1 May 1846, and Letter 17, to James Allan Grahame, 1 May 1847, from the McLoughlin letter book. Courtesy of the National Park Service, Fort Vancouver National Historic Site

McLoughlin's home and mills, Oregon City, 1857. Photograph by Lorenzo Lorain, army officer and amateur photographer. Courtesy of the Oregon Historical Society

Oregon City as seen from the east side heights, 1857. Photograph by Lorenzo Lorain. Courtesy of the Oregon Historical Society

you wish to make a Contract I wrote to know what price they would charge pr Barrel for any quantity under three thousand Barrels. The Reply was I could have one thousand Barrels at nine Dollars pr Barrel. This is too high unless the demand is as great as When David was with you. However he will touch at Vancouver as he passes and make further Enquiry and Communicate the Result to you and you will be able to Judge — Mrs Rae and the Children Request to be Remembered to you and I am

Dear Sir

Yours Respectfully

John McLoughlin

6. To [George Pelly]

Oregon City 11th April 1847

Dear Sir

I Beg to inform you that I have drawn on you in favour of Captain Couch for the sum of two thousand Dollars at ten Days sight which please Honor and Charge to my Account. My Son David is leaving for California and from there proceeds to Oahu when he will arrange my Account and you will please let him have what Money he Requires out of my funds.

Mess Pomeroy and Hedges have a large Quantity of Lumber which they trust you will avail yourself of the first opportunity to Enable them to send it to you for Sale.[25]

I am

Dear Sir

Yours Respectfully

Jn McLoughlin

25. McLoughlin had bound Pomeroy and Hedges to send their lumber to the agents of the Hudson's Bay Co. in Hawaii, for in 1843 he had contracted to send twelve hundred yellow pine logs to Hawaii to enable them to compete with American lumber, since fir from the Columbia River was considered to be inferior. Peter Skene Ogden, writing to Sir George Simpson from Fort Vancouver on 15 March 1847, said that Pomeroy had undertaken to fulfill McLoughlin's log contract, which "had been made when extravagance was the order of the day at the Falls and it was so far fortunate for us the contract has been assumed by him and thus we escape a heavy loss. . . ." McLoughlin, *Letters, Third Series*, pp. 159n and 155–56.

7. To David McLoughlin

Oregon City 10th April 1847

My Dear David

I Received yours of the 8th by Mr Norris at least the man who delivered it told me so.

I am surprised there should be only 39 Barrels flour as there are 40 Charged. You told me there were 40, and Mr Fenton[26] says there were 40 and I must pay for forty.

As you say I think it will be better to Remit my funds at the Islands to my Agent George Moffatt Esqr of Montreal on Account of the Exchange as I will be able to Remit from here sufficient to pay for What I Require. But of course you must pay all you owe and When Pettygrove and Co[27] pay up they can Remit to A G Benson & Co.[28]

Yours affectionately
Jn McLoughlin

form of Letter

To

Honble G Moffatt

Sir

I take the Liberty to Remit the Enclosed   amounting to which please draw and carry to the Credit of John McLoughlin Esqr and oblige. Yours Respectfully

S D McL

PS I had the pleasure to leave the family Enjoying Good Health on the 8th Apr When I left Oregon City.

S D McL

PS You might get Mr Stark[29] to forward this letter to A G Benson & Co and Request them to forward it to Mr George Moffatt.

26. John Fenton, a miller and millwright employed by the Hudson's Bay Co. It would appear that Fenton may have left the Company before his official retirement in 1849. See Letter 83, to Messrs. Albert Pelly & Co., n. 148.

27. The firm of Francis W. Pettygrove and Albert E. Wilson (see Appendix C), in which young McLoughlin was a partner.

28. A. G. Benson & Co. (also called A. G. and A. W. Benson or Benson and Bro.) was the New York mercantile house which Pettygrove represented when he arrived in Oregon in May 1843. Pettygove, "Oregon in 1843," pp. 1–3.

29. Benjamin Stark. See Appendix C.

8. To David McLoughlin

Oregon City 10th April 1847

My Dear David

You will ask Mr Douglass if he will give me Cash in Exchange for Cash at the Islands as very probably I will Require Cash to purchase Wheat this fall. But this is for your own information and as McKindlay[30] is gone to the Fort you can send me an answer by him.

Yours affectionately

Jn McLoughlin

I Understand the Stockton will carry from 7 & 800 that would have made your freight as Cheap as pr Toulon.[31] The Season in Summer is fine for navigating between this and San Francisco all will depend on the price Mess O & D[32] ask and the price flour will sell in California. Keep in Mind that Lumber can be had here perhaps you may in with some [sic] who would come to Buy Lumber. I will write pr Henry[33]

30. Archibald McKinlay. See Appendix C.

31. The *Toulon*, a bark of 272 tons commanded by Nathaniel Crosby, Jr., arrived in the Columbia on 14 October 1845 with a cargo of merchandise consigned to F. W. Pettygrove by Benson and Bro. of New York. During the next two years she made six trips from the Columbia to Oahu and San Francisco. She frequently carried wheat or lumber for McLoughlin, and he considered purchasing a half interest in her in the summer of 1847 because of a temporary lack of shipping on the Northwest Coast. (See Letters 22 and 23, to George Pelly.) The freight charges on the *Toulon* between the Columbia and Honolulu were $24 per ton and $3 per barrel. During the summer of 1846, the charge for lumber sent on the *Toulon* to Honolulu was raised from $16 per ton to $24 per ton. By comparison, the price on freight from New York to Oregon was $25 per ton and $3 per barrel. *Oregon Spectator*, 23 July 1846.

32. Peter Skene Ogden and James Douglas.

33. The *Henry*, an American brig of 153 tons, cleared the Columbia River on 1 May 1847 bound for Honolulu with a load of lumber. She had first arrived in Oregon about 1 March 1847 with a cargo of merchandise, mostly used furniture, with which her captain, William K. Kilborne (see Appendix C) opened a store in Oregon City. In the following seventeen months, she made five trips to Oahu and San Francisco, carrying wheat, lumber, and produce. On 9 August 1848, Kilborne, aboard the *Henry*, brought the formal news of the discovery of gold in California to Oregon. Letter from the Bishop Museum, Honolulu, to W. R. Sampson, 24 December 1963; *Oregon Spectator*, 18 March, 1 April, 13 May 1847, 7 September 1848.

to meet you at Oahu and will then Instruct you what to do with my funds. Mess O & Douglass I think would do well to send their Money to California to purchase U S Bills But that is their Business.

J McL

9. To Peter Skene Ogden and James Douglas

Oregon City 12th April 1847

P S Ogden ⎫
James Douglass ⎬   Esqr

Gentlemen

Will you please send me the following Articles

    20 Sheet strong tin
    4   " Iron No 17
    6 Yds. Canvas
    1 Cwt spikes 4½ Inch
    ½" 6d Nails Cut[34]
    6 Ct [cwt] 8' do
        and Charge
        Yours
        Jn McLoughlin

10. To James Douglas

Oregon City 15th April 1847

James Douglass Esqr

Dear Sir

I Received yours of 13th Instant with the Extract from the Governor and Committees Dispatch of 7th Oct 1846 for which please to Accept my thanks.[35] I observe what the Board wrote But the Censure or applause

34. McLoughlin's several orders for quantities of nails reflect the building boom in Oregon as immigrants opened farms and constructed homes and shops. As early as 19 February 1846, the *Oregon Spectator* had announced that there was a great need for nails and paint.

35. McLoughlin refers to the governor and committee's comments on the Warre and Vavasour report. See letter 3, n. 10.

[16]

of Men cannot alter facts and some the Directors of the Hudson Bay Company are convinced the Measures I took were Right the Least they could have done in Justice to themselves and their Concern over which they preside (after acting as they have to me) was to have communicated to me on the subject themselves.

As to the treaty[36] It seems to me the British subjects in the Country have every Reason to be satisfied with it and I do Believe that the Conduct we pursued has tended to our obtaining such favourable terms and prevented Britain and the United states being Involved in Horrors of War.

As to the flour our differance of opinion arises from your Viewing it as a speculation and my Viewing it as a Business and this is the light my Correspondent wrote me as an outlet to the produce of the Country. David has no authority from me to make any Contract he was to get your price and Communicate it. Your Remark[s] about him are I Believe Correct. I was happy to see Jane[37] she has grown Greatly. On Enquiring about Cecil[38] and why she had not come I was sorry to learn Mrs Douglass was unwell. I hope she is better please Remember Mrs McL Mrs Rae Mrs E to her not forgetting

Yours Respectfully

Jn McLoughlin

NB I sent a Copy of your & Mr O Letter to me about the flour to my Correspondent.

36. The Oregon Treaty, which established the boundary between the United States and British North America at the 49th parallel and guaranteed the "possessory rights" of the Hudson's Bay Co. and the Puget's Sound Agricultural Co., was signed at Washington, D.C., on 15 June 1846 and ratified by the United States Senate on 18 June 1846. News of the ratification reached Oregon with the *Toulon* late in October, and on 4 November the *Oregon Spectator* printed an "Extra" issue to report the boundary settlement; but not until the following year were the provisions known to anxious Oregonians. On 4 March 1847, the *Oregon Spectator* published an erroneous version of the treaty which made no mention of the "possessory rights" question. On April first, the correct version was published, but its authenticity was doubted by the editor. In the issue of 15 April, however, the editor announced that the Hudson's Bay Co. bark *Cowlitz* had arrived with a true copy of the treaty which was the same as the version published two weeks previously.

37. Jane Douglas, a daughter of James Douglas, married Alexander Grant Dallas, successor to Sir George Simpson as governor of Rupert's Land.

38. Cecil (Cecilia) Douglas, another daughter of James and Cecilia Douglas, married Dr. J. S. Helmcken of Victoria, B.C. She died in 1865.

11. To David McLoughlin

Oregon City 16th April 1847

My Dear David

I paid on order of yours in favour of A McKindlay Esqr which he presented himself for thirty Six Dollars and twenty Cents But Mr Campbell[39] returned me the Money.

I wish you to purchase for me

100# Sperm Candles
300# Oahu Sugar
200 Gall Syrup
100# Rice
50 Bus Salt[40]
3 pair strong shoes (for myself)

and you will out of my funds on your hands and those of Mr Pelly pay the Draft I drew on Mr Pelly In favour of Captain Couch and all you owe and the Remainder of my funds you will Remit to Mess A G Benson and Company New York, City old Slip to the Credit of your firm[41]—for this you will have to pay me Cash here in course of the Season As I will have to purchase Wheat for Cash to carry on my Milling Operations and you will have to pay me Interest on the Amount I will pay for you at Oahu at the Rate of 6 p Cent pr Annum in Cash payable here and the principal to be repaid in two Years. I do this that you may have no calls on you at Oahu and to Enable you to lodge funds at New York to order Goods from there. Mess Pettygrove &c will of

39. John G. Campbell, who came to Oregon with Lt. John C. Fremont in 1843, was assistant to Archibald McKinlay at the Hudson's Bay Co. store in Oregon City. McLoughlin, *Letters, Third Series*, p. 138.

40. In 1845 there was a scarcity of salt in Oregon, and McLoughlin raised the price from $ .625 to $2.00 a bushel. Pettygrove and Stark saw an opportunity for securing a monopoly of the salmon trade by withholding their salt, a cash commodity, from the market. By 1847 their monopoly was broken, and salt was down to $1.00 a bushel. Bancroft, *History of Oregon*, 1:19; *Memorial of J. Quinn Thornton Praying the Establishment of a Territorial Government in Oregon, and for Appropriations for Various Purposes* (25 May 1848), 30th Congress, 1st Session, Senate, Miscellaneous Document no. 143, serial 511, p. 16.

41. F. W. Pettygrove & Co.

[18]

course Instruct you what to purchase and which ought to be only what you find a Ready Market for and for which you can pay Immediately as I think there will be a Vessel here with Goods from the states this season. The family send you their Love.

Yours affectionately
John McLoughlin

PS I also Want you to purchase for me
    1 Keg 6' [d] Cut nails
    2 " 8d   "   "
    4 " Shingle Nails as p Sample

12. To George Pelly

Oregon City 19th April 1847

To
George Pelly Esqr

Dear Sir

    I have written a Letter to my son David which I have desired to be Enclosed to you. But in case he is not at Oahu I Beg to inform you I send ten Barrels flour Marked 1M for sale. I send no More from the Want of freight and I wrote my son to purchase for me
    1 Keg 6d Cut Nails
    2 —— 8" ————
    4   " Shingle Nails
and to this you will please add
    1 Cwt 4½ Inch spikes
    3 Bags Coffee
    2 Cut Glass Lamps/small
of course if he is not at Oahu you will please pay the freight for the flour and do the Needful.

I am
Yours Respectfully
Jn McLoughlin

2 Doz Cups & Saucers

[19]

13. TO GEORGE PELLY

Oregon City 21st April 1847

George Pelly Esqr

Dear Sir

I wrote you on the 19th Inst that I had written to my Son to purchase for me

    1 Keg 6d Cut Nails

    2 " 8d

    4 " Shingle Nails

and to this you would please add

    1 Cwt Spikes 4½ In

    3 Bags Coffee

    2 Cut Glass Lamps

    2 Doz Cups and Saucers

But I forgot to state that I had also given him the following [*note*] Memorandum

    100# Sperm Candles

    300# Oahu Sugar

    200 Gall Syrup

    100# Rice

    50 Bushels Salt

    3 pair strong shoes

and to this please add also

    3 Cwt White paint

    12 Gall Linseed oil But if Tartaric [?] oil will Answer for out of door Work send it in place of the Linseed oil.

Yours Respectfully

Jn McLoughlin

[Written vertically across the left-hand side of the letter is the following:]
June 9th 1847
This Letter reached Fort George one Day after the sailing of the Henry[42] and this Letter was returned.

Jn McLoughlin

42. The *Henry* was piloted across the Columbia Bar on May first. *Oregon Spectator*, 13 May 1847.

14. To Nathaniel J. Wyeth[43]

Oregon City 20th April 1847

N J Wyeth Esqr

Dear Sir

I have the pleasure to Acknowledge the Receipt of your Esteemed favour of 25th Oct 1845 with the Cuttings seeds Newspapers and Thiers life of Napoleon[44] to page 568 for all which please to accept my thanks, — The Cuttings I am sorry to say are all Dead and as yet none of the fruit trees have appeared above Ground But they may yet. You know perhaps by this time that I only came to Reside here permanently spring 1846 When I Retired from the Charge of the HB Co Business and have only now begun to get my place in a little order to do which I have had a good deal of trouble about this place with persons who followed the Example of the Methodist Mission[45] however now the Boundary is settled I hope the Government will soon be here to Maintain order and Establish the Rights of Individuals as most certainly if I had

43. For biographical information on Wyeth, see Appendix C.

44. Louis Adolphe Thiers (1797–1877) was a French historian and statesman. Between 1824 and 1855 he published twelve volumes on the history of the French Revolution and the life of Napoleon. In 1840 he was prime minister of France and later served as president of the Republic (1871–73).

Wyeth had long known of McLoughlin's interest in the career of Napoleon, and it is not surprising that he chose Thiers' biography as a suitable gift for his friend. George Traill Allan, a clerk at Fort Vancouver from 1831 to late 1841 or early 1842, wrote his reminiscences of life at Fort Vancouver in 1841, in which he related the following incident. "Doctor McLaughlin was fond of argument and especially on historical points connected with the first Napoleon of whom he was a great admirer and often entered them with Captain Wyeth and upon one occasion which I well remember he happened to be dressing my hand which I had lately got hurt and when in the height of debate on the Peace of Amiens he treated my poor hand so roughly that I heartily wished Napoleon and the Peace of Amiens far enough." George T. Allan, "Reminiscences of Fort Vancouver"; for a slightly altered published version, see *Transactions of the . . . Oregon Pioneer Association for 1881*, pp. 77–78.

45. McLoughlin is here referring to the continuing and generally successful efforts of the Methodist missionaries, particularly Rev. Alvin E. Waller, to deprive him of his land claim at the Falls. Their most persistent argument for the legality of their actions was based on the fact that McLoughlin was a British subject representing the interests of a foreign corporation.

[21]

not been so forbearing as I have there would have been dreadful troubles in this Country. But when I considered the Immense Evils that would arise out of it that troubles among us here would inspite of the two Governments Involve Both Countries in the Horrors of War I put up with injuries that caused me to Incur great Expense confident that time would do me justice. As to the Methodist Mission you certainly did put me on my Gaurd [*sic*]. But I thought you like others of my Worthy friends were prejudiced against Missionaries and if it was not on Account of my friends I would publish An Account of their Whole proceedings towards me and I may do so Yet.[46] But I will do so here when it can be done without Exciting tumults and publish it first here because here the facts are known and it will give them an opportunity of Rebutting them if they can.

I will do myself the pleasure to attend to your Claim[47] there are

---

46. At least twice during his lifetime, McLoughlin published lengthy defenses of his efforts to secure the land claim at the Falls and of his contributions to the settlement of Oregon. In seeking to avoid increasing the antagonism of certain Americans toward him, he evidently did not publish a direct charge against the Methodist missionaries, but rather blamed Congress, the territorial legislature, and unnamed "men high in authority" for the troubles of his declining years. Long after his death, a more vigorous account of his troubles with the Methodist Mission, in his own handwriting, was discovered and printed. *Oregon Spectator*, 12 September 1850; "Letter of John McLoughlin, June 8, 1852," pp. 295–99; John McLoughlin, "Copy of a Document Found among the Private Papers of the Late Dr. John McLoughlin," pp. 46–56.

47. In 1834 Wyeth established claims to two locations in the Willamette Valley. On 22 September 1834 he located a farm on a prairie fifteen miles long and seven miles wide on the south bank of the Willamette about twenty miles south of the falls of the Willamette, but by 1847 he seems to have relinquished this claim. Wyeth's second claim was on Sauvie Island (then called Wappato or Multnomah Island), a low, swampy area of some 24,000 acres formed of rich alluvial deposits at the mouth of the Willamette River. During the winter of 1834/35, Wyeth's men constructed Fort William in the northwest section of the island. Wyeth's fur and salmon enterprise was a failure, and in the autumn of 1836 he left the Oregon country. On his departure, he instructed Courtney M. Walker, in whose care he left Fort William, to lease his claim to "some trusty person" for fifteen years. Hearing nothing from Walker for some years, Wyeth directed McLoughlin to enter his name at the Provisional Government's land office and to have the property leased. Nathaniel J. Wyeth, *The Correspondence and Journals of Captain Nathaniel J. Wyeth, 1831–6*, ed. F. G. Young, pp. 233, 255.

The Provisional Government of Oregon was organized on 5 July 1843, and

several Squatters on it — On the Receipt of your letter I applied to a Lawyer to Enforce your Claim But he told me you could not Claim more than a Mile under the organisation though you had taken your Claim before and this seems to be the General Opinion and in that case considered it Better to wait till the Government took possession. I send you a Copy of the Record so as to Enable you to do what you can at Head Quarters. In the Mean time I will when the Government comes put in your Claim and as I said before take Legal advise and follow such Measures as may be considered most condusive to your Interests. The Island is Worth little at present as you know in high Water It mostly overflows But it will rise in Value as the Country settles which it is doing Rapidly though last year the greatest part of the Immigrants went to California. But as this is the Best Agricultural Country of the two When the fact is Well known the tide of Emigration will again turn to this.

But when the Rail Road is Run across this Continent and Which I think it must soon beyond a Doubt it will Rendor this the finest portion of North America and I think it will not be long before this is done.[48] But you have seen the Country and you can Judge if it is

---

that same day a report on land claims was adopted. This report provided that within one year anyone already in possession of a claim should file a description of it in the recorder's office. It further provided that individual claims were to be limited to 640 acres, in square or oblong form, and that no person could hold more than one claim. These provisions were retained in the new land laws passed in 1844, but in 1845 the law was amended to exclude nonresidents. David C. Duniway and Neil R. Riggs, eds., "The Oregon Archives, 1841–1843," p. 267; Bancroft, *History of Oregon*, 1:478; McLoughlin, *Letters, Third Series*, pp. 237–38.

To protect Wyeth's interests, McLoughlin leased the claim in his own name and allowed the Hudson's Bay Co., which had established a dairy on the island about 1838, to pasture cattle on it. However, jumpers moved onto the claim, and McLoughlin could do little to remove them (see Letter 56, to Nathaniel J. Wyeth). For Wyeth's statement on the matter, see his letter to J. G. Palfrey, a member of Congress, dated 13 December 1847, in Wyeth, *Correspondence and Journals*, pp. 253–56.

48. As early as 3 September 1846 the *Oregon Spectator* reprinted an article from the 8 January 1846 issue of the *New York Sun* in which the writer proposed that a railroad be constructed as far as South Pass to facilitate emigration from the East and North to the West. In late September, delegates were appointed to determine public opinion on a railroad to Oregon, and on 2 November they met to draft a memorial to Congress on the subject, but were somewhat

feasible and when this takes place What an Immense intercourse will there not be Between this and the East side and I think one of the finest Watering places in the World will be the Soda springs[49] in the Mountains which will be Resorted to also on account of the Salubrity of the Air.

By Last a/c from Mexico Monterey was taken But California was quiet and subdued. I wrote you formerly that I had stated to the officers of the Exploring Squadron[50] your having taken possession of your Island and I took purposely a Mr Dayton or Drayton[51] an artist attached to the Expedition to point it out to him and show him where you had Built which I mention in case of its being of use to you. With Best Wishes Believe me

Yours Respectfully
Jn McLoughlin

I have not learnt of any place on the North West Coast that will suit for Ice[52]— But I have Enquiries on foot —   JMcL

---

distracted by the issue of land claims. In December a memorial to Congress from the provisional legislature commended the transcontinental railroad proposed by George Wilkes. In February 1847 the *Spectator* again reminded Oregonians of the railroad issue by reprinting Asa Whitney's proposal for a transcontinental railroad to Oregon first made in 1845. *Oregon Spectator*, 3, 17 September, 1, 15 October, 26 November, 24 December 1846, 18 February 1847.

49. Soda Springs, in southeastern Idaho, is located on the east side of the Bear River at the point where it turns south to flow into the Great Salt Lake. The springs may have been discovered by the returning Astorians in 1812. Located about fifty miles east of Wyeth's Fort Hall, the springs were an important stopping point between Fort Bridger and Fort Hall on the Oregon Trail. The springs, called "Beer Springs" by the trappers, were deep pots in the earth which vented suffocating fumes and effervescent soda water. Perhaps the first to recognize the spalike qualities of the area was Lansford Hastings, who saw the springs in 1842. He later wrote that the region about the springs was "a very extraordinary section of country, and is destined, beyond any kind of doubt to become immensely important and valuable; because of its peculiarly favorable locality; its extraordinary, wonderful, and delightful scenery; and perhaps, the medicinal properties of its inexhaustible mineral waters." Lansford W. Hastings, *A New History of Oregon and California*, p. 37.

50. The United States Exploring Expedition under the command of Lt. Charles Wilkes, U.S.N., surveyed part of the Antarctic coast, many of the islands of the Pacific, and the Northwest Coast during its trip around the world, 1838–42. Part of the expedition was at Fort Vancouver from April to October 1841, while surveying the lower Columbia and Willamette rivers. Chapters

[24]

15. To George Moffatt

Oregon City 1st May 1847

To

The Honble George Moffatt
Montreal

Sir

On the 10th Ult I drew on you for three thousand Dollars in favour James Douglass Esqr which please pay and Charge to

Yours Respectfully
Jn McLoughlin

The Honble George Moffatt
Montreal

16. To Captain Thomas Baillie[53]

Oregon City 1st May 1847

To

Captain Baillie
HM Ship Modeste[54]

Dear Sir

I am this moment informed the Modeste Sails on Monday next. Allow me to Wish you a pleasant Voyage home and a happy meeting with

on the Columbia River country are to be found in the fourth and fifth volumes of Wilkes' *Narrative of the United States Exploring Expedition.*

51. Joseph Drayton was one of two artists and draughtsmen attached to the Wilkes expedition.

52. Following his business failures in Oregon in 1832 and 1834, Wyeth had returned to his association with Frederic Tudor of Boston in the lucrative ice trade with the West Indies and Calcutta. In 1840 he severed his connections with Tudor and established a profitable trade in refrigerated garden produce and fruits with the tropics. William R. Sampson, "Nathaniel Jarvis Wyeth," p. 399.

53. Thomas Baillie (1811–89) was captain of H.M.S. *Modeste.* He entered the Royal Navy in 1827, and by 1845 he had been promoted through the ranks to captain. He commanded the White Sea Squadron of the British fleet during the Crimean War and was made a rear admiral in 1863. In 1870 he was promoted to the rank of vice-admiral, and in 1873 he was placed on the retired list. McLoughlin, *Letters, Third Series,* p. 1n.

54. H.M.S. *Modeste,* a sloop of 568 tons and 18 guns, arrived at Fort Van-

your friends and to assure you that I consider that the presence of HMS Modeste at Vancouver Your Conduct and that of your officers the Good Behaviour and Discipline of your Crew have been the Means of preventing trouble in the Country and With Best Wishes for your and their Wellfare Believe me to Be yours Respectfully

Jn McLoughlin

PS Permit me to state a fact that since I am in the Country I have known no ships Crew Conduct themselves in so orderly a Manner as that of HM Ship Modeste under your Command.

J McLoughlin

17. To James Allan Grahame[55]

Oregon City 1st May 1847

Mr Graham

Sir

Will you Please send me by first opportunity half a Ream letter as p Sample also if you have any 4½ In spikes I would wish to have 100#.

Yours Respectfully

Jn McLoughlin

---

couver on 7 July 1844, and remained in the river until early August, when she sailed for California. In late November 1845, the *Modeste* resumed her station off Fort Vancouver and remained there until she sailed for Oahu on 3 May 1847. Her presence in the Columbia lent valuable support to the Company and to Mc-Loughlin, who feared that the Americans might attempt to push the British out of Oregon by force. During her long stay in the Columbia, the officers and crew of the *Modeste* enlivened the social life of the residents by providing the first theatricals in the Oregon country as well as the first horse race and curling match. Ibid., pp. liii–lv; *Oregon Spectator*, 19 February, 20 August 1846, 4 February, 13 May 1847. See also Priscilla Knuth, ed., "HMS *Modeste* on the Pacific Coast, 1843–47," pp. 408–36.

55. McLoughlin is probably addressing James Allan Grahame who was a clerk at Fort Vancouver. He entered the Company's service in 1843 as an apprentice clerk, and in 1845 he was one of nine Company employees who were registered as holders of claims in and around Fort Vancouver. This fiction was a maneuver by which the Company hoped to maintain its lands in the event that foreign corporations were excluded from possession in the expected boundary treaty. By 1874 Grahame had risen to the rank of chief commissioner at a salary of £ 1,500 exclusive of traveling expenses. He retired in 1884 and died in 1905. McLoughlin, *Letters, Third Series*, p. 107.

18. To Peter Skene Ogden and James Douglas

Oregon City 2nd June 1847

P S Ogden ⎫
James Douglass ⎬ Esqr

Gentlemen

The Bearer of this Spagnole's[56] time is out and leaves my Service. He has applied to me to be allowed to settle in the Willamette. But of course as I had him from the Company I could not agree to his proposal and therefore return him. If you could let me have Another Sandwich Islander it will Accomodate me much I Expect an Islander or two from the Islands.

Yours Respectfully
Jn McLoughlin

19. To Peter Skene Ogden and James Douglas

Oregon City 8th June 1847

P S Ogden ⎫
Jas Douglass ⎬ Esqr

Gentlemen

Yours of 3rd Instant came duly to hand and I beg to inform you that I am Willing to Renew the Lease of my premises which you at present Occupy[57] for two Years on the present terms Except that when

56. Spagnole was evidently a Kanaka, or Hawaiian, of which there were many employed by the Company on the Columbia. The Sandwich Islanders were usually employed on a three-year contract, and in addition to their subsistence they were paid about £ 17 (roughly $85) per annum during the 1840s. Kanakas were frequently employed in the Company's sawmills east of Vancouver, and McLoughlin seemingly was permitted to take over the contracts of some of them for labor in his own mills during 1846–47. (See Letters 21 and 53, to Peter Skene Ogden and James Douglas.) For the usual terms and conditions of the employment of Hawaiians in the Columbia Department, see Appendix A, John McLoughlin's Bond for Dr. Ira L. Babcock.

57. In 1846 the Hudson's Bay Co. had decided to close its business and dispose of its property in Oregon City. On June first, the beginning of the Company's business year, McLoughlin assumed ownership of the property, his share of the year's profits at the Falls (£ 1,053) representing the purchase price. In preparing to close out the business at the Falls, Ogden and Douglas had found that a large inventory of goods remained which could be removed to

[27]

I find it Inconvenient to Allow flour to be retailed in the Mill you can arrange a place for it in Wallers[58] Old house.

I am Gentlemen
Respectfully Yours
Jn McLoughlin

20. To Peter Skene Ogden and James Douglas

Oregon City 9th June 1847

P S Ogden
James Douglass ⎬ Esqr

Gentlemen

I wish to know if you could spare a pair or two of Burr stones[59] and the price you demand.

I am Gentlemen
Respectfully Yours
Jn McLoughlin

Fort Vancouver only at considerable expense. As the prospects for business at Oregon City were good, they determined to retain a store there with Archibald McKinlay in charge. On 19 March 1846 they informed Governor Simpson that they had rented a store, a dwelling house, and a granary for storage from McLoughlin for two years at £ 121 per annum. McLoughlin, *Letters, Third Series*, pp. lxi, 138n. McLoughlin is evidently agreeing to a renewal of this lease a year in advance.

58. The closing of the Methodist Mission in April 1844 enabled McLoughlin to settle his dispute with Waller at a cost of $500. Waller retained for his use his house and other lots which the mission had used, but in August McLoughlin was able to secure the undisputed ownership of all lots and improvements formerly used by the mission within his Oregon City claim at a cost of $5,400. Waller subsequently moved to The Dalles, where he was living in 1847. Ibid., pp. xlvi, 150; *Oregon Spectator*, 18 March 1847.

59. McLoughlin is requesting millstones for his flour mill. French buhr (or burr), which came from Bergerac near Paris, was preferred for such stones since an irregular network of quartz cavities in the stone kept its grinding surfaces sharp as the stone was worn. John Storck and Walter D. Teague, *Flour for Man's Bread*, p. 102. The stones used by the Hudson's Bay Co. on the Columbia were generally about four and a half feet in diameter. In 1841 millstones ordered from Messrs. James Abernethy & Co. of Aberdeen, Scotland, had cost £ 28 per pair. McLoughlin, *Letters, Second Series*, pp. 160–61n.

PS Will you please send me the two Beech logs which came this year by the Cowlitz[60]

JMcL

Will you please send me the two Beech Logs which came by the Cowlitz and if there are in the last Dispatches from the Governor and Committee of the Hudson Bay Co any Remarks on the Measures I pursued or suggestted [sic] I would thank you if you consider it consistent with your Duty to send me a Copy of them.[61]

Jn McL

21. To Peter Skene Ogden and James Douglas

Oregon City 16th July 1847

P S Ogden }
Jas Douglas }   Esqr

Gentlemen

I duly Received yours of 13th Inst and I Beg to Observe in Regard to the two Beech Logs if you Require them you are Welcome to keep them. I only applied for them because I had ordered them for my Mills and I am afraid they might Remain on your hands. I find young Oak answers my purpose.

Yours Respectfully
Jn McLoughlin

PS Do you Expect any Mill Stones Next Year since I wrote I fell in with a Kanacka who came with Mr Cooper[62] and Engaged him for a Month or two as I was afraid you might not be able to meet my Request and send you your Kanacka with Many Thanks.

JMcL

60. The bark *Cowlitz* (289 tons) was built in England for the Hudson's Bay Co. Her first voyage was from London to Fort Vancouver (1840–41), and from then until she was sold in London in June 1851, she was primarily engaged in the coasting trade to Sitka and the Sandwich Islands. McLoughlin, *Letters, Second Series*, p. 35n.

61. McLoughlin refers to the governor and committee's comments on the Warre and Vavasour report. See Letter 3, to James Douglas, n. 10.

62. Captain Cooper commanded the Company's brig *Mary Dare* which had arrived in the Columbia River from England via the Sandwich Islands on 26 June 1847. *Oregon Spectator*, 8 July 1847.

22. TO GEORGE PELLY

Portland 2nd July 1847

George Pelly Esqr

Dear Sir

I Beg to Acknowledge the Receipt of your favour of 30th April 22 and 29th May last. Yours of 30th April by May Dare [*sic*][63] only reached me to day though she arrived in May at Victoria and I Received my London Letters a long time ago as the Captain sent them across Land But why he detained yours I cannot say.

I am Extremely obliged to you for the trouble you took to collect the information you sent me in your Letter and it was Judicious in you for the Reasons you state not to Charter the Mount Vernon as before she came a large ship the Brutus[64] Capt Adams came here from California (my Son David came on her) and Mr Pomeroy (Mr Hedges has retired from the Concern) sold about 100 M feet Lumber to the Captain at Eighteen Dollars pr M feet which he preferred to do than to pay twenty Dollars pr M feet for freight and I Believe he has not [*sic*] the same quantity remaining which if he can he will ship to California in the Mount Vernon or Else to you if an opportunity offers as two more American Vessels are Expected from the states and a third supposed to be a french Vessel[65] with the Revd Bishop Blanchette and twelve Roman Catholic Missionaries.

63. The *Mary Dare* was a brig belonging to the Hudson's Bay Co.

64. The *Mount Vernon*, a New York ship of 446 tons, arrived in the Columbia River on 27 June 1847 from Oahu and departed for San Francisco, Oahu, and Manila on 15 July. Her captain was J. O. Given. Letter from the Public Archives of Hawaii to W. R. Sampson, 23 January 1964; *Oregon Spectator*, 8, 22 July 1847.

The *Brutus*, a Boston ship of 470 tons, arrived in Oregon on 14 June 1847 from Boston, via San Francisco, and sailed for Oahu on 15 July 1847. James Adams was her captain. Letter from the Public Archives of Hawaii to W. R. Sampson, 23 January 1964; *Oregon Spectator*, 24 June, 22 July 1847.

65. The bark *L'Etoile du Matin* (Morning Star) arrived in the Columbia on 14 August 1847 with Bishop Francis N. Blanchet and a Catholic reinforcement of three Jesuits, five priests, three lay brothers, two deacons, and seven Sisters of Notre Dame de Namur. On leaving the Columbia, she sailed to Tahiti and back to France. In July 1849 she returned to the Columbia, but in attempting to cross the bar without a pilot she became stuck in the shifting sands. She was finally floated, but the damage was so extensive that upon her arrival at

[30]

The Non Receipt of your letter to my Son pr Mary Daer [*sic*] in time made him and his partners suppose you could not send him the Articles he had requested and made them purchase to the Amount of about seventeen hundred Dollars from Captain Adams which they paid in produce and I Believe they now send you a hundred thousand feet Lumber and Barrels Salmon.

I am Extremely obliged to you for paying the Draft for two thousand Dollars which I drew on you in favour of Captain Couch as when I drew I Believed you had not drawn Captain Mervines Draft as I Understood from my Son when he Returned last fall from Oahu that he was to pay for his supplies in produce and that he was to have Credit for one Year and that the Draft I gave him on my Agent would Remain with you as Collateral security which I mention to show you I supposed I had funds in your hands as most certainly if at the time I had been aware that such was not the case I would not have taken the liberty to have drawn on you and though I have a hundred Barrels flour and Mr Pomeroy owes me Lumber to the Amount of fifteen hundred Dollars[66] yet I have no means of shipping the last nor can I send you the flour as I Require it to supply my Customers at Oregon City. However as my Son left flour &c to the Amount of Between 6 and 8 thousand Dollars with Mr Leidsdorff for Sale and the proceeds were to be remitted to you I presume before this Reaches you you will have the means of paying yourself.

And I Beg to Observe if an opportunity offers that I will ship my flour now on hand and the Lumber Mr Pomeroy owes me to California which I mention that you may be aware of my Means as I do not want to draw on my Agent till I hear from him so as not to damage my Investments and as I am Cramped for the want of a Vessel if you think the Toulon is worth twelve thousand Dollars and what you will take one fourth Captain Crossby the other 1/4 I am willing to take the half provided I can raise the funds without drawing on my Agents and Besides the funds I have in California and the flour and Lumber at Present here

---

Portland her hull was burned for the salvage of the copper and iron. Her captain on both trips to Oregon was François Marie Menes (see Letter 44, to Captain François Marie Menes, n. 94). Bancroft, *History of Oregon*, 1:326; *Oregon Spectator*, 19 August 1847, 4 October 1849, 18 April 1850.

66. Walter Pomeroy, who leased McLoughlin's sawmills for $1,000 per year, was evidently paying McLoughlin in lumber.

to send there I have funds here to purchase Wheat to make four hundred Barrels flour after harvest. If we purchase the Toulon I wish my share to be Insured and to be Understood that she is to be Employed between this California and Oahu and to go if deemed proper to Manilla for a Cargo of sugar Coffee and molasses. I Understand these articles are Cheap at Manilla and they will sell well here and California.

In Regard to the Cadboro[67] she is not here and will not be sor [for?] some time. But she is Old and I am told Mess Ogden and Douglass demanded one thousand pounds for her which is a great Deal more than I consider her Value.

I am Dear Sir
Respectfully Yours
Jn McLoughlin

23. To George Pelly

Oregon City 8th July 1847

George Pelly Esqr

Dear Sir

If this Reaches you before you purchase half of the Toulon on my Account I beg you will not do so as it is certain there will be a sufficient Number of Vessels here to take away the Lumber and produce.

I will be obliged to you to send me by first opportunity on my Account

1 Keg 6d Cut Nails
2 Kegs 8d Cut Nails
2 " Shingle "
100# Sperm Candles
400# Oahu sugar   100# Soap
200 Gall Syrup   6# Snuff
50 Bus. Salt

As I wrote you in Mine of the 2nd Instant you will pay yourself out of the Monies Mr Leidsdorff will Remit to you — from the proceeds

---

67. The little schooner *Cadboro* of about seventy tons was purchased by the Hudson's Bay Co. in 1826. She was sent to the Columbia, arriving in 1827, and thereafter she was engaged in the Sandwich Island and coasting trade. The Company disposed of her about 1850. McLoughlin, *Letters, First Series*, p. 42n.

belonging to me which my Son left in his hands and the surplus you will detain till you hear further from me. I am

Dear Sir
Yours Respectfully
John McLoughlin

24. To Lansford W. Hastings [Extract]

Oregon City 14 July 1847

Extract of a Letter to Mr Hastings at San Francisco

"There is a Man of the Name of Wornbough[68] who ran away from this in my Debt. I made him advances to Build a Shingling Machine he sold it Never paid me one farthing and Ran away to California he Owes me $403.80. If you would do any thing for me in the Way of Business you would oblige me.

Yours Respctfully
Jn McLoughlin

25. To William A. Leidesdorff

Oregon City 16th July 1847

Wm A Leidesdorff Esqr

Dear Sir

I have the pleasure to Acknowledge the Receipt of yours 29th May and I approve of my Son leaving my flour &c with you for better times and I hope you have been able to sell all before this and Remit my funds to George Pelly Esqr where I will want them as soon as you can Remit.

In Regard to Mr Knights Mill Irons I presented his Order which you sent me to Mr Abernethy[69] who informed me he had taken a Mill Crank belonging to Mr Knight at the suggestion of a Mr Keys[70] which you will see fully Explained in the letter Mr Abernethy Writes to Mr

68. See Letter 4, to David McLoughlin.

69. George Abernethy. See Appendix C.

70. Possibly Robert C. Keyes, who had come from California in 1846. Bancroft, *History of Oregon*, 1:552.

Knight and which will be further Explained By Capt Gilston of the Whitton[71] By whom I send these packages as pr Bill of Lading which I Enclose and you will also see that according to your Instructions I paid Mr Abernethys Account Amounting to $85.98 which you will please place to my Credit.

I have some flour but I cannot send any by this opportunity as it is not yet packed.

The Janet[72] Capt Dring is come here for a Cargo of Lumber for Mess Grimes[73] which she is to take to California. But I think Mr Grimes's Agent has not the Lumber to Load her. But on Landing her Cargo at California she is to come here for a Cargo from me. But Whether I will send it to you or to Oahu depends on the information I Receive from you — as I trust you will give me every information in Regard to the Demand for lumber flour and Beef.[74]

Yours Respectfully
John McLoughlin

NB The Crank is too Bad to be sent. A Crank will be sent by the Henry.

J McLoughlin

71. Roland Gelston, captain of the *Whiton* (see Appendix C). The bark *Whiton* arrived in Oregon on 22 June 1847, after a passage of 162 days from New York. She departed for San Francisco on 15 July and returned to the Columbia on 11 September 1847. On 19 October she cleared for San Francisco and Panama. *Oregon Spectator*, 8, 22 July, 30 September, 28 October 1847.

72. The *Janet*, an English bark of 333 tons commanded by David Dring, arrived in the Columbia on 6 July 1847 following calls at Tahiti and Oahu (see Appendix B). Her cargo of general merchandise was consigned to John H. Couch. *Oregon Spectator*, 22 July, 5 August 1847. In 1849 the *Janet*, arriving in the Columbia from San Francisco, carried as passengers Joseph Lane and Joe Meek who were returning home from Washington, D.C., with appointments as governor and U.S. marshal of the newly created Oregon Territory. E.W. Wright, ed., *Lewis and Dryden's Marine History of the Pacific Northwest*, p. 24.

73. McLoughlin refers to the San Francisco firm of E. & H. Grimes. See Eliab Grimes in Appendix C.

74. Drought and consequent crop failure, increased immigration, and the disruptions of the Mexican War all combined to make California a lucrative market for Oregon's produce in 1847. Shortly before McLoughlin wrote this letter to Leidesdorff, concrete news of California's increasing demands reached Oregon. In June 1847 the *Oregon Spectator* published a letter from C. E. Picket stating that California wanted twenty thousand barrels of flour and several

[34]

26. To William A. Leidesdorff

Oregon City 19th July 1847

W A Leidesdorff

Dear Sir

I Beg you would have the Goodness to inform me what prospects you think your Country affords this fall for the sale of flour and Lumber and after remitting as soon as you can thousand Dollars to Mr Pelly you will Remit the Remainder to me. But if you find an Earlier opportunity to Remit all my funds here than to Oahu you can do so. You know I have no Goods and I want cash to purchase Wheat.

Yours Respectfully

Jn McLoughlin

I have sent for Goods to London and Expect them in 1848. Send me a statement of my a/c. I have taken in my Account the supplies my son got from Oahu and left with you to the Amount of $1870.92—in addition to what I sent from this.

JMcL

27. To Peter Skene Ogden and James Douglas

Oregon City 21st July 1847

Mess Ogden and Douglass

Gentlemen

On settling my Account last spring with this post there was an order of the Revd Mr Demers[75] of three thousand Dollars to my Credit. But

---

thousand bushels of white wheat for sowing from Oregon. Lumber, potatoes, and butter were also in demand, and it was anticipated that California would have to depend on Oregon and Chile for the next two years. Of great interest in Oregon, which was chronically short of cash with which to conduct business, was the news that all payments for goods sent to California would be made in specie. Flour brought from $15 to $30 per barrel in California during the spring of 1847, while pine lumber sold for $50 a thousand feet and beef, which sold for about the same price as in Oregon, brought $6 per hundred pounds. The *Toulon*'s cargo of flour, shipped from Oregon in April 1847, was sold at $15 per barrel, realizing a profit of about $10 per barrel. *Oregon Spectator*, 25 June 1846, 10 June 1847.

75. Modeste Demers (1808–71) accompanied Father F. N. Blanchet to Oregon in 1838. The two priests were the first of their faith to reach Oregon.

[35]

on your Receiving Intelligence from London that the Revd Gentlemans order of last year had not been paid you sent me the Draft and I paid it by a Draft on my Agent. At the time it Escaped me that the Discount allowed in turning Currency into Cash had not been made on this Sum.[76]

I am Gentlemen
Respectfully Yours
Jn McLoughlin

28. To Peter Burnett[77]

Oregon City 28 July 1847

P Burnet

Dear Sir

Mr Abernethy has begun to haul logs for the Road over my Dam[78] to Which I called Mr Lovejoy's[79] Attention four Days ago and he then

---

Blanchet was stationed at the French-Canadian settlements on the Willamette, while Demers was stationed north of the Columbia at the Hudson's Bay Co. Cowlitz Prairie farm. During 1842–43 Demers acted as a missionary to New Caledonia and in 1847 he was consecrated bishop of the newly created diocese of Vancouver Island where he remained until his death. McLoughlin, *Letters, Second Series*, pp. 165–66n.

76. Cash was in short supply in Oregon, and a premium favoring cash over currency prevailed between 1846 and 1848. In the winter of 1847 the Hudson's Bay Co. sold flour at $3.00 per hundredweight if payment was in currency, or $2.50 for cash. Normally, however, the rate of exchange in favor of specie was 33 1/3 percent. Throckmorton, *Oregon Argonauts*, p. 60; *Oregon Spectator*, 4 February 1847.

77. Peter H. Burnett (1807–95) left Missouri, where he had been a district attorney, in 1843 for Oregon. He was one of the original founders of Linnton at the mouth of the Willamette River, but later moved to the Tualatin Valley which he represented in the legislature of the Provisional Government. Following his election to the legislature in May 1844, Burnett was made a member of the standing committee on roads, and in 1845 he was elected supreme judge, the office he held at the time of this letter from McLoughlin. In 1848 he led a company to the California gold fields, and in November 1849 he was elected the first governor of California. Bancroft, *History of Oregon*, 1:393–96, 427–28, 431, 496.

78. George Abernethy acquired full control of the Methodist-sponsored Island Milling Co. in 1846, and from that time until 1861 his mills occupied Governors or Abernethy Island opposite McLoughlin's mills on the mainland. During low water, Abernethy's mills were separated from the mainland by a forty-foot channel, easily dammed in the summer. (During high water, much of the island was awash.) The outcome of this trespass case is unknown; however, by Sep-

told me he was Watching them and as I Understood would do the Needful. They have now five sticks on the spot and to day Mr Lovejoy tells me that Mr Abernethy has been speaking to him and called to his Mind that he Mr Lovejoy was previously Engaged to him (Mr Abernethy) and of which most assuredly I was not aware however I state to you how affairs are and hope you will do the Needful.

Yours Respectfully
Jn McLoughlin

29. To James Douglas

Oregon City 30th July 1847

James Douglass Esqr

Sir

I Beg you would send me as soon as Convenient a Copy of my Letter to you in Reply to the Extract you sent me of Messr Warre & Vavasours Report to Government and I owe it to myself to apply to you for a Copy of your Report on my Reply.[80] I am Sir

Respectfully Yours
Jn McLoughlin

James Douglass Esq
    Chief factor HB Co
       Vancouver

30. To Peter Skene Ogden and James Douglas

Oregon City 9th Augst 1847

P S Ogden }
Js Douglass }

Gentlemen

Will you do me the favour to inform me if you think you will have any

---

tember 1847 a public bridge from the end of Main Street to the island mill was open, and the *Spectator* declared it "a decided improvement." McLoughlin, *Letters, Third Series*, p. 218; Throckmorton, *Oregon Argonauts*, p. 50; *Oregon Spectator*, 16 September 1847.

79. Asa L. Lovejoy. See Appendix C.
80. See Letter 3, n. 10.

Wheat this Season for Sale and the price you think you will demand for it.[81]

I have a small Quantity due me by the settlers and though they are obliged to deliver it here still as I may find it Necessary to take it on the Willamette I would be obliged to you to Instruct Mr McDonald[82] to Receive it for me.

> I am Gentlemen
> Yours Respectfully
> Jn McLoughlin

31. To Captain John H. Couch

Oregon City 12th Augt 1847

To
Captain Couch

Sir

I Beg to inform you [*that*] in Compliance with Instructions from Captain David Dring of the Janet that her lay Days are up this Evening[83] and I am directed to apply to you for fifty Dollars pr Day to be placed to the Credit of Captain Dring on the Books of Mess Pettygrove and Co for Every Day that she may be detained in demurrage According to Charter.

> I am
> Respectfully Yours
> Jn McLoughlin

81. No figures are available for the amount of wheat grown or purchased by the Hudson's Bay Co. in 1847. However, in 1846 the Company received 30,256 bushels from the Willamette settlers at its three granaries south of the Columbia River, and it was estimated that the production of its own farms amounted to an additional ten to twenty thousand bushels. The Company was under contract to supply 12,000 bushels annually to the Russian-American Co. at Sitka; the remainder was sold in Oregon or shipped to the Sandwich Islands. *Oregon Spectator*, 4 March, 15 April 1847.

82. McLoughlin sent Angus McDonald, a Scotsman who had served the Hudson's Bay Co. as a clerk at Stikine and Nisqually, to Champoeg to collect the harvest of 1843. At the beginning of the 1844/45 business year McDonald was appointed clerk in charge of the Company's warehouse and granary at "Campment de Sable" (Champoeg), and was evidently still there in 1847 when McLoughlin was asking the Company's officers to act as his receiver. John A. Hussey, *Champoeg: Place of Transition*, pp. 113–14.

83. The *Janet* arrived from Oahu on 6 July 1847. *Oregon Spectator*, 22 July 1847.

32. To Captain David Dring

Oregon City 12th Augst 1847

To Captain D Dring

Dear Sir

I Beg to Acknowledge the Receipt of yours of 12th Instant and I will with pleasure attend to your Request and apply as you state after this Day Daily to Captain J Couch to pass the Demurrage on the Janet fifty Dollars pr Day to your Credit in the Books of Messr Pettygrove & Co. But as Captain Couch is at present absent and Will be so for a few Days I will have to Manage with his agent Mr Brooks.[84] I Understand they consider the lay Days as Not Expired and that they are Entitled to the time you took to go from Portland to the Mouth of the Willamette to this I observed even allowing that you had to Remove from Portland to the Mouth of the Willamette still with that allowance you had plenty of time to take the Cargo on Board if they had had it alongside to Keep you agoing receiving Cargo. But I told Mr Brooks Captain Couchs Agent that I mentioned this merely as a Remark and I would as you direct apply for Demurrage and only Mention this that you may Know what I have Done and Will do. At the same time I Understand that Mr Abernethy is going to see you on the Business.

Mr Pomeroy will attend to your suggestion and Will have the Lumber &c Ready to deliver Where you Mention.

I am Dear Sir
Respectfully Yours
Jn McLoughlin

NB Pray do not forget to send Back the Key for the piano. I Enclose you a Copy of my Letter to Captain Couch and According to the tenor of it I will apply to morrow and Every Day after for the Demurrage till I hear from you. This Moment I Received the Accompanying Letter from Mr Brooks. But to Repeat what I said before I will apply to morrow Evening for the Demurrage and do so Daily till I hear from you. As to applying as you direct to a Soliciter I know of none here. But I will apply by Letter.

JMcL

84. John P. Brooks, Couch's Oregon City agent, taught the first school in Oregon City in 1844/45 and was the first secretary of the Oregon Printing Association, which published the *Oregon Spectator*. George H. Himes, "History of the Press of Oregon, 1839–1850," pp. 336, 342.

33. To Captain David Dring

Oregon City 13 Augst 1847

To
Captain Dring

Sir

I Beg to send Back the Documents you sent me as Mr Abernethy who takes them is going down to see you and you may Require them.

Will you Enquire as to the Demand for Lumber the sort Required and the price in California (and also of flour as if it suited you it might Answer better to send it There than to Oahu. Shingles could also be sent from this.

Yours Respectfully
Jn McLoughlin

34. To William A. Leidesdorff[85]

Oregon City 13th Augst 1847

W A Leidesdorff Esqr

Dear Sir

I presume by this time you have Received mine of 19th Ult and I hope that you have Been able to Remit the Amount I stated to Mr Pelly. But that if you have not you will soon as I owe him a small Balance which I wish to settle and I hope you will be able to remit me by first opportunity the sum I mentioned and if not then By Captain Dring the Sum I mentioned. I have no Goods and as I have to do my Business in purchasing Wheat by orders on [illegible] Stores — a little Cash faciliates the transaction.

Our Crop this year is lighter than last year owing to the Drought in the beginning of the Season and if there is as large an Immigration as Expected We Will have little Wheat to spare and it will be dearer than last year.[86]

85. This letter was probably not sent, for the following letter to Leidesdorff of the same date is almost a verbatim copy with certain additions and clarifications.

86. Wheat production for 1846 was estimated at 150,000 bushels, of which 25,000 bushels were grown north of the Columbia. Fifty thousand bushels, the equivalent of 10,000 barrels of flour, were estimated as surplus to domestic needs, and therefore available for export. *Oregon Spectator*, 7 January 1847.

Reliable production figures for 1847 have not been located, but one estimate

I hope you will state to me by first opportunity the prospect for flour Shingles and Lumber in California and the sort of Lumber most [*Required*] in Demand. If Government Required Lumber and would state the [*Dimensions*] would Require they could have it (But give us time according to quantity) at $[blank] Dollars p M feet — Deliverable at my Mills or $[blank] deliverable at Portland and $[blank] deliverable at the Mouth of the Willamette on Columbia River.

I have flour but as the Janet is Chartered by Mess Grimes and I suspect there will be some difficulty about demurrage I ship none — Indeed I might have sent per her 100 M feet of Lumber But the Reason alluded to prevented me. On her Return I Expect there will [be] 200 M feet lumber for her But Whether she will proceed to California will depend on the Demand in your Market and the Will of the Captain whom I have taken the liberty to Introduce to you. Mrs Rae sends her Respects to you and the Children still Remember you and all prefer California to this Country.

Yours Respectfully
Jn McLoughlin

35. To William A. Leidesdorff

Oregon City 13th Augst 1847

W A Leidesdorff Esqr

Dear Sir

I presume by this time you have received mine of 19th Ult[87] and I hope that you have been able to remit the Amount I stated to Mr Pelly But that if you have not done so yet you will [*as soon as possible*] before long. I owe him a small Balance which I wish to settle and I hope you will be able to remit me by first opportunity (if not then) by Captain Dring the sum I mentioned As I have no Goods And as I have to do my Business in purchasing Wheat by Order on the stores a little Cash faciliates the transaction. Our Crop this year is lighter

gives total production as 180,000 bushels, with a surplus of 50,000 bushels. Bancroft, *History of Oregon*, 2:2n.

At least 4,500 immigrants arrived in Oregon in the fall of 1847, and by December wheat, which had become scarce, had risen to $1.00 per bushel from the high of $ .80 of the previous winter. W. J. Ghent, *The Road to Oregon*, p. 91; Throckmorton, *Oregon Argonauts*, p. 63.

87. See Letter 26, to William A. Leidesdorff.

than last owing to the Drought in the Beginning of the season and if there is as large an Immigration as Expected We Will have little Wheat to spare and it will be dearer than last year.[88]

I hope you will state to me by first Opportunity the prospect for flour Shingles and Lumber in California and the sort of Lumber [*Required*] most in Demand. If Government Required Lumber and Would state the dimensions they Require they could have it (But give us time according to the Quantity) at $16 P M feet deliverable at my Mills $18 deliverable at Portland and $19 deliverable at the Mouth of the Willamette on the Columbia.

I have flour But as the Janet is Chartered by Mess Grimes And I suspect there will be some difficulty about demurrage I ship None. Indeed I might have sent by her 100 M feet Lumber But the Reasons alluded to prevented me. On her Return I hope there Will be 200 M feet Lumber for her But Whether she will proceed to California Will depend on the Demand in your Market and the Will of the Captain. And it may be Contrary to Law for a British Vessel to go there — pray inform me of this.

I have taken the liberty to Introduce Captain Dring to you. Mrs Rae Begs to be remembered to you and the Children still Remember you and Both prefer San Francisco to Oregon.

Yours Respectfully
Jn McLoughlin

[Written vertically on the left side of the page is the following:] Pray how would Squared Lumber sell in California? What is the price p foot Cubic Measure and the Sizes most in Demand?

36. To Captain David Dring

Oregon City 13th Augst 1847

Captain Dring

Dear Sir

Will you have the Goodness to give me a memorandum of the Dimensions of the Lumber most suitable to the Tahitian Market and the price it Brings there and oblige

Yours Respectfully
Jn McLoughlin

88. See Letter 34, to William A. Leidesdorff, n. 86.

37. To John P. Brooks[89]

Oregon City 13th Augst 1847
6 PM

Mr J P Brooks

Sir

I Beg to Acknowledge the Receipt of yours of Yesterday and to inform you that I am Instructed by Captain David Dring of the Janet to state that he considers he has to Look to Captain Couch for the Demurrage and that he cannot Recognise Mr Abernethy in the Business and in compliance with Captain Drings Instructions Request Captain Couch to cause the sum of fifty Dollars to be placed to the Credit of Captain Dring in Mess Pettygrove and Co Books for the Demurrage of the Janet this Day.

I am
Yours Respectfully
Jn McLoughlin

38. To William A. Leidesdorff

Oregon City 13 Augst 1847

Most Confidential and Private
W A Leidesdorff Esqr

Dear Sir

I Intend if I can collect enough of my funds in the Country and Captain Dring is Willing I propose to Charter his Vessel to go to Manilla for a Cargo of Coffee Sugar Molasses and Rice. I think 30 M would suffice for the purpose. I think it should be in Cash as I am afraid flour and Lumber will Not sell — after all It depends on the funds I am able to Collect and the information I may get. Would such a Cargo sell Well in California? I am told Coffee Costs 7 Cents p lb Sugar 2 Cents p lb and Molasses 7 Cents p Gall at Manilla.[90] Pray

89. John P. Brooks was the Oregon City agent for Captain John H. Couch (see Letter 32, to Captain David Dring, n. 84).

90. McLoughlin could rightfully expect to make a large profit on such a venture. Jessy Quinn Thornton, who left Oregon in October 1847 aboard the *Whiton* to memorialize Congress on the necessity for the establishment of territorial government in Oregon, quoted the following prices then prevailing in Oregon: coarse brown sugar per pound, $ .125; molasses, indifferent, per gallon, $ .60; coffee, indifferent quality, $ .333; rice, per pound, $ .125. United

[43]

have you any information on [*the subject*] the price of these articles there — And What think you of such a Speculation? Would you join in it — There are some here who would join in it — There are some here who will also join in the trip — If the Janet Returns to California, you might ship your funds then But if she Cannot you would have to have your funds at the Island — But after all as for me it Entirely Depends on the funds I can collect — as My funds on the other side of the Continent are Loaned on Mortgages — and I can only draw the Interest. I have mentioned the subject to Captain Dring. You talk to him about it. JMc

[I] sent a Copy to Captain Dring — and wrote to him as follows. The above Extract speaks for itself — and it may be of use to you and us here to have you go to Manilla for a Cargo of these Articles during the Winter Months — as these articles will sell here and at California and you would in the Summer — find Employment in transporting Lumber. Yours Respectfully

Jn McLoughlin

39. To John P. Brooks

Oregon City 14th Augst 1847
6 PM

To Mr J P Brooks

Sir

I Beg to Acknowledge the Receipt of yours of Yesterday in Reply to Mine of same Date to you And in Regard to your reference to Mr Abernethy I am Instructed by Capt Dring to state that I am to apply to J H Couch Esqr and Beg to apply to you as J H Couchs Agent to cause the sum of fifty Dollars to be placed to Capt Drings Credit in Mess Pettygrove & Co Books as the Amount due for the demurrage on the Janet for the last twenty four hours. And as you have not Complied with my Request of yesterday I Beg to Repeat my demand.

Yours Respectfully
Jn McLoughlin

Mr. J P Brooks

States 30th Congress, 1st Session, Miscellaneous Document No. 143, p. 16. In California during the summer of 1846, the only period for which figures are available prior to the gold rush, coffee and sugar sold for $ .50 a pound. *Oregon Spectator*, 25 June 1846.

40. To John P. Brooks

Oregon City 15 Augst 1847

Mr J P Brooks

Sir

I Beg to Acknowledge the Receipt of yours of yesterday And Notice its Contents But it is my Duty to Repeat my Request that the sum of fifty Dollars be passed to the Credit of Capt Dring in Mess Pettygrove & Co Books for demurrage for the Ship Janet for the last twenty four hours.

Yours Respectfully
Jn McLoughlin

41. To Captain David Dring

Oregon City 16 Augst 1847

To Captain Dring

Dear Sir

[*The foregoing are*] With this you will Receive Copies of my Application for the daily demurrage on the Janet to Capt Couch through his Agent Mr J P Brooks and I send you also his Answer as Referred to And I will continue to apply Daily till I hear from you. Indeed I Expected an answer to my last by Mr Abernethy before this as he left Saturday forenoon to call on you as I Understood about his affair.

Yours Respectfully
Jn McLoughlin

NB since Writing the above to You I wrote the following to be delivered to Mr Brooks this Evening

Sir

Yours of Yesterday came Duly to hand and in Regard to your reference to Mr Abernethy I Beg to Repeat that Capt Dring has Instructed me to state that he Cannot Know Mr Abernethy on the Business And to Repeat my Application to you As Agent for J H Couch Esqr to cause fifty Dollars to be placed to the Credit of Capt Dring in Mess Pettygrove & Co Books due [for the] Demurrage of the Janet for the last twenty four hours.

Yours Respectfully
Jn McLoughlin

[45]

7 PM I this moment Received the Answer No 5 and Captain Couch told me Verbally that he had informed you that he would have Nothing to do with the Business in Question Except to hand Mr Abernethy Eight Hundred Dollars.

Jn McLoughlin

There are no Solicitors here or Else I would have applied to one before this. I hope to hear to day from you or at least to morrow.

42. To Captain David Dring

Oregon City 24 August 1847

Extract of a Letter to Capt D Dring

"Mr Pomeroy is absent and I cannot say definitively if he will be able to send his Lumber to Tongue point[91] But still I hope you will Examine and let me know if there is a suitable place and you may depend I will do all I can to send it there.

Jn McLoughlin

Of course you will drop me a Note from Fort George[92] to inform me if you have found a suitable place for Lumber at Tongue point.

Jn McLoughlin

91. Tongue Point, a high, steep peninsula of about seventy acres, is located about five miles upstream from the modern city of Astoria, Oregon. Jutting from the south bank of the Columbia River, it commands the ship channel. By rafting lumber to Tongue Point from the Willamette, sawmill owners saved ship captains the trouble and expense of making the long, tortuous trip up the Columbia. For those captains unfamiliar with the shifting channels of the river, the charges for having their vessels piloted to Portland could be costly. The schedule of pilotage fees was published at the time of the appointment of Selah C. Reeves as the first official pilot on the Columbia in April 1847. From outside the Columbia's bar to Baker's Bay just east of Cape Disappointment the fee was $4 per foot (draft), and from Baker's Bay to Astoria the fee was $1 per foot. From Astoria to Astoria Mills thirty miles east, the charge was also $1 per foot, and the same amount was charged for pilotage from Astoria Mills to Vancouver or Portland. *Oregon Spectator*, 15 April 1847.

92. Fort George, modern Astoria, was the Hudson's Bay station near the mouth of the Columbia River. Built by the Astorians in 1811, it was purchased by the North West Co. in 1813 and renamed Fort George. In 1821 it was transferred to the Hudson's Bay Co., but after the removal of the principal Columbia River depot to Fort Vancouver in 1824–25, it became only a minor trading post.

43. To William A. Leidesdorff

Oregon City 25th Augst 1847

W A Leidesdorff Esq

Dear Sir

I am this Moment informed that Mr Abernethy according to promise sends by the Janet Capt Dring a Crank to your address to replace the Crank he took belonging to Mr Knight.[93]

I am sorry to inform you our harvest is very poor and as to other points of Business I Beg to refer you to my Last. In the Expectation of hearing from you I am

Yours Respectfully

Jn McLoughlin

44. To Captain François Marie Menes[94]

Oregon City 1st Sept 1847

Cap Menes

Mon tres Chere Capitaine

Ayoz la Bonté s'il vous plait de livrer la lettre Inclus a Monsieur Birnie[95] et il vous livrera deux Barrels de Saumon lesquels Je vous prie

93. See Letter 25, to William A. Leidesdorff.

94. François Marie Menes was captain of *L'Etoile du Matin*, which arrived from Brest, France, on 14 August 1847. In July 1849 Menes returned in *L'Etoile du Matin*, but the ship ran aground while trying to enter the Columbia without a pilot and was so badly damaged that she could not be repaired (see Letter 22, to George Pelly, n. 65). With the goods salvaged from the ship, Menes opened a French store in Oregon City for the ship's owners, V. Marzion & Co. of Le Havre-de-Grâce, France. According to Hubert H. Bancroft, McLoughlin became a partner in Menes' firm in 1850 and remained in the firm until 1853 when it was closed. Menes then settled on French Prairie near Champoeg, where he lived until his death in 1867. Bancroft, *History of Oregon*, 1:326–27, citing the *Oregon City Enterprise* of 21 March 1868.

95. James Birnie (ca. 1799–1864) was born in Scotland and entered the service of the North West Co. as an apprentice clerk in 1818. During 1820–21, he was stationed at Fort George, and after the coalition of 1821, the Hudson's Bay Co. retained his services. Following service in New Caledonia he was placed in charge of Fort George in 1839 and remained there until his retirement in 1846, when he moved to Cathlamet on the north bank of the Columbia where he lived until his death. Fleming, ed., *Minutes of Council Northern Department*, pp. 428–29.

d'Accepter, ils serviront a vous faire Connaitre la qualitie du Saumon de La Colombie. Vous souhaitant un heureux Voyage et le plaisir de Vous Voire ici dans le Cours du Mois de Mars prochain.

Je Suis avec le plus profond Respect

Votre tres humble Serviteur
Jn McLoughlin

Editor's translation:

Cap[tain] Menes

My very dear Captain,

Have the goodness, if you please, to deliver the enclosed letter to Mr. Birnie and he will deliver to you two barrels of Salmon which I beg you to accept. They will serve to make known to you the quality of the Columbia Salmon. Wishing you a happy trip and the pleasure to see you here in the month of March next.

I am with the deepest respect

Your very humble servant
Jn McLoughlin

45. TO JAMES BIRNIE

Oregon City 1st Sept 1847

To
James Birnie Esqr

Dear Sir

Please deliver to Captain Menes of the Morning Star two Barrels of your Best Columbia Salmon.

Yours Respectfully
Jn McLoughlin

NB It will serve to make him Acquainted with the quality of our Columbia Salt Salmon.[96]

96. Salt salmon was produced in quantity on the Columbia for domestic consumption and for trade with the Sandwich Islands. When the fish were landed, Indian women cut out the backbones and chopped off the heads. The salter then placed them in a large hogshead with a quantity of coarse salt, and there they remained for several days until they became quite firm. The pickle produced from this process was boiled in a large copper kettle, and the blood, which was floated by the boiling process, was skimmed off, leaving the pickle perfectly clear.

The salmon were then taken from the hogshead and packed in tierces (casks

46. To Edward Roberts

Oregon City 2nd Sept 1847

Mr Edward Roberts

Dear Sir

Yours of the 25th Sept 1846 with the late Mr Raes[97] Will &c came duly to hand and I Return them signed &c According to Instructions and Which I hope will prove satisfactory And Enable you to do the Needful.

> I am
> Dear Sir
> Yours Respectfully
> Jn McLoughlin

---

holding forty-two gallons) with a little more salt. The tierces were then sealed and laid on their sides with the bunghole left open. The pickle recovered from the boiling process was poured in until the tierce was full, and a circle of clay, about four inches high, was made around the bunghole into which the oil from the salmon rose. The oil was skimmed off, and as the salmon absorbed the pickle, more was poured in. When the oil had ceased to rise, the clay circle was removed and the cask was sealed. It was said that salmon cured in this manner would keep for three years. John Dunn, *History of the Oregon Territory and British North American Fur Trade*, pp. 163–64.

97. William Glen Rae (ca. 1809–45) was McLoughlin's son-in-law. He was engaged by the Hudson's Bay Co. in 1827, and in 1834, following service at York Factory and in the Red River District, he was sent to the Columbia District. In November 1837 he was appointed a clerk at Fort Vancouver, and in 1838 he married Eloisa McLoughlin. When Stikine was acquired from the Russian-American Co. in 1840, Rae was placed in charge. In November 1841 he was promoted to the rank of chief trader, and the same year he was sent to San Francisco to open a Company store and trading house.

Rae was not a strong character, and he was known to drink to excess. The lack of news and support from either McLoughlin or the London office, the intense competition in the California trade, and his involvement in an unsuccessful revolt against the Mexican government all served to agitate the young trader. Rumors that he was unfaithful to his wife began to circulate in January 1845, and Rae, overcome with mortification and disgrace, shot himself. From the time of Rae's suicide until December 1845, British Vice-Consul James A. Forbes managed the Company's affairs. Rae's suicide, coming after the murder of John McLoughlin, Jr., in 1842, further embittered the elder McLoughlin against his employer, for he felt that with more adequate support from the Company, both tragedies would have been prevented. McLoughlin, *Letters, First Series*, pp. 353–55; ibid., *Third Series*, pp. xxvii–xxix; William Heath Davis, *Seventy-five Years in California*, ed. Douglas S. Watson, p. 94.

[49]

47. To Edward Roberts

Extract of a letter to Mr Edward Roberts

"If such Hats as you sent me stand Rain and Cost no more than 4/[98] send me forty of them.

Jn McLoughlin

3rd Sept 1847

NB you will apply to the Hudson Bay Co to pay you for the Hats on my a/c.

JnMcl

48. To Archibald McKinlay

Oregon City 17th Sept 1847

Archibald McKindlay Esqr

Sir

I Beg to inform you that I consider all within the space on the plat of Oregon City[99] Marked as Mill Reserve as a place Not to be Intruded on for the purpose of trade by any But myself of Course leaving Every Access to the Granary According to Lease and to the Mill for any Business connected with it. If Any Creditors of the Hudson Bay Company Land Wheat on the plat form they can pass it through the Mill to the Granary As my only object is not to allow myself to be opposed on my own premises And in Every other Respect I am Willing and Ready to give Every facility to the Company which the place affords.

If any man Brings Wheat to my Mills who is Indebted to the Hudson Bay Co you have a perfect Right to go there to ask him for his debt and Use Every advantage the place affords to Enable you to Recover the debt. All I want is merely the first chance to purchase from him after he has paid his Debt.

Yours Respectfully
Jn McLoughlin

98. Four shillings, worth about eighty cents in the 1840s. McLoughlin, *Letters, Second Series*, p. 11.

99. Jesse Applegate, an immigrant of 1843 who had been a deputy surveyor in Missouri (see Letter 60, to William L. Marcy, n. 123), surveyed and platted McLoughlin's Oregon City claim in the winter of 1843/44. The "Mill Reserve" was on the mainland opposite Abernethy Island. The original plat is in the collections of the McLoughlin Memorial Association in Oregon City, Oregon; and a certified copy dated 2 December 1850, with corrections to 1927, is filed in the office of the county clerk, Clackamas County, Oregon City, Oregon.

49. To Captain David Dring

Oregon City 20th Sept 1847

Capt Dring

Dear Sir

I have not been able to find any one whose management I could trust to take a Raft down to tongue point. Mr. Pomeroy Intends to go with Rafts to the Lower Mouth of the Willamette and When there he will see what he can do But he cannot Engage to go farther. As to tongue point Channel it is never Lower than when you Crossed it so that it will be Necessary for you to come Up. In the Mean time I will do all I can to Induce Mr Pomeroy to drop down with his Rafts When he Learns you are in the River so as you would pick him Up before he got to Tongue point Channel as it is crossing to tongue point that he dreads and I think justly as though I think crossing with a Raft perfectly feasible and safe with proper hands But I do not think he can find such hands. My Respects to Mrs and Miss Dring and Believe me to Be

Yours Respectfully
Jn McLoughlin

50. To Alexander Lattie[100]

Oregon City 21st Sept 1847

Mr Lattey

Dear Sir

Enclosed is a letter for Capt Dring which I would be obliged to you if you Deliver it to him as soon as possible after he Crosses the Bar.

100. Alexander Lattie, also spelled Lattey (1802–49), was a Columbia River pilot. He arrived in Oregon in 1831 as an employee of the Hudson's Bay Co. and worked in the Company's coastal service for the next fifteen years. He was the first accepted bar and river pilot, and in March 1836 he piloted the steamer *Beaver* to Fort Vancouver on her maiden voyage. Sometime during the winter of 1845/46, Lattie settled at Fort George, where he was James Birnie's assistant. Lattie succeeded Birnie in charge of Fort George, but in the fall of 1846 Lattie left the Company's service and moved across the river to Chinook, where he was close to the northern channel and possible piloting jobs. In May 1849 he piloted the U.S. steam transport *Massachusetts*, carrying the first American troops to Oregon, to Fort Vancouver. In July he went to the rescue of the French ship, *L'Etoile du Matin* (see Letter 22, to George Pelly, n. 65), and helped work her upriver to Portland. He was accidentally drowned on

It is to inform Capt Dring that Mr Pomeroy cannot undertake to take his Lumber to tongue point But is to take it to the Lower Mouth of the Willamette and I will do my Utmost to Induce Mr Pomeroy to drop down the River when he hears that Capt Dring is in the River as he will trust to meeting Capt Dring before he (Mr Pomeroy) gets to tongue point Channel as it is Crossing to Tongue point that he dreads and I think very Justly as though I know it to be perfectly safe and feasible with proper hands Yet I do not see where he can get proper hands.

Yours Respectfully
Jn McLoughlin

51. To Peter Skene Ogden and James Douglas

To   Oregon City 21st Sept 1847

P S Ogden   }
James Douglass }

Gentlemen

On the 21st last July I wrote you the following Letter "On settling my a/c last spring with this post there was an Order of the Revd Mr. Demers of three thousand Dollars to my Credit. But on your Receiving Intelligence from London that the Revd Gentleman's Order of Last year had not been paid you sent me the Draft and I paid it by a Draft on my Agent. At the time it Escaped me that the Discount allowed on turning Currency into Cash had not been Made on this sum."[101] In your Reply Dated the 2nd Augst you wrote "having no statement of your Shop a/c at the falls here We cannot say Whether Discount was Allowed you nor not on the Mission Bill which you gave last spring in payment of your Account. If not the transaction will of course be settled in the same manner as if you had made payment in Cash to the Amount of three thousand Dollars in question and We Will now Write Mr McKindlay on that subject." But since the Receipt of this Letter I have heard no more on the subject and I would be happy to learn your decision. I am

Yours Respectfully
Jn McLoughlin

9 September while crossing from Portland to Vancouver. Alexander Lattie, "Alexander Lattie's Fort George Journal, 1846," ed. Thomas Vaughan and Priscilla Knuth, pp. 197–209 *passim*.

101. See Letter 27, to Peter Skene Ogden and James Douglas.

52.. TO GEORGE PELLY

Oregon City 23rd Sept 1847

George Pelly Esqr

Dear Sir

Since I wrote you on the 2nd And 8th July[102] I Received yours of the 10th June and 13th August and I am much obliged to you for sending the Janet. By her I Received the Goods you sent me according to Invoice #90. She Crossed the Bar of the Columbia about the 1st Sept bound to San Francisco with a Cargo of Lumber for Mess Grimes at San Francisco. The Captain Expects to be back about the 10th Oct When he will Load with Lumber and flour and proceed to Oahu Unless I Receive certain information *Very Certain* of better prices than you quote and Immediate payment in San Francisco. In this case she will sail to that place (if a British Vessel can go from here to that place and Capt Dring consents) and the proceeds will be remitted to you and I trust it will be sufficient to meet all your Demands. But though I mention the probability of the Janet going to San Franciso [*sic*] still I see very little probability of such being the case as it is subject to so many Contingences [*sic*] and merely mention it — in case from Circumstances it might be advisable.

I was much surprised to learn by yours of 13th Augst that Mr Leidesdorff has made no Remittance to you and still more so to find by his Letter to me of the 24th Augst by Capt Gelson of the Whitton (which sailed from this in July with flour and Lumber) that he (Mr Leidesdorff) had been Unable to Effect any Sales When I see by the public papers that they state flour was selling there at $12 pr Barrel in Retail and Capt Gelson sold his for that price and in Whole sail at $10 p Barrel which shows you were Correct in your surmises however I wrote him by the Janet Capt Dring to sell and Remit to you — and I trust to have more satisfactory Intelligence in a short time by the Janet.

My Son is in the french settlement[103] collecting his Debts and two Days ago an Express came here from Portland for Mr Wilson[104]— as

102. See Letters 22 and 23, to George Pelly.
103. McLoughlin refers to the Champoeg district. Champoeg, about twenty miles above Oregon City on the southeast bank of the Willamette River, had since about 1827 been the home of retired servants of the Company, many of whom were French-Canadians, hence the name "french settlement."
104. Albert E. Wilson.

Mr Pettygrove was taken suddenly Very ill and reports received to Day state that Mr Pettygrove I am Extremely sorry to say is beyond all hopes of Recovery and I hope this will Account for their Silence (if Mr Wilson has not written — and I can only say that they received Supplies you sent by the Toulon — which is now at Portland.

Our Crop is poorer than I ever knew it and the Emigration much larger than it ever has been And the farmers Are ploughing diligently for Next Year — But this year We Will Export less flour than Usual. Please Remember me to Mess Allen and McLeod[105] and Believe to be Yours Respectfully

Jn McLoughlin

NB There are ten Barrels flour of mine missing at Portland. They are supposed to have been shipped on Board the Brutus Capt Adams. Did he give them to you? He also was to pay you about twenty Dollars for me. I have not my Books in the house to refer to to state the Exact sum.

Jn McL

As stated in mine of 8th July last I do not wish to purchase a share of a Vessel at present.

Jn McLoughlin

53. To Peter Skene Ogden and James Douglas

Oregon City 26th Sept 1847

P S Ogden ⎫
James Douglass ⎭   Esqr

Gentlemen

An American offers to sell me two hundred and ninety five Bushels Wheat in the Cowlitz.[106] If I purchased it how many Bushels Wheat will you give me in Exchange at this place for it.

Yours Respectfully
Jn McLoughlin

105. George Traill Allan was Pelly's assistant at the Honolulu agency of the Hudson's Bay Co. The McLeod referred to has not be identified.

106. The Cowlitz settlement was located at the portage between the Cowlitz and Chehalis rivers about thirty miles north of the Columbia. There, in 1838, the Hudson's Bay Co. established a farm which was transferred to the Puget's Sound Agricultural Co., a subsidiary of the Company, in 1839. The arable land was limited to about three thousand acres of which the Hudson's Bay

NB of course I will Expect no Wheat to be delivered me at this place till the Wheat is delivered into the Companys store at the Cowlitz. Tom has applied to me for his Wages from 1st June 1846 to 1st June 1847 saying he had been referred to me by the officers at Vancouver. Now in settling my a/c with the Hudson Bay last spring I was Charged with Tom's Wages from 1st June 1846 to 1st June 1847[107] and he left me at that time.

JMcL

54. To Albert E. Wilson

Oregon City 1st Oct 1847

Private & Confidential
A E Wilson

Dear Sir

It will be necessary you would give me an Idea as soon as possible What quantity of Cargo you will have to send by the Janet[108] so as not to Retain more space in her hold than is Required. As you know the Vessel will be here soon and Every thing Must be Ready and we must send all that we can to Market and therefore must take precaution in time. Waiting your Reply

I am
Yours Respectfully
Jn McLoughlin

NB The fact is Mr Pomeroy I think will have more than a Cargo for the Janet — and if you had any other Means of sending your produce to Market It would be Well that Mr Pomeroy should fill the Janet — as

---

Co. farmed half. Galbraith, *The Hudson's Bay Company*, pp. 200, 455. It was estimated that eight to nine thousand bushels of wheat were grown at the Cowlitz farms in 1846. *Oregon Spectator*, 15 April 1847.

107. The charge to which McLoughlin refers must have been made on the accounts at Fort Vancouver, for no record of such a charge appears on the London accounts of McLoughlin. John McLoughlin, *The Financial Papers of Dr. John McLoughlin*, ed. Burt Brown Barker, p. 76. "Tom" was very likely a Hawaiian (Kanaka) loaned by the Company for employment in McLoughlin's mills.

108. The *Janet* arrived about November 1847 from California and departed for Oahu in January 1848.

it Realizes funds — But this cannot be decided on at the present moment. I am sorry I did not see you yesterday before you left to have a full conversation on the subject. Remember me to Mr Pettygrove and if he is sufficiently — well to attend on Business let him see this Letter. If [I] could absent myself from my Mill I would go to see him. [JnMcL] I am told the Eveline[109] is Bound to this place if she comes she will afford means of Exporting. But of this only among ourselves.

55. To George Pelly

Oregon City 7th Oct 1847

George Pelly Esqr

Dear Sir

Since I last wrote you on the 23rd Ult I Received a letter (by the Brig Henry Capt Bray[110]) from Capt Dring Dated San Francisco 7th Ult in which he States he Expects to be here by the 20th Inst and I can only say there are Now 200 M ft Lumber Ready for the Janet But if Mess Pettygrove cannot ship by the Toulon I will have to make Room for them and therefore will not be able to send that quantity of Lumber. I will send more than sufficient to meet my Liabilities and feel duly the handsome Manner you Acted in taking up my Draft which certainly I would not have drawn if I had been aware you had no funds of Mine.

In my Last I stated I supposed there were ten Barrels of flour of Mine Missing and supposed they were sent by the Brutus — but it is a Mistake they are found.

Mr Leidesdorf did not write me by Capt Bray. It is Reported here that he has sold his property to Norris and Shelly for $75,000. What does this Mean? However I think he will answer the letter I wrote him by Capt Dring. Yours Respectfully

Jn McLoughlin

109. The *Eveline*, an American brig, arrived in the Columbia from Newburyport, Massachusetts, in April 1848. (See Letter 85, to Charles L. Ross, n. 151.)

110. Bray was captain of the *Henry* on two trips during 1847, after which William K. Kilborne, who had brought the ship from Newburyport in March 1847, resumed command (see Appendix B).

56. To Nathaniel J. Wyeth

Oregon City 10th Oct 1847

N Wyeth Esqr

Dear Sir

I have the pleasure to Acknowledge the Receipt of your Esteemed favour of 1st April last and beg to Return you my thanks for the Copy of the Boundary treaty which you sent me and also the other important information which you Communicate. In Regard to your claim as our organisation allows a claim of Land to Actual settlers only[111] It is evident our Constituted Authorities can afford you no protection against our Jumpers as they are Called. But to secure your Claim I had it Recorded as soon as I could and that was before any had attempted to infringe your Rights and I stated before & Since to Every one [since and before] I Recorded it — that it was yours particularly to the officers of the U S Exploring Squadron and took Mr Drayton an artist or rather a Member of the Scientific Corps to the place and pointed out your houses and improvements with the Expectation this might be Useful to you which I state in case of your being able to avail yourself of it and for the same Reason I sent you the Copy of the Lease. But as I said your Only Chance of getting your Claim is from the supreme Government. As for my proceedings I will do Nothing more till the United States Government Extends its Authority over Us But Continue as I have done to state that you Claim it and that I lease it from you. When in Charge of the Hudson Bay Companys affairs I placed Cattle on it for Which alone it is adapted as though there [are] some spots [?] of fertile Soil Yet as you know they are almost Every year overflown in June Except in years of very Low Water, and they cannot be depended on for Agricultural purposes and as the Hudson Bay Co have cattle on it with Herdsmen to Gaurd [sic] them It is possessed by Company as much as it can be

111. On Wyeth's claim, see Letter 14, to Nathaniel J. Wyeth. By "our organisation" McLoughlin refers to the Provisional Government of Oregon. In August 1845 McLoughlin, on behalf of the Hudson's Bay Co., concluded an agreement with the Provisional Government whereby the authority of the government was recognized and the rights of British subjects were protected. Robert Carlton Clark, "The Last Step in the Formation of a Provisional Government for Oregon in 1845," p. 315. The revised land law of 1845 prevented nonresidents from holding claims in Oregon. *Oregon Spectator*, 23 March 1848.

and I therefore hope The US Government will admit your Claim. And as it is Your Right though of no Great Value at present as those Men who have Jumped it have done so from a desire to annoy and in the Expectation of being Bought off as if they had taken Claims in the Willamette Valley they would have been more than ten times more Valuable to them than any they could get on your Island still your Island though of no great Value at presant [sic] will become of some Value when the settlement of the Country Increases and as I Believe your Right to use the Words of a Great Authority "Unquestionable" [112] I consider it Worthy of being maintained provided it does not Lead to too great Expense which I think cannot be the case. As to the course I intend to pursue — I will put in your Claim when the U S Extend their Jurisdiction over Us and if that fails as you suggest I will put in my Claim as your tenant and if that is of use I will be happy of it on your Account as it was only [to] serve you that I took the lease in my Name as the HB Co would have refused to do it in theirs if I had applied to them for it and I am certain would have objected to my doing it in Mine if they had known it though what I did was known to all the officers about me. I think Neither the soil or Climate about Fort Hall[113] is adapted to Raising Grass But is is said the Mormons have begun a settlement in the Vicinity of Bear River[114] on a Rich

112. McLoughlin has reference to James K. Polk's inaugural statement that "our title to the country of the Oregon is 'clear and unquestionable.' " . . . (4 March 1845). James D. Richardson, ed., *A Compilation of the Messages and Papers of the Presidents, 1789–1897*, 4:381.

113. Fort Hall, on the east bank of the Snake River near the mouth of the Portneuf in southeastern Idaho, was built in 1834 by Nathaniel Wyeth. The fort was sold to the Hudson's Bay Co. in 1837 for five hundred dollars, and it continued to be used by the Company until 1856. Located some two hundred miles from Fort Bridger, Fort Hall was a major resting place on the Oregon Trail, and the hospitality of Chief Trader Richard Grant who was in charge from 1842 to 1851 was widely known to the weary travelers. Soda Springs, the junction of the Oregon and California trails, was located some eighty miles southeast of Fort Hall. Richard G. Beidleman, "Nathaniel Wyeth's Fort Hall," pp. 209, 248; Louis S. Grant, "Fort Hall under the Hudson's Bay Company, 1837–1856," pp. 35, 38.

114. Bear River flows north from the Uinta Mountains some eighty or ninety miles to Soda Springs where it turns to the southwest and south to discharge into Great Salt Lake. The Mormons had originally considered settling in the Bear River Valley, but finding it unsuitable they moved on to the shores of

tract of Country and I Understand they are very Disagreeable Neighbours and I have as I informed you had to do too much to do with pagans and Sectarians — to Venture among them again and therefore have No Relish for your Speculations. But you may depend if the projected Rail Road from the States to this place is carried into Effect which I Believe it will be before long the Soda springs will be resorted to by Convalescents and particularly by those affected with pulmonary Complaints for the Salubrity of its Air. As Every patient that I have known has been greatly Benefitted by Residing there in Summer and some were Actually Cured and it will be the Watering place most resorted to in North America and a Splendid City will be Built there. Indeed two or three Claims of 640 Acres Each are already Recorded. But as for me I have had too much trouble in opening new Countries to attempt again. You know what I did to Introduce Civilisation into this Country and you know how I treated the Methodist Missionaries and how they Acted to me and the Manner I treated all who came to the Country and Wanted Assistance and When I could afford assistance I never denied it. Yet what troubles have I not had [at] this place first with the Methodist Mission though as you know I had Worked and improved it for years before they came and last year a Man of the Name of Vickers[115] Jumped

---

Great Salt Lake. The Mormons were camped at Sulphur Spring on the Bear River near the present site of Evanston, Wyoming, during the early part of July 1847, and it may be that this encampment is the "settlement" to which McLoughlin refers. Leland Hargrave Creer, *The Founding of an Empire*, p. 86.

115. In the fall of 1846, one A. J. Vickers occupied 274 acres on the Willamette River adjacent to Oregon City. Although McLoughlin had sown oats and timothy on about ten acres of the land in question, Vickers considered the land to be "unencumbered by the laws of Oregon, or the improvement of Indian or White Man," and on 16 October 1846 he registered his claim at the Recorder's Office in Oregon City. McLoughlin forbade Vickers to cut timber or make improvements on the land and instituted legal proceedings against the trespasser which were almost immediately abandoned for unexplained reasons. On 15 April 1847 McLoughlin placed a notice in the *Oregon Spectator* forbidding all persons to trespass on his land claim as surveyed by Jesse Applegate and registered at the Recorder's Office on 16 December 1843. He cautioned all prospective purchasers against buying any land within the claim from anyone except himself. On 29 April, Vickers countered with a similar notice disclaiming any rights of McLoughlin to the land in question.

On 14 May, William K. Kilborne, captain of the *Henry* and Oregon City merchant, chaired a meeting to discuss methods of dealing with "jumpers."

half of my Claim Under the pretence first that no one could get from Congress more than 320 Acres and then that as the first organisation in [1843] Reserved all town sites and Water Privileges Except for Missionaries. My Record though I did so in 1843 and first a Survey with Record in 1844[116] is not Valid as they say I ought to have Recorded again in 1845 when this clause in the first Record was Repealed. This man has got three or four Men to join him and has caused me a good Deal of trouble and Expense and though the Community Disapprove their Conduct still it is Extremely harrassing to be Annoyed in this Way. The Country is settling fast. The population was in July about ten

---

It was resolved that a committee of five should be appointed to select twelve men to investigate and adjudicate such a dispute. The resolutions adopted at this meeting also deprived claim jumpers of the right to vote. McLoughlin signed the resolutions, but Vickers refused to do so. According to G. W. Bell, one of Vickers' supporters, another lawsuit was begun, but there is no evidence of this in the pages of the *Spectator*. During November 1847 and January 1848. the matter was actively discussed in the columns of the *Spectator* by the supporters of both Vickers and McLoughlin; but unfortunately the outcome of the dispute was never recorded. *Oregon Spectator*, 15, 29 April, 27 May, 25 November 1847, 6 January 1848.

116. On 5 July 1843 the newly organized Provisional Government adopted a report from the Committee on Private Land Claims, which called for the registration of land claims with the territorial recorder. Those persons already in possession of land were allowed one year in which to file a description; within six months from the time the claim was recorded, improvements were to be made; and the claim was to be occupied no later than one year after filing the description. No individual was to be allowed to hold a claim of more than 640 acres in a square or oblong form. Lastly, and most importantly for McLoughlin, the act provided that "no person shall be entitled to hold such a claim upon City or Town sites, extensive water privileges or other situations necessary for the transaction of Mercantile or Manufacturing operations and to the detriment of the community — provided that nothing in these laws shall be so construed, as to affect any claim of any Mission of a Religious character made previous to this time of an extent not more than six miles square.—" Duniway and Riggs, eds., "Oregon Archives," p. 279 (quoted from the May 1844 copy of the Organic Laws of 1843).

McLoughlin first had his land claim at Willamette Falls (Oregon City) surveyed by J. M. Hudspeath in 1842, but after the passage of the land law of 1843, he hired Jesse Applegate to make another survey. Applegate's survey was filed at the territorial recorder's office in Oregon City on 13 December 1843, and the plat was filed in the following spring. *Oregon Spectator*, 6 January 1848; copy of a "Plat of Oregon City" on file with the county clerk, Clackamas County, Oregon City, Oregon.

thousand it said on the 21st August about a thousand Wagons had passed from the states Bound here and in my Opinion though the Soil is not so fertile as Missisouri's [sic] nor is there so great an Extent of Country fit for Cultivation as is Reported in the Newspapers As you Well Know yet taking it altogether I think from the Mildness of the Climate it is the most comfortable Residence for Civilised Man in North America. But the Government must take good care in selecting proper officers particularly their Indian Agents for whom they ought to seek here Among the Old traders Who know the Indians And have to deal with them and are Respected and Esteemed by them. But to Return to the Business of the Country this summer we have sent ten Cargoes of Lumber and produce to Market and the trade must Increase Rapidly once the U S Establish a Government which will give a Spur to Business. With Best wishes Believe me to Be

Yours Sincerely

Jn McLoughlin

P S The following Clause was part of Organic Compact formed in 1843 "No person shall be Entitled to hold such Claim Upon City or town sites Extensive Water privileges or other situations Necessary for the transaction of Mercantile or Manuffacturing [sic] operations to the Detriment of the Community Provided that Nothing in these Laws shall be construed as to Effect any Claim of Any Mission of a Religious Character made previous to this time of an Extent of not more than Six Miles Square." The late Jason Lee[117] got the late Le Breton[118] to Bring in

117. Jason Lee (1803–45) led a group of Methodist missionaries to Oregon in 1834. From St. Louis, the party traveled west with Nathaniel Wyeth's second expedition to Oregon. Lee's first mission was established near the upper (southern) settlements on French Prairie; but after the arrival of reinforcements in 1840, Lee moved mission headquarters to Chemeketa, the site of modern Salem, and established a branch at Willamette Falls on land claimed by McLoughlin. Lee was influential in the establishment of the Provisional Government of Oregon in 1843, and the mission clause in the 1843 land law was aimed at dispossessing McLoughlin of his Oregon City claim. For a more complete discussion of McLoughlin's land dispute with the Methodists, see particularly Charles H. Carey, "Lee, Waller and McLoughlin," pp. 187–213; Holman, *Dr. John McLoughlin*, pp. 101–20; McLoughlin, *Letters, Third Series*, pp. xl–li, 195–219.

118. George W. Le Breton, who arrived with Captain John H. Couch as supercargo on the *Maryland* in 1840, was active in the formation of the Provisional Government of Oregon. In 1841 he served on the Committee of Arrangements in the first abortive attempt to establish a government of the Columbia. He was one of the secretaries at the historic Champoeg meeting of 2 May

[61]

this Clause to dispossess me if possible. What can you think of a Man — a Missionary acting in this Manner to a person who has Acted towards him as you know and I never Acted otherwise than as you saw. In 1845 the Convention formed a New Compact

Article 3 —

"Any person now holding or hereafter wishing to Establish a Claim to Land in this Territory shall Designate the Extent of his Claim by Natural Boundaries of such Claim or By Marks at the Corners And Upon the Lines of such Claims and have the Extent and Boundary of such Claim Recorded in the office of the Territorial Recorder in a Book to be kept by him for that purpose within twenty Days from the time of making such Claim provided that those who shall be already in possession of Land shall be allowed twelve Months from the passing of the Act to file a Description of his Claim in the Recorders office and provided further that the said Claimant shall state in his Record the size shape and Locality of such Claim and Give the Names of the adjoining Claimants and the Recorder may Require the applicant for such Record to be made to Answer on his Oath touching the facts — " At the time this Law passed my Claim was Recorded and a Survey with the Notes of the Survey in the Record Book. The Book is kept and I never thought the new organisation Intended or Could obliterate Acts performed Under the Old and as far as my information goes None of those who had Recorded Under it Recorded again Under the last.

JnMcL

57. To WILLIAM A. LEIDESDORFF

Oregon City 16 Oct 1847

W A Leidesdorff

Dear Sir

Yours of 24th Augst by the Whitton[119] Capt Gelston came duly to hand and I must say having seen previously in the California papers that flour was selling in Retail at \$12 pr Barrel I was disappointed

---

1843 at which the Provisional Government was organized, and at that same meeting he was elected to serve as clerk of court or recorder. He continued to hold that office until his death. In early March 1844 he was mortally wounded during an Indian alarm in Oregon City. Bancroft, *History of Oregon*, 1:282–83; Duniway and Riggs, eds., "Oregon Archives," pp. 216, 236–37.

119. The *Whiton* had arrived in the Columbia on 11 September 1847.

to find you had not sold mine Especially as Capt Gelston sold his after you had Received my Letter. But as you have Received my letter 13th Augst by the Janet Capt Dring I presume that long before this you have done as I Requested sent me a thousand Dollars by Capt Dring and Remitted the Balance to George Pelly Esqr Oahu.

Yours Respectfully
Jn McLoughlin

NB The Account you sent me is not the one I meant as my Son had handed me the Copy you gave him I presumed when I wrote that you had effected the Sale of the property my Son left with you — for that purpose and this is the account I Requested. Jn McLoughlin
NB On the Receipt of this if you have any flour of Mine in your possession you will please deliver it to Capt Gelston and take his Receipt for the same and deliver him the Goods unsold. Of course Capt Gelston will pay the Storage. J McLoughlin

58. To Captain Roland Gelston

Oregon City 16th Oct 1847

To Captain Gelston

Dear Sir

Will you please to Receive any flour and Goods of mine from W A Leidesdorff Esqr. Dispose of them and Remit the proceeds to George W Pel[ly] [Three lines which include the complimentary closing and signature have been clipped from the manuscript.]

59. To Captain Roland Gelston

Oregon City 17 Oct 1847

Capt Gelston

Dear Sir

According to promise I wrote you by the Henry Capt Kilborn But have[ing] Nothing to add in Regard to my Affairs with Capt Leidesdorff But hope you will get it Settled.

I Enclose my letter to the Secretary[120] Whom I Understand is the

120. See the following letter to William L. Marcy, secretary of war. The Indian Bureau was in the War Department until 1849, when it was transferred to the newly created Department of the Interior.

proper officer to be addressed in Regard to Indian affairs and leave it open for your own private perusal then Seal and do the Needful. You see I have Been Brief and urged only We get the Most urgent — that is to send an agent with men to Meet the Immigrant at Fort Hall as Unless this is done there will be trouble with the Indians which Besides the loss of Valuable lives will cause great Expense and Retard the improvement of this Country and which I think the Best Country for Agricultural operations in North America and It Entirely depends on ourselves reclaiming it [?] to make it a happy Residence for men [*Civilised*]. Wishing you a pleasant Voyage home and a happy meeting with your family and friends to[o] and to have the pleasure of seeing you Back as soon as possible Believe me to Be

Yours Respectfully

[The signature and three lines of the postscript have been clipped from the manuscript.]

[Three lines of the postscript missing] Immigrants safely to the Country and opening the Communication Between this and Fort Hall and Between this and San Francisco as they are the most Urgent points. The 2nd is to secure the trappers and their families on their Claims as if they are deprived of them they will have to take refuge among the Indians and this will Excite such a feeling of hostility to the Whites as may Bring on trouble and retard greatly the settling of the Country.
NB I came to the Conclusion not to write to the Secretary of War as I have written to Government to the same purpose through Another Channel.
JMcL

60. To [WILLIAM L. MARCY][121]

Oregon City 16th Oct 1847

To
The Secretary of War
Washington

Sir

My Residence in this Country and the situation I held as officer in Charge of the Hudson Bay Co Business in it from 1824 to 1846 has

121. William L. Marcy (1786–1857) was secretary of war during the administration of James K. Polk, 1845–49.

afforded me opportunity to acquire some Knowledge of the Character and Disposition of the Indians in this Territory and I am convinced that the Manner in which the Immigrants travel from Fort Hall to this place will lead to trouble with them Unless as I stated to Dr White[122] in 1845 when he left this to go home that Every Company leaving Missisouris [sic] Bound to this Country ought to have a Conductor well

122. Dr. Elijah White (1806–79) was born in New York and educated at a medical college in Syracuse. In 1836 he was appointed physician to the Methodist Mission in Oregon and sailed from Boston with seven other adults bound for Oregon in July. The reinforcement group was delayed in the Sandwich Islands until the following April and did not arrive in the Columbia until 18 May 1837. Stationed first at the Methodist Mission at French Prairie near Champoeg, White helped to move the mission to Chemeketa (modern Salem) during the summer of 1840 following the arrival of the "Great Reinforcement" aboard the *Lausanne*. For reasons that are not quite clear, White resigned from the mission after a dispute with Jason Lee over policy and financial matters. He returned to New York aboard the *Lausanne*, which sailed from the Columbia in the summer of 1840.

In 1842, with the help of the "Friends of Oregon" in New York, White obtained an appointment as Indian subagent for Oregon, and as such he organized the immigration party of 1842 at Elm Grove, near Independence, Missouri. Inclined to be officious, if not imperious, White was replaced as leader of this the first wagon train to use the Oregon Trail by Lansford W. Hastings at the end of the first month. During 1842 and 1843 White sought to appease the Cayuse and Walla Walla Indians who were threatening to destroy the Whitman Mission, and he persuaded the Nez Perces to accept a code of conduct which he had formulated. In April 1844 White, with Major William Gilpin (later to be first governor of Colorado Territory) and James Douglas, represented McLoughlin as arbitrators in the settlement of McLoughlin's dispute with Alvin F. Waller and the Methodist Mission over the land claim at Oregon City.

White was prominent in the formation of the Provisional Government of Oregon. In 1845 he was asked to carry a petition to Washington, D.C., for the extension of American jurisdiction over Oregon; and, his drafts on the treasury having been questioned, he departed for the east to clear up the matter. Before he could return, representations by his political enemies in Oregon reached Washington, and White's appointment was not renewed. The vacancy thus created was the reason for McLoughlin's correspondence with Marcy. White did not return to Oregon until 1850, and in 1861 he was commissioned as a special Indian agent for the territory west of the Rockies; but soon afterward he moved to California where he was living at the time of his death. Howard M. Corning, ed., *Dictionary of Oregon History*, p. 263; Bancroft, *History of Oregon*, 1:154, 223, 254, 268–80, 290–91; and McLoughlin, *Letters, Third Series*, pp. 214–15.

Acquainted with the percautions [sic] Necessary to be taken by persons travelling from there to Fort Hall where the Government should Establish a post and place an Indian Agent who during the Summer ought to have ten or twelve steady Judicious Men well Acquainted with the Indians Between this and that place and the Agent should put one of these men with Every Company comeing here who would Act as Conductor and Manage Any Business the Immigrants might have with the Indians till they Reached this Valley. And as it is found the Best Route from Fort Hall to this place is by the Road Explored Summer 1846 by Mess Applegate[123] and party as the Immigrants who came by it this Season were here long before those who came by the Old Route and as it passes out of the Range of the Nez perces Cayouses and Walla Walla tribes the Best Armed Most Numerous and the Most Warlike tribes on this side of the Rocky Mountains and as the Applegate Road[124] passes in a Country thinly [Inhabited] populated and Badly Armed for these Reasons Every Exertion ought to be made to get the Immigrants to pass by this Route and a post ought to be Established at Rogues River Valley Garrisoned by forty or fifty Men to keep these Indians in Check and the Communication open Between this and Fort Hall and Between this and San Francisco. An Indian Agent ought to be placed at this post

123. Jesse Applegate (1811–88) led the famous "cow column" to Oregon in 1843 and later that year surveyed McLoughlin's claim at Oregon City. In 1845, as a member of the Legislative Committee of the Oregon Provisional Government, he drew up the oath which permitted both American and British subjects to support the government. In 1849 he moved to the Umpqua Valley in southern Oregon, where he farmed and raised beef cattle. Corning, ed., *Dictionary of Oregon History*, pp. 9–10; Bancroft, *History of Oregon*, 1:473.

124. The Applegate Road, correctly termed the South Road, was pioneered in 1846 by Levi Scott, Jesse Applegate, and thirteen others as a shorter, less troublesome route from Fort Hall to the Willamette Valley than the northern route along the Snake River to the Whitman Mission and thence through the rugged mountains along the Columbia River by the Barlow Road. Starting from the Willamette Valley, the explorers went south to the Rogue River, followed the base of the Siskiyou Mountains to the summit of the Cascades and thence to Lower Klamath Lake, across northern California to the Humboldt River and on to Fort Hall through Thousand Springs Valley a short distance west of the Great Salt Lake. Although actually longer than the northern route, the South Road was less rugged, and once past the alkali deserts of the Great Basin, the grass for stock grazing was more plentiful than to the north. Bancroft, *History of Oregon*, 1:544–62.

with an Indian trader with Goods to carry on trade with the Indians as the sure Means of Reconciling them to the presense of Whites on their Lands.

But as the Hudson Bay Companys Establishment at Fort Hall would serve as it has hitherto the purpose of a post there for the present the post of Rogues River might be dispensed with for a Season. But it is of Urgent Necessity the Agent with the Necessary Authority to Act and his twelve Conductors were at Fort Hall Summer 1848 in time to Meat [sic] the Immigrants.

As the Agent and Men Ought to Be persons Well Known to the Indians and Respected by them such persons can only be found Among the Rocky Mountain traders and trappers Now Residing on the Willamette and I would take the liberty to Recommend Mr Robert Newel[125] an Old

125. Robert Newell (1807–69) spent eleven years in the Rocky Mountains as a trapper before going to Oregon with his brother-in-law, Joe Meek, in 1840. He first settled in the Tualatin Valley, but in 1843 or 1844 he took a land claim at the edge of French Prairie near the Champoeg settlement, where in 1850 he platted a townsite. In addition to farming, he operated the keelboats *Mogul* and *Ben Franklin* between Oregon City and Champoeg. He was a founding member of the Oregon Lyceum in January 1844, and helped to organize the Oregon Printing Association in 1845.

In 1845, following the revision of the organic law of the Provisional Government, Newell was elected to the legislative assembly, in which he served until 1849. Shortly after the Whitman Massacre in November 1847, Newell was appointed as one of two commissioners to join the superintendent of Indian affairs, General Joel Palmer, in attempting to prevent a coalition of Indians against the white settlers. In March 1849 Newell received a federal appointment as one of three United States Indian subagents for the newly organized Oregon Territory. He was also elected to the territorial legislature from the Champoeg District. However, he failed to qualify for either office, for the news of the California gold discoveries lured him south. He was back in Champoeg in 1850, however, and in 1860 he was elected to the first state legislature.

In the winter of 1861/62, a flood swept most of Champoeg toward the sea, and Newell's properties were destroyed. He moved to Lapwai, Idaho, where his first wife's people, the Nez Perce, were becoming restive under reservation discipline and the intrusion of miners. Until shortly before his death in 1869, he served as special commissioner, interpreter, and Indian agent at the Lapwai reservation. Robert Newell, *Robert Newell's Memoranda*, ed. Dorothy O. Johansen, pp. 11–12, 81–92 *passim*.

Newell, the most influential man in the French-Canadian settlement at Champoeg, was less antagonistic toward the Hudson's Bay Co. than most of the early American settlers. He was also an admirer of John McLoughlin. Newell

Rocky Mountain trader as a person well qualified for the office of Agent at Fort Hall and he should select the Conductors and if these suggestions are approved by Government Instructions might be here in time to Enable Mr Newel to proceed to Fort Hall to meet the Immigrants.

As Mr Newel and the Men he Would take are settled in the Willamette on their Claims they would demand what some Might consider great Wages. But my Experience convinces me that it is Economy to get men who can and Will Manage the Business as it ought, Especially as it is most important to begin the Business Well and in three years the Road will be Established and the Expenses can be Reduced.

As I am informed you are the proper officer to be addressed on Business Relating to the Indian Affairs my duty as a Christian to do all I can to Avert Evil from my fellow Men And my Desire to promote the prosperity of the Country will I am Certain be considered as An Apology for troubling you and if [the following is written across the left-hand side of the sheet] I can be of any further use command me

who am

with the Greatest Respect

Your Obedient

humble Servant

Jn McLoughlin

To The Secretary of War
    Washington
        US

---

supported McLoughlin in the latter's land claim dispute with the Methodists at Oregon City, and in 1845 McLoughlin proposed to the Company that Newell be employed to collect the debts of the Willamette settlers. McLoughlin, *Letters*, *Third Series* (McLoughlin to the Governor and Committee, 20 November 1845), p. 139.

Newell's first wife, who died in 1845, was a Nez Perce; and he seems to have had great influence among her people, for they made it a condition of their treaty with the United States in 1867 that Newell be confirmed in the possession of a parcel of land between the Snake and Clearwater rivers which they had given to him in 1861. Newell, *Memoranda*, p. 91. His relations with the Nez Perce no doubt motivated McLoughlin to recommend his friend for the Indian agency at Fort Hall. And, although Newell did not get the appointment, McLoughlin's recommendation may have had some influence in the subsequent appointment of Newell as subagent to the Indians of Oregon Territory in 1849.

61. To [William L. Marcy]

Oregon City 21st October 1847

To
The Secretary of War
    Washington City

Sir

Since I did myself the Honor to address you on the 16th Inst a Report reached this that a party of Immigrants had been pillaged of their property By the Indians between Walla Walla and the Dalles and Most certainly this would not have happened if the Immigrants had known how to Act and shows the Necessity of the Measure I Recommended in my Last as if their [sic] had been An Agent at Fort Hall he would have made the Immigrants keep in Numbers Sufficiently Numerous to be Respected By the Indians and placed a Conductor with them who would have prevented the Whites doing any thing which might justly offend the Indians and thus the Whites will be Respected and peace and Harmony Maintained between them and the Natives. It is thus I always Acted in Managing the Hudson Bay Co Business — and Never to send a party through the Country Without putting an officer in Charge Who knew how to Conduct any Business they might have with the Indians and Who had Authority to keep his Men in Order and in Justice to the Indians I must say I have known Many and Many a White Man as Ready to impose on the Indians when in their power as Indians in Similar situation to impose on Whites. But by Acting as I suggest though at first it Required Sixty Well Armed Men to travel from Fort Hall to Vancouver — the Indians were Brought to that state that ten men could perform that Journey in perfect safety Because when we became Acquainted with them if any did us Wrong we could point him out and thus discriminate Between the Innocent and the Guilty As even Among Indians the Majority will support Right — and Reprobate and punish Wrong.

I would Beg also to call the Attention of Government to the situation of the half Breed population now settled in the Willamette Valley. When I came here fall 1824 the following Winter the plough might have been kept going during the Whole Season and as from the first coming of the Whites to that year not a single case of fire had been known after Examining the Country I came to the conclusion from the Goodness of the Soil in Willamette Valley the Mildness of the Winter and the Salubrity of the Climate that it was the place Best Adapted for the Residence of Civilised man farming in North America and Immediately took Every Measure in my power which could tend to promote the facility of Whites settling in the Country. For this purpose I Encouraged the Old trappers to open farms in the Willamette Valley as it is the Best place to farm a settlement to have a Beneficial Effect on the Whole Country. But as it was Well Known that the Williamette Valley Would Belong to the United States the Canadians Observed that they and their Children would not be allowed the same advantage as American Citizens When the United States Extended Their Jurisdiction over the Country and Wished to be allowed to Reside among the Relations of their Wives in different parts of the Country. But as this would scatter them over the Country and their Children would become Indians I considered it a duty to prevent this and to persuade them to settle in the Willamette where they could be collected to gether and their Children Instructed in the principles of the Christian Religion and taught to farm And Brought up with the Sympathies And feelings of Whites and throw their influence on the side of the Whites and in fact make them Hostages for the Good Behaviour of their Indian Relatives as Indians Judging of Us By themselves would be afraid if injuries were inflicted on Whites on their Lands that we would Retaliate on their Relations among us. But there is a Report that the Half Breeds will not be allowed to have Claims of Land by the United States Government if such Unfortunately is the Case It will Blast the prospects of these persons and force them with their parents to Retire Among the Indians Where they will Excite disaffection to American Interests When by allowing them to hold their Claims as American Citizens they would faciliate Immensely the settling of the Country by their influence over their Indian Relatives and of which Indulgence they are Worthy as all who know them must admit they are as peaceable orderly and Industrious as any settlers in the Country. Indeed the Grandmother of the most Extensive Cultivator in the Country[126] was a pure Indian. This Man sold Winter 1846 two thousand

126. McLoughlin probably refers to his stepson, Thomas McKay (1797–ca. 1850), who was descended from a Cree Indian grandmother. McKay, the son of Marguerite Wadin McKay McLoughlin and Alexander McKay, went to Oregon with his father on Astor's ship *Tonquin* in 1811, and remained in the

[70]

Bushels Wheat he has been a trapper began to farm Nine Years ago with a Capital of only two hundred and fifty dollars and six or Seven Horses and this Year he has Built a [*Saw and*] Grist Mill with one Run of Stones — and in a few days will have a saw Mill in operation. And I am certain it is sufficient for their Conduct to be known and the facilities they have afforded to settle this Country to secure them the Justice to Which they Are Entitled as I may say by subduing the Indians they have Been the means of this Country being peaceably settled by the Whites and When its Remote situation and all connected with it taken into Consideration fully as Easily as any other part of America and at Not one hundreth part of the Expence it would have cost the United States if these Men had not prepared the Way.

I am
Your Obedient
humble Servt
Jn McLoughlin

To
The Secretary of War
     Washington

Oregon Country after his father's death aboard that ill-fated vessel. After several years spent with Peter Skene Ogden's Snake country fur brigades during the 1820s, he retired temporarily from the Company in 1833 or 1834 and settled on a land claim opposite Sauvie Island near Scappoose, Oregon. In 1834 McLoughlin outfitted McKay to trade with the American trappers at their annual rendezvous, and in 1835 McKay built Snake Fort (Fort Boise) to compete with Nathaniel Wyeth's traders at Fort Hall. McKay was placed in charge of Fort Hall after its purchase by the Hudson's Bay Co. in 1837, and in 1838 he was sent to the Umpqua Fort to set its affairs in order. He spent the winter of 1838/39 at Fort Hall, and then retired again from the Company. He invested his accumulated savings in a farm and millsite at French Prairie, where he built a gristmill and dam worth an estimated seven to ten thousand dollars. In the Cayuse War following the Whitman Massacre, McKay led the company raised at French Prairie. In 1849 he conducted Peter Burnett's wagon train to California, but was back in Oregon in November. He died sometime between 18 November 1849 and 19 April 1850. Annie Laurie Bird, "Thomas McKay," pp. 1–14 *passim*; Thomas J. Farnham, *Travels in the Great Western Prairies, the Anahuac and Rocky Mountains, and in the Oregon Territory*, p. 93; Hussey, *Champoeg*, pp. 92–99; McLoughlin, *Letters, First Series*, pp. 347–49.

62. To Captain Roland Gelston

Oregon City 2nd Nov 1847

To
Captain Gelston

Dear Sir

In mine of 16th Ult I Requested you to Receive any flour and Goods of mine from W A Leidesdorff Esqr dispose of them and Remit the proceeds to George Pelly Esqr But in case of his having disposed of the property you will please apply to him for any funds he may have of mine in his hands and Remit the same to George Pelly Esqr Oahu of course it can be Easily ascertained how we stand by getting the Accounts from —

Yours Respectfully
Jn McLoughlin

Capt Gelston

63. To David McLoughlin

Oregon City 5th Nov 1847

My Dear David

Mr Pomeroy told me he was to sel [*sic*] Lumber to Mess Pettygrove for Cash if so I wish the Cash to be remitted to George Pelly Esqr and let me know the Amount so as I may send Mr Pelly a Draft for the Remainder of my Balance so that in the Event of Leidesdorff not having sent him the proceeds of my property which he has for Sale or that the Janet does not come here Mr Pelly be not put to any Inconvenience for me.

Yours Affectionately
Jn McLoughlin

64. To George Pelly

Oregon City 7th Nov 1847

George Pelly Esqr

Dear Sir

I Understood a few Days ago that the Toulon was only to sail on the 11th Instant But I am this moment informed she drops down to

[72]

morrow and I merely write at present (in case the Letter I may write a few Days Ago may not overtake her) to inform you that there is a Report that the Janet is off the Bar and that Mr Pomeroy is off with 180 M feet Lumber in Rafts to meet her. He will go as far as Portland and wait till he hear the Janet is in and will drop down with the Rafts to meet her. I saw Mr Wilson of Pettygrove & Co and who told me they would remit to you Lumber flour & Beef to meet their Liabilities with you. But what they have done I do not know at the time he spoke he wanted to Retain part of the Janet But this I told him would depend on Circumstances — I meant if Leidesdorff has remitted my funds to you they may purchase Pomeroys Lumber and Remit to you But if Leidesdorff has not done so I must Remit you Pomeroys Lumber to meet my Liabilities to you which I mention for your information. I wrote by Captain Dring on the 13th Augst and though he had an opportunity to write by the Henry he has not done so and there is a Report here that he has sold his property to Norris and Shelly therefore I wrote him the following Letter.

Oregon City 16th Oct 1847

W A Leidesdorff Esqr

Sir

On the Receipt of this if you have any flour of mine in your possession you will please deliver it to Capt Gelston and take his Receipt for the same and deliver him the Goods Unsold of course Capt Gelston will pay the Storage.

Yours Respectfully
Jn McLoughlin

Oregon City 16 Oct 1847

To Captain Gelston

Dear Sir

Will you please Receive any flour and Goods of mine from Capt Leidesdorff dispose of them and Remit the proceeds to George Pelly Esqr.

I am
Yours Respectfully
Jn McLoughlin

[73]

Oregon City 2n Nov 1847

To
Captain Gelston

In mine of 16th Ult I Requested you to Receive any flour and Goods of mine from W A Leidesdorff Esq dispose of them and Remit the proceeds to George Pelly Esqr. But in case of his having disposed of the property you will please apply for any funds he may have of mine in his hands and Remit the same to George Pelly Esqr Of course it can be Easily ascertained how Mr Leidesdorff and I stand by getting his a/o [a/c — accounts].

Yours Respectfully
Jn McLoughlin

By the foregoing copies of my Letters you can see What I have done and form your Opinion of Leidesdorfs [accounts?].

Yours Respectfully
Jn McLoughlin

65. To Archibald McKinlay

Oregon City 30th Nov 1847

Archibald McKindlay Esqr

Dear Sir

I certainly did use the Words the Immigrant states in the 127 Page of his Journal "Are you aware the Spanish are inferior to your American Cattle. Mr McKindlay did Wrong and I will not consent to profit by your Reliance on our Good faith."[127] As I was Naturally enough surprised to learn that people had given American for Wild California Cattle,

127. McLoughlin is referring to George Wilkes' *An Account and History of the Oregon Territory; together with a Journal of an Emigrating Party across the Western Prairies of America, and to the Mouth of the Columbia River* (London: William Lott, 1846), originally published in New York in 1845 with the title, *The History of Oregon, Geographical and Political, With an Examination of the Project of a National Rail Road, from the Atlantic to the Pacific Ocean, also an Account of the Characteristics and Present Condition of the Oregon Territory, by a Member of the Recently Organized Oregon Legislature.* The final section of the book is a reprint of the journal of Peter H. Burnett, an Oregon immigrant of 1843, which was published in the New York *Herald*, December 1844 to January 1845. Henry R. Wagner and Charles L. Camp, *The Plains and the Rockies:*

It struck [me] they must not have been aware how inferior the latter were to the former And at the time I Believed you yourself were not aware of it and that you meant by Wild Spanish or California Cattle cows of that Breed Unaccustomed to be Milked and Males Not accustomed to Work But Both of which could be driven from one place to Another. Whereas the California Cattle at Vancouver were as Wild as deer and could not be approached so that when we Wanted to kill any for Beef We had to hunt them as deer and What I meant by saying you had

A Bibliography of Original Narratives of Travel and Adventure, 1800–1865, pp. 168–70.

Burnett arrived at Fort Walla Walla on 16 October 1843 and before leaving for Fort Vancouver arranged with McKinlay for the care or disposition of his cattle. "We found a Mr. McKinley, a very intelligent scotchman, in charge of this post, and at his hands received every civility and attention. This gentleman proposed to us a conditional arrangement, subject to the ratification or refusal of Doctor McLaughlin, his superior, at Vancouver, in regard to our cattle. He represented the impossibility of our conveying them to Vancouver, and to save us any loss, offered to take them for himself, and give us an order on the Doctor for an equal number of Spanish cattle of the same age and gender, in the possession of the latter at the before-mentioned station. If Dr. McLaughlin disapproved of the arrangement, Mr. McKinley was to hold our cattle subject to our order, and to receive one dollar per head for their keeping. This was a pretty acute arrangement of his, as we afterwards found, but as it eventuated in nothing but a temporary deprivation of our beasts, we did not have occasion to regard it as a very serious matter." Wilkes, *An Account and History of the Oregon Territory*, pp. 109–10.

Burnett continued his journey down the Columbia by boat, arriving at Fort Vancouver on 10 November. Anxious to settle the matter of his cattle, he went to see McLoughlin. "On the morning after my arrival, I therefore opened my business to the Doctor, and presented him with the aforementioned gentleman's order. The old gentleman at once gave evident signs of displeasure. He saw in a moment that Mr. McKinley had taken advantage of our ignorance to drive a sharp bargain, and gave an immediate and decided dissent to the whole proceeding. 'Are you aware,' said he to me, 'that our Spanish cattle are much inferior to yours?' I told him I thought they were from the specimens I had seen at his place. 'And you have learned,' continued he, 'that cattle may be safely driven from Wallawalla to this post?' I admitted that the success of our emigrants in bringing through their stock, had convinced me of the fact. 'Mr. McKinley has done very wrong,' said he, shaking his head, 'very wrong indeed! Your cattle are superior to those I should be obliged to give you, and you would be much the losers by the arrangement. I will not consent to profit by your reliance on our good faith. I will write to Mr. McKinley to take good care of your animals, and to deliver them to you whenever you have settled upon your final residence. If you should decide upon settling near

[75]

done Wrong I meant you had Erred and Never thought or had the least Idea that you had Intended to take advantage of their situation Which you had no Interest to do did not do and could not mean to do as you made the Bargain subject to my Approbation — But of which I would have been Guilty if I had kept them to it as I knew the Injury it would do them and neither you nor they seem to have been aware of it at the time the Bargain was made and it would have been a Breach of the confidence put in us to have kept them to it — and it is this I meant by the Expression I will not consent to profit by your Reliance on Our Good faith — and I can also observe there can be no foundation for the Immigrant stating you drove a hard Bargain with them as I always Understood the Bargain was at their Request and to take care of their Cattle during the Winter at a dollar pr Head cannot certainly be considered by any Acquainted with the Country as a hard Bargain. The Very statement of the Case refutes the Charge and With Great Pleasure I take this opportunity to state that Every Immigrant who conversed with me on the subject Expressed himself in the Warmest terms of Gratitude for the Very Kind Manner you had treated them.

I am
Dear Sir
Yours Respectfully
Jn McLoughlin

us, we shall have the advantage of improving the breeds by them. . .' " Ibid., p. 127.

The incident to which McLoughlin alludes in his letter to McKinlay is indicative of the manner in which McLoughlin treated the American immigrants, particularly those of 1843 whose arrival so severely strained the resources of the small settlement on the Willamette. Although he sent boats to The Dalles to bring the immigrants down the Columbia and was eventually to give credit to the immigrants to the value of £ 6,606, McLoughlin was not acting from purely humanitarian motives. He defended his actions against the criticism of Lieutenants Warre and Vavasour by saying that his generosity to the immigrants was not only humanitarian but had been in the best business interests of the Company, and that they had thereby avoided troubles which might have involved the United States and Britain in war. (See Letter 3, to James Douglas, n. 10.)

Although some of the American immigrants later turned against McLoughlin because of their resentment of the economic domination of the Hudson's Bay Co. in Oregon, many of them appreciated his kindness. Peter H. Burnett was among these latter, and in 1844 and 1845 he supported the interests of McLoughlin and the Company in the restructuring of the Provisional Government. McLoughlin, *Letters, Third Series*, pp. xxxviii, 296.

[76]

66. To George Pelly [not in McLoughlin's handwriting]

Oregon City
10th Decr 1847

G Pelly Esquire

Dear Sir

You will receive with this a Cargo of Lumber as per enclosed Bill of Lading, shipped to you by Mr Pomeroy which you will please sell as soon as possible and pay Capt Dring for the freight and pay yourself the Balance I owe you and let me know how we stand. I hope Capt Adams paid you $18.80 which he owed me. I wish you to complete my memorandum of 8th July last as follows

    1 Keg 6dy [penny] Cut Nails
    2 " 8   "   ditto
    2 " shingly [sic] ditto
  100 lbs sperm Candles
  400 " Oahoo Sugar
  200 gns Syrup
   50 bus Salt
  100 lbs Soap
    6 " Snuff
excuse my indisposition for not writing to you more fully.

I am
Sir
Yours respectfully
Sd John McLoughlin

As Capt Dring intends to follow this business it will not be necessary for you to charter a vessel for me.

Sd John McL

67. To Captain David Dring [not in McLoughlin's handwriting]

Oregon City
10th Decr 1847

Capt Dring

Dear Sir

I beg to acknowledge the receipt of yours 3rd Decr/47 and though I approve the way you suggest of carrying on business; as no doubt it would be advantageous to us both, yet, I cannot enter into it at present being too unwell — but I can insure you of a Cargo in the spring and I believe full employment for the Summer and I hope when I have the pleasure to see you this spring we will by verbal communication to settle Matters to our Mutual Satisfaction as I rely so fully on your coming back that I do not write to Mr Pelly to send me a vessel. In the mean time I wrote to Mr Pelly to receive this Cargo [and] sell it.

In regard to the Thousand Dollars you have of mine I wish it to be laid out in the purchase of syrup sugar and American Plug Tobacco and bring it back with you.

I am

Yours truly

(Sd) John McLoughlin

68. To Captain David Dring

Oregon City 18 Dec 1847

Capt Dring

Dear Sir

I this moment Received yours of the 14th and my only Reason for not answering Definitively in mine of 10th the proposal you made in yours of the 3rd is that I do not know that I understand you Correctly and which can only be ascertained by Verbal communication in the mean time if in Verbal communication I find your Views do not suit me that you will have a Cargo of 180 M feet Lumber in freight at $20 prM and I hope the Business can be arranged to our Mutual advantage. Mr Pomeroy has managed his Business very Badly. He told me when he left this the first time that he had as you Specified 180 M ft when he Returned he told me he had not so much as he mentioned But that you had told him you were satisfied and would only Charge him for the quantity he then had Below. But Saturday Mr Hunt[128] told him you Required 40 M ft more he Immediately left this with a Raft of

128. Henry H. Hunt of Smithfield, Indiana, arrived in Oregon in 1843. Together with Tallmadge B. Wood (or Benjamin T. Wood) of New York, Hunt brought mill irons across the plains, and in 1844 the two began to construct two sawmills and a gristmill on the edge of a small stream which fell seventy feet into the Columbia River. The mill was located on the south bank of the river some thirty miles east of Astoria and opposite the lower end of Puget Island. By early 1845 the mills were ready, and in a good day's run as much

the said 40 M ft But his Clerk tells me he has not more than 20 M however David will be able to fill you on my Account from Pettygrove & Co Lumber at Hunts Mill. I give you Pomeroy statement to me that you may compare Notes — as you ought not to suffer for the Errors of others. My Respects to Mrs and Miss Dring and with Best Wishes I am

Yours Respectfully
Jn McLoughlin

69. To Captain David Dring

Oregon City 24th Dec 1847

Capt Dring

Dear Sir

On second thoughts I find I will not require to Employ the thousand Dollars in the purchase of Sugar Molasses and Tobacco as stated in mine of 10th Inst — and I will deffer [*sic*] to get what I want by your next trip. Therefore please pay to Mr Pelly the Thousand Dollars which you Received from Mr Leidesdorf for me — taking Mr Pellys Receipt for the same.

Yours Respectfully
Jn McLoughlin

---

as three thousand board feet were cut, most of which was sold in the Sandwich Islands for around $20 per thousand.

Albert E. Wilson, who was managing the Cushing store during Couch's absences, bought Wood's interest in the mill in 1844 or 1845 to give the new concern the advantage of reasonable freight rates on the Cushing ship *Chenamus*. That same year, a yoke of oxen for hauling logs was taken by scow from Oregon City to the mill, and five Kanakas were contracted from King Kamehameha at $5 a month plus board consisting of salmon and potatoes. Early in 1845, James Birnie bought a one-fourth interest in the mill for $1,000, but he seems not to have retained it, for on 30 June 1848 a new firm at Astoria Mills was announced with Henry H. Hunt and Henry Marlin as partners. After leaving J. P. Cushing & Co., Wilson, in 1846, became a member of the firm of F. W. Pettygrove & Co. Through his connections with Hunt's mill, Wilson was able to secure lumber for Pettygrove's trade with the Sandwich Islands and San Francisco. But in March 1847 Wilson sold his share in the mills to Hunt, who, his fortune made, left Oregon for California in 1851 and was not heard from again. John Minto, "From Youth to Age as an American," pp. 128–29; Tallmadge B. Wood, "Letter of Tallmadge B. Wood (April, 1844)," p. 397; Throckmorton, *Oregon Argonauts*, p. 39; McLoughlin, *Letters, Third Series*, p. 189; *Oregon Spectator*, 29 April 1847, 12 October 1848.

70. To P. C. Michaud[129]

Oregon City 1st Feb 1848

To
Mr P C Michaud
River du Loup Below Quebec
Canada East

My Dear Nephew

I hope I need not say that I am Extremely sorry to learn by yours of 1st April last that my poor Sister your Affectionate Mother is no more and that she died in debt. I allowed my Mother (and I Believe your Mother lived with her) for a Number of years before her Death £ 150 pr Annum and the Revenue of my farms at River du Loup on Condition of her paying the Annual Rent to the Seigneur. Since my Mothers Death I allowed your Mother Enjoy the Revenue of my farms on the same Condition as I did to my Mother and certainly it ought to be sufficient to support an old Woman and therefore I cannot see how she can be in debt and her being in debt makes me afraid that the Seignorial Rent is not paid. All that I can do in this state of Ignorance of my Affairs is to Authorise you to hold Lands on the same terms as my Mother held them and which I do by these presents (and Write me on the Receipt if the Seignorial Rent is paid or Not and I will then see what further is to be done. The Revd Mr Proulx writes in his postscript to yours that the fabrique holds a Lot of Land which is surrounded by Mine. I know nothing of this But I presume it is so

129. P. C. Michaud, one of McLoughlin's nephews, was the son of Julienne McLoughlin (1788–ca. 1847) and Jean Marie Michaud of St. André, Quebec. McLoughlin owned three farms at Rivière-du-Loup totaling 676 acres, most of which he inherited at the time of his father's death in 1813. McLoughlin's mother, Angélique Fraser McLoughlin, occupied the "Big Farm" (the subject of this letter) until her death on 31 July 1842, after which time Julienne lived there. In July 1856 McLoughlin empowered his older daughter Marie Elizabeth (Eliza) Eppes to act as his attorney in selling or renting the Rivière-du-Loup properties. She sold the farms on 9 September 1856 for £ 1,350 to John Fraser of St. Mark near Montreal. However, McLoughlin seems not to have been aware of this transaction, for in his will, dated 21 February 1857, he gave Eliza a lifetime interest in the lands; and there is no record of the farms or the income from their sale in the inventory of McLoughlin's estate. Barker, *The McLoughlin Empire*, pp. 26, 39, 60, 296–99, 302, 311–13.

[80]

and you see by the Postscript what I write him and you will be pleased to act accordingly. My Love to the family

Yours Affectionately

Jn McLoughlin

PS

To The Revd Mr Proulx

Curé River Du Loup Below Quebec

Revd Sir

In the postscript to Mr P C Michauds letter you inform me that the fabrique of River du Loup — think they have a Right to a piece or Lot of Land on my farm. I know nothing of this But please settle with Mr P C Michaud My Attorney and I will Ratify what he does. But if you and he cannot settle it let you Chuse two persons Mr P C Michaud will Chuse two these four will Chuse a fifth and the fabrique and I will be bound to Ratify what the Majority of these five decide. In this way the Affair can be settled without Difficulty and I hope this will satisfy the Hihabitants [sic] of my Native parish River du Loup and with the Greatest Respect Believe me to Be your Obedient

humble Servant

Jn McLoughlin

71. To Nathaniel J. Wyeth

Oregon City 15th Feby 1848

N J Wyeth Esqr

Cambridge Boston

Massacussetts [sic]

Dear Sir

I have the pleasure to Acknowledge the Receipt of your Esteemed favour 19th April and I am much obliged to you for the trouble you take about my Claim. As to the Memorial I sent you by Mr [Francis] Ermatinger it was merely for your information and you may show it to whom you please though I do not wish to have it printed and Circulated till the Government comes and then if Necessary I will publish it, with the facts as stated Attested Under Oath so that the public may Judge and Decide. I am much obliged to you for your offer of fruit seeds,

[81]

But I have been so Unfortunate with those you were so kind as to send me as not one of them Vegetated, that I am afraid to trouble you, the fact is as our late friend Douglass[130] told me, that Unless seeds are kept above the Water Line on a long Voyage they will lose their Vegetative power and to do this Requires more care and attention than most Captains will Bestow. Your affairs in Regard to your Island are in status Quo. Our Organization can do Nothing to protect your Rights and you must get them secured by the General Government and When its officers come I will support your Right to Wapatoo Either as your Claim or as your tenant. But I trust you will write me by the Government Officers. With Best Wishes Believe me To be

Yours Respectfully
Jn McLoughlin

NB You are aware before this that Ermatinger was not sent Back to this quarter and since such is the Case I am surprised that he did not come Back and Open a Shop at this place on his own account. If he had come with a Vessel of three hundred Tons and Goods I would have given constant Employment to his Vessel — in transporting to Oahu and California, there will be Business done here and in California.

72. To George Moffatt

Oregon City 5th March 1848

George Moffatt Esqr

Dear Sir

I send you the Deeds of trust of the Mortgages on Mr Jarvis's[131]

130. David Douglas (1798–1834) was an English botanist who visited Fort Vancouver and the Pacific Northwest intermittently between 1825 and 1833. He identified the fir that bears his name and the sugar pine as well as numerous other species of trees and plants in the Northwest. While traveling in the Sandwich Islands he mysteriously fell into a pitfall in which a bull had been trapped and was gored to death. Athelstan George Harvey, *Douglas of the Fir*, pp. ix–x, 232–37.

131. Simon Talbot, who was called Gervais (McLoughlin spells it as it is sometimes pronounced), married McLoughlin's sister Margarite in 1820, and at the division of their father's estates in 1821 Margarite shared in the partition. Barker, *The McLoughlin Empire*, pp. 165, 312.

property in favour of Mrs Eppes.[132] I thought I had sent them But to my surprise I found them Among my papers last Summer. You can now do with them as you proposed.

Yours Respectfully

John McLoughlin

73. To William A. Leidesdorff

[The letter is not in McLoughlin's handwriting, there is no signature, and the entire letter has been crossed out.]

Oregon City 1st Mar 1848

Wm Leidesdorff

Dear Sir

I received yours of the 6th Oct last and a thousand Dollars by the Janet Captain Dring and also yours 5th Jany P Henry Capt Kilborn enclosing Capt Gelston receipt for ninety three Barrels Flour delivered him by you for me — your account of the sale of two hundred and fifty three Barrels flour and ninety five Blankets and Capt Kilborn's receipt for eighteen hundred and forty Eight Dollars from you on my account.

You account for 346 Barrels flour (your letter states 348 but in your write [written] account it is 346) there is certainly a mistake somewhere as by my Millers account and my own account I shipped 354 Barrels flour on Board the Stockton Capt Young. You say you have sold the Oahu Goods at nine months credit and that the time will soon be up. I am disappointed at your not sending me an Invoice of the Sales so as I might know what I had to expect.

Capt Kilborns receipt is for Eighteen hundred and forty Eight Dollars but he says he only received three hundred and twenty eight Dollars in cash which he handed me on arrival and that you paid him fifteen hundred and twenty in goods and that he will pay me as he effects sales and indeed has since that time paid four hundred and six Dollars.

132. Marie Elizabeth (Eliza) McLoughlin (born 1814) was the older daughter of John and Marguerite McKay McLoughlin. She remained in eastern Canada when her father assumed his duties on the Columbia River in 1824, and about 1832 she married William Randolph Eppes, an assistant commissary general in the British army. Ibid., pp. 128–29.

[83]

74. To WILLIAM A. LEIDESDORFF [not in McLoughlin's handwriting]

Oregon City 1st March 1848

William Leidesdorff Esqr

Dear Sir

I received yours of the 6th Oct last and a thousand Dollars by the Janet Capt Dring and also yours of 5th Jany per Henry Capt Kilborn enclosing Capt Gelston receipt for 93 Barrels flour delivered by you to him and your Account of the Sale of two hundred and fifty three Barrels four [flour] and ninety five Blankets and Capt Kilborns receipt for eighteen hundred and forty Eight Dollars from you on my account.

Your Account for 346 Barrels Flour your letter states 348 but you write Shelly and Norris claim having had 62 Barrels and as there was only 408 on Board consequently there could only be 348 on your Account." This is a mistake in the figure as it is only 346 agreeing with the account you last sent. By my Miller and my Clerk's accounts I shipped 354 Barrels Flour on board the Stockton. There must be a mistake somewhere but who made I cannot say. You write you have sold the Oahu Goods at nine Months Credit and that the time will soon be up. I am disappointed at your not sending the account of the Sales — so as I might know what I had to expect. Capt Kilborn's receipt is for eighteen hundred and forty eight dollars but he says he only received three hundred and twenty eight in cash which he handed me on arrival and that you paid him fifteen hundred and twenty Dollars in Goods and that he will pay me as agreed between you as he effects sales and has since paid me four hundred and six dollars which I mention that you may be aware of the state of the case. This will be handed you by Mr A E Wilson to whom I request you will please pay any Balance of mine you may have in your hands and also hand him the account of the Sales of the Island Goods and oblige.

Yours respectfully
Sd John McLoughlin

75. TO MESSRS. STARKEY, JANION AND COMPANY[133]
[not in McLoughlin's handwriting]

Oregon City 11th Mar. 1848

Messrs Starkey, Janion & Co

Gentlemen

I am requested by Mr Pomeroy a person who rents my saw Mills to inform you that he has a hundred and fifty thousand feet of Lumber which he will be happy to despose off [sic] at twenty Dollars pr M feet delivered alongside of the Vessel at Portland or lower down if the Vessel could not come so high up the River but I would beg to observe that from the 15th May to the 1st August any Merchant Vessel that can enter the Columbia can safely come up to Portland.

I am
Gentlemen
Respectfully Yours
Sd John McLoughlin

76. TO MESSRS. STARKEY, JANION AND COMPANY
[not in McLoughlin's handwriting]

Oregon City
12th March 1848

private & Confidential

Messrs Starkey, Janion & Co

Gentlemen

I did myself the Honor to address you yesterday on the part of Mr Pomeroy stating that he would be happy to despose of a Cargo of Lumber. I beg to observe that Mr Pomeroy's lease of my Mills expires on the

133. Messrs. Starkey, Janion & Co. was established in Honolulu in September 1845 and was one of three English commercial firms operating in the Sandwich Islands at that time. About 1847, the firm opened a branch in San Francisco with offices in Leidesdorff's City Hotel, where the firm of Shelly & Norris also had quarters. R. C. Janion, one of the partners, was apparently the representative of the firm in San Francisco from 1847 to 1849. Starkey moved to San Francisco in 1848 and died there about 1850. As recently as 1938 the firm was still in business in Honolulu under the name of Theo. H. Davies & Co., Ltd. Ralph S. Kuykendall, *The Hawaiian Kingdom, 1778–1854*, p. 302; Bancroft, *History of California*, 4:691, 5:680, 732.

12th June and that though Mr Pomeroy is a good honest man and has done me justice, still at the expiration of his lease I may take them into my own hands as I think I can do better by them. My two present saw Mills could supply unless the Winter should be uncommonly cold 1 Million feet of Lumber per annum and my water power could allow to erect three or four more and I think I could supply any quantity of Lumber that you may require and as Calefornia is a rising Country —

I think we might do a business to our Mutual advantage. If this meets your views I would require the enclosed list of Goods from England as soon as possible for which I will allow you an advance of 40 per cent on prime Cost payable in Lumber at fifteen Dollars per M delivered alongside the Vessel either at Portland or on the Columbia River as the state of the Water will admit. It is necessary you should let me know by the present opportunity what time you expect the Goods will be here and as you could not take all the Lumber at once — it would be delivered as fast as you could take it or else I may pay the Money down in Dollars at 4/2[134] or in Bills on London or Canada and you would agree to take that amount in Lumber from me at $15 pr M payable in money or Bills of Exchange at 4/2 per Dollar. I have also a good flour Mill, with three run of Stones.[135] I could also supply a large quantity of Flour, if there was a demand for it, as the farmers have soun [sic] a large quantity and it has a fine appearance, but for this I would require further information and procure an additional quantity of Goods to purchase Wheat as at present I limit myself to Grinding for toll.[136] Your answer by the first opportunity will oblige

Yours respectfully
Sd John McLoughlin

134. That is, an exchange rate of four shillings two pence per dollar.

135. This was the flour mill with three pairs of buhrstones which the Hudson's Bay Co. had ordered from Messrs. James Abernethy & Co. of Ferryhill Foundry, Aberdeen, in March 1841. The mill and machinery, which were originally ordered for the use of the Puget's Sound Agricultural Company, were delivered to Fort Vancouver in 1842, but remained in storage until McLoughlin had them erected at the falls in 1844. The mill machinery had cost about £ 490, while the millstones were £ 28 a pair. One pair of stones could grind about one hundred bushels of wheat daily. McLoughlin, *Letters, Second Series*, pp. 160–61n; Palmer, *Journal of Travels*, p. 159; Schafer, ed., "Documents Relative to Warre and Vavasour's Military Reconnaissance," p. 46.

136. Joel Palmer reported that the mills above the falls were grinding for a toll of one-eighth in the spring of 1846. Palmer, *Journal of Travels*, p. 189.

PS But in the mean time if you want Lumber before I receive my Goods I will be happy to supply you and also to sell you the flour I have on the current prices of the Country but as I have no Vessel you would have to send for it and if your Vessel brought Tea Sugar Coffee and Slops,[137] suitable to the wants of the Country I would take it in payment. There is not much flour in the Country and what there is at seven Dollars per Barrel cash in the Mills which is about the general price of Flour in the Country. I am sorry this state of my business will not admit of my going to see you.

JMcL [initialed by McLoughlin]

77. To George Moffatt

Oregon City 15th March 1848

To
Honbl George Moffatt

Dear Sir

In settling my Account Spring 1848 at Vancouver I gave Messr Ogden and Douglass a Draft for three thousand Dollars which I Received from a person to whom I sold Lumber to that Amount. But this persons Draft returned protested after the Express left and I was called upon for payment and Gave a draft on you for this sum with a letter of Advice and as I thought it would not be sent till next spring on Receiving payment I applied for the Draft to settle it But I was informed it had been sent to Canada Via Mexico which I consider rather sharp Work and which will account for my addressing you Merely a letter of Advice.

I am

Dear Sir
Yours Respectfully
Jn McLoughlin

78. To Francis Ermatinger

Oregon City 15th March 1848

Francis Ermatinger Esqr

Dear Sir

To morrow Catherine and Fanny leave this to go to Vancouver from

137. "Slops" were cheap or inferior grades of ready-made clothing.

Whence they will proceed with the Express if the Route is safe and as usual in Boats to join you. But if the Reverse is the Case or that danger is apprehended they will Return here and proceed with the Summer Brigade which I Understand will go by Fort Langley and proceed in the fall with Lewis to Boat Encampment Where she will Receive Instructions from you. It has been suggested to me by Mr McKindlay that she could go by New Caledonia But to this I objected and if it depends on me she will go in the Way I Mention and no other Unless I receive orders from you to the Contrary by the Spring Express.

Since I last wrote you We Received Via Oahu a Bedstead, a Cooking stove with pans &c Kettles But the Damper I Believed it is called is Broken a Box containing Carpet or Carpets five Kegs which seem to be paint and 8 Cases — one of which has been opened and Contained 12 Bottles Brandy which I Believe was sold at $2 pr Bottle and the Money given to Catherine. If the other Cases Contain Brandy and I can get the same price or Even less I will sell. Indeed I sent for your letters to Vancouver and if I had seen any in Wyeths hand Writing I would have opened it in the Expectation of finding the Account and I would have sold all that he sent you as soon as I could. I will therefore Wait for your Instructions before putting all he sent you up to sale Except the Brandy which I will sell for what I can get. But I must Remark the Damper of your Cooking stove is Broken But I suppose I will be able to get one Cast here this Summer as we have two foundaries in operation. I suppose you will also consider it advisable to sell your house and Catherines two Lots. I think they will Bring next year between two and three hundred Dollars Each and I have made Catherine leave the Deeds. The House on your Lot is a poor Concern besides a Corner infringes on the street. In fact I think the house Worth little But the Lot is a Good one But you will never get two thousand Dollars the price you asked for it — Nor even half that money as all that is Valuable is the lot the house is a Nuisance. Give your full instructions on these points. Applegate Sold his Lots on two years Credit for two hundred and fifty Dollars Each. They are alongside of yours But he will have to Wait more than double that time in my Opinion. But to Return to your Goods here I have kept them at the present price Because there are none Else on the Market. If they do not sell in the beginning of Summer I will Lower the price. Mrs E has left with me

[88]

Nesmith & Hedges[138] note for 333..50 payable 1st March 1848
    D   D   "   333. 50 "   1st March 1847
  Robert Newel[1]   "   228"   1st Feby 1847

79. To George Pelly

Oregon City 15th March 1848

George Pelly Esqr

Dear Sir

I Beg to Acknowledge the Receipt of your favour 13th Dec 1847 and I hope I need not say that I am Extremely sorry to learn that you are so Unwell But I fervently hope that long before this you are restored to the Enjoyment of health. I see by your statement that Lumber has fallen in your Market But I think if there are Vessels to take lumber from this to California that you will not Receive much as last year and that it will rise again.

I hope the Janet has reached you and safely delivered her Cargo. I was Unwell when she sailed and wrote David to write you that the Cargo was mine. This is not Exactly what I ought to have said. The Cargo is Mr Pomeroys. He wanted to sell it to me But I would not purchase it. It is to be sold on his Account and the proceeds carried to my Credit in your Books in part payment of the advances I made him. If he comes here before the Cowlitz leaves I will get him to Write You Accordingly. Mr Pomeroy has now nigh three Cargoes on hand. One of these I presume will be sent you by the Janet on her Return

138. James W. Nesmith and Absalom F. Hedges. James Willis Nesmith (1820–85) was born in New Brunswick but educated in New England and Ohio. He went to Oregon with Marcus Whitman in 1843, where he became a supreme court judge under the Provisional Government of Oregon. He served in the legislature in 1847–48 and was a captain in the Cayuse War, which followed the massacre of the Whitmans. In 1848 he went to California but returned to Oregon in 1849. He succeeded Joe Meek as U.S. marshal in 1853, served in the Rogue River and Yakima Indian wars, and from 1857 to 1859 was superintendent of Indian affairs. He served in the U.S. Senate from 1861 to 1865 where, although he was a Democrat, he strongly favored abolition. He was a U.S. representative from Oregon from 1873 to 1875. Corning, ed., *Dictionary of Oregon History*, p. 174.

and I presume the Morning Star will be here from Otaheite[139] for Another Cargo and the accounts I Receive from you will dicide if he sends any more to the Islands. Indeed by the first of June his lease Expires and the state of the Market Will Dicide whether I take them in my own hands or not.

I sent you ten Barrels flour by the Brig Henry which left this the 19th April last But I never Received an Acknowledgement of your Receiving them though the Captain says he delivered them. With Best Wishes Believe me To Be

Yours Respectfully
Jn McLoughlin

80. WALTER POMEROY TO GEORGE PELLY
[The entire letter is in McLoughlin's handwriting.]

Oregon City 15th March 1848

George Pelly Esqr

Sir

I consigned to you by the Janet Capt Dring 168 M feet Lumber and you will oblige me after paying the freight and Expense of Sale to transfer the Balance to the Credit of John McLoughlin Esqr.

I am Sir
Your Obedient
humble Servant
[*Jn McLoughlin*]
Walter Pomeroy

81. TO SIR WILLIAM DRUMMOND STEWART[140]

Oregon City 15th March 1848

To
Sir W Stewart

Dear Sir

The foregoing is a Copy of a letter I addressed you as you see on the 16th July 1846 and as I have had no Account from [you] I presume

139. Tahiti.

140. For biographical information on Sir William Drummond Stewart, see Appendix C.

you have not yet given up your Wandering propensity or that the letter has Miscarried.

Our population in the Territory is about fifteen thousand, Our last Immigration brought the Measles which they communicated to the Natives and it carried many of them off and the Survivors supposing it was Bad Medicine thrown on them by the Americans to kill them and get their lands the Cayouses Massacred Dr Withman [*sic*] and his Wife and nine other Americans at Walla Walla which has thrown the Whole Country into trouble and how this will End God only knows.[141] A large party of Americans and half Breeds with Thomas McKay are gone to punish the Indians But we have no Accounts of them Since their departure. With Best Wishes

Believe me to Be
Yours Respectfully
Jn McLoughlin

Sir W D Stewart Bt Murthly Castle N Britain

[The following is written vertically across the left-hand side of the page:]

NB I have requested my Agent Edward Roberts Esq of the Hudson Bay house to forward this to you to whom I would be happy you would communicate on the Subject.

141. The tragic massacre at Waiilatpu, the site of the Whitman Mission, began on 29 November 1847. By the following day nine people, including Marcus and Narcissa Whitman, lay dead at the mission, and in the following days five more either were killed or died from the effects of their treatment by the Cayuse Indians. Clifford Merrill Drury, ed., *First White Women over the Rockies,* 1:161–70.

News of the massacre was sent down the Columbia to Vancouver by a Hudson's Bay Co. courier, where it arrived on 7 December. The following day, James Douglas sent word of the murders to Governor George Abernethy of the Oregon Provisional Government; on 9 December the legislative house passed a resolution authorizing the formation of a regiment of Oregon volunteers, and the first company of riflemen left for Walla Walla and the scene of the massacre that evening. During the next few weeks other companies of thirty to fifty men each were raised, and on 12 January 1848 the Canadian citizens at Champoeg resolved to send one company of riflemen. Thirty men volunteered, and Thomas McKay, McLoughlin's stepson, was chosen captain. On the fourteenth, four companies, totaling 230 men, left Portland for Walla Walla. *Oregon Spectator,* 10 December 1847, 6, 20 January 1848. The Cayuse War dragged on until 1850 when the demoralized Indians surrendered five of the participants in the massacre. The end came with their hanging in Oregon City on 3 June 1850.

82. To Edward Roberts

Oregon City 15th March 1848

Edward Roberts Esqr

Dear Sir

Enclosed is a letter for Sir W D Stewart Bt Murthly Castle N Britain it speaks for itself. This Gentleman Visited the Columbia in 1834 and handed a Circular from the Right Honbl E Ellice[142] addressed to the Mess Gerrard and Allen[143] of Lower & Upper Canada to Sir G Simpson and the factors & trader [sic] of the Hudson Bay Company. He passed part of the Winter at Vancouver got Supplies out of the Store for which he paid in Drafts which were duly honored in consequence of Which in compliance with his Request I made advances and gave a passage to London on the Hudson Bay Co Vessel to a Mr Gyer[144] who gave

142. Edward Ellice, Sr. (1781–1863), was early connected with the London firm that supplied the North West Co. In 1820–21 he, with Simon McTavish and William McGillivrays, was active in bringing about the coalition of the Hudson's Bay Co. and the North West Co. He was a member of the committee of the Hudson's Bay Co. from 1824 to 1837, and it was as such that he wrote the letter of introduction for Stewart which McLoughlin quotes. He served in the House of Commons as the member from Coventry from 1818 to 1826 and from 1830 to 1863, and was secretary of the treasury (1830–32) and secretary of war (1832–34) in the government of Lord Grey. Robertson, *Correspondence Book*, pp. 210–11; Wallace, ed., *Documents Relating to the North West Company*, pp. 437–38.

143. The letter was more correctly addressed to "John Allan Esquire York, Samuel Gerrard Montreal, Governor Simpson and The Chief Factors & Chief Traders Hudsons Bay Company." Samuel Gerrard (1767–1857) went to Canada from Ireland and became a partner in the Montreal supply house of Parker, Gerrard, & Ogilvy, later Gerrard, Gillespie & Co., which George Moffatt entered about 1811. He had an indirect interest in the North West Co., and when the firm of McTavish, McGillivrays & Co. failed in 1825, Gerrard was appointed a trustee with the responsibility of unraveling the tangled finances of the defunct North West Co. McLoughlin, *Letters, First Series*, p. 126; Wallace, ed., *Documents Relating to the North West Company*, p. 447.

144. Karl Andreas Geyer, also known as Carl or Charles (1809–53), was an eminent German botanist who came to the United States about 1835 to conduct a botanical study of the Missouri River country. In 1838–39 he was botanist for the Nicollet expedition to survey Iowa, Minnesota, and the Dakotas. He taught botany to John C. Fremont on that expedition, and in 1841 he accompanied Fremont to the Des Moines River as botanist. In 1843 Geyer was one of four distinguished naturalists who accompanied Sir William Drummond Stewart to the Rocky Mountains. At Sandy Creek, a tributary of the

[92]

Drafts on Sir William D Stewart which were protested and Charged to my Account after perusal will you do me the favour to forward the Enclosed (if he has not already paid the Amount informing that you are Requested to do so by me and to apply to him for the Amount and oblige.

Yours Respectfully

Jn McLoughlin

83. TO MESSRS. ALBERT PELLY AND COMPANY[145]

Oregon City 16 March 1848

Mess Albert Pelly & Co London

Gentlemen

I take the liberty to Request you would have the Goodness to get

---

Green River, Geyer left Stewart to accompany a party of Jesuit missionaries to the Flathead country of Montana, and late in 1843 he crossed the Rockies to spend the remainder of the winter at Elkanah Walker and Myron Eells' Tshimakain Mission on the Spokane River. During the summer of 1844, he collected specimens in the Nez Perce country, and in June he spent some time with Henry H. Spalding at Lapwai Mission on the Clearwater River. Armed with an introduction from Sir William, Geyer arrived at Fort Vancouver on 29 October 1844 and there he secured passage on the Company bark *Columbia* which sailed for the Sandwich Islands and England on 13 November. Most of his collections were sent to the Royal Botanical Gardens at Kew, and some were sent to Dr. Asa Gray, a distinguished Harvard botanist.

Stewart had asked McLoughlin to charge any assistance given to Geyer to the former's account, and McLoughlin accordingly submitted a bill for £ 122 19s. 9d. which included £ 22 19s. 9d. for goods and £ 100 for passage on the *Columbia*. Stewart, however, refused to pay the bill, for he claimed that he had remitted the money directly to McLoughlin. In 1845 the Company therefore charged McLoughlin's account for the advances made to Geyer. McLoughlin did not receive a remittance, if Stewart sent one; and, as this letter indicates, he was attempting to collect the debt as late as 1848. McLoughlin, *Financial Papers*, p. 76; Frederick V. Colville, "Added Botanical Notes on Carl A. Geyer," pp. 323–24; Clifford M. Drury, "Botanist in Oregon in 1843–44 for Kew Gardens, London," pp. 182–86 *passim*; John Charles Frémont, *Narratives of Exploration and Adventure*, ed. Allan Nevins, pp. 14, 41, 80; Mae Reed Porter and Odessa Davenport, *Scotsman in Buckskin*, pp. 215, 237; McLoughlin, *Letters, Third Series*, pp. 53, 67, 160–61, 193.

145. Messrs. Albert Pelly & Co. was a London firm with which the Hudson's Bay Co. had considerable dealings. It was organized by the third son of Sir John Henry Pelly, the governor of the Company from 1822 until his death in 1852.

the Enclosed Requisition fulfilled for me the Costs and Expences of which you will please draw from My funds in the Hands of the HB Co.

I wish if possible this Memorandum to be shipped to me by the Hudson Bay Co Vessel which leaves England this fall for Fort Vancouver Columbia River But if this Cannot be done I wish them to be Consigned to George Pelly Esqr Oahu which will obli[ge] Gentlem[en]

Your Obedient

Humble Servant

Jn McLoughlin

I trust you will Insure the Articles to Fort Vancouver.

J McLoughlin

Memorandum for Jas Abernethy[146] ferry Hill Aberdeen 3 pair Mill Stones.

Dimensions of Mill Stones & Gearing. 3 Mill stone spindles 7 ft Long 3 Inch Diameter — the Toes to 1 3/4 Inch Diameter to have brass slips fitted to them the Brasses to have Cast Iron Boxes with four punching [Holes] Screws the sole plates of the Boxes to have four holes 5/8 Inch Square for Bolting them down to Wooden Bridges. The top of the Spindles to have Balance Rhynes [Rynes] with Stone Gearing Complete. The Pinions to be 17 1/2 In Diamer [sic] 24 teeth 8 Inch Broad to be fitted on tapering Blocks. The Blocks to be Keyed on the Spindles. Each pinion to be supplied with hand Gearing for disengaging the Pinion.[147] The Gearing to be on the principle of the Puget Sound Mill.

The Mill stones to be 4 1/2 ft Diameter French Bur[r].

Sd John Fenton[148]

146. See Letter 76, to Messrs. Starkey, Janion & Co., n. 135.

147. The best work on early nineteenth-century flour mills is Oliver Evans, *The Young Mill-Wright and Miller's Guide.*

148. John Fenton was engaged by the Puget's Sound Agricultural Co., a subsidiary of the Hudson's Bay Company, in June 1841 on the recommendation of Messrs. James Abernethy & Co. from whom the Company had ordered machinery and stones for a gristmill. Fenton, who was a millwright and miller, was to supervise the erection of the flour and barley mill in the Columbia Department. The mill was put into storage when it reached Fort Vancouver, and Fenton was employed as a miller at the Company's existing mills five miles east of the fort. Fenton's contract was transferred to the Hudson's Bay Co. for Outfit 1843–44, and he retired from the Company's service in June 1849. McLoughlin, *Letters, Second Series*, p. 161n; ibid., *Third Series*, pp. 122–23n.

84. To George Pelly

Oregon City 28th March 1848

George Pelly Esqr

Dear Sir

The Janet Capt Dring Entered the River 12 or 14 Days ago and Mr Campbell[149] Reached this Nine Days Ago But I am disappointed at Receiving no Communication from you or Capt Dring. In this absence of information I cannot say otherwise than I have already done that Mr Pomeroy has transferred the proceeds of the Cargo of Lumber sent by the Janet to my Credit as he wrote you and that he has three Cargoes on hand But Whether he will send them to Oahu or California depends on Circumstances though from what Capt Dring wrote me before sailing I presume he will take a Cargo to Oahu But I am sorry to learn By Last Accounts that the Janet was aground in tongue point Channel. I Beg you would [do] me the favour to Attend to the Enclosed Memorandum and send it by first opportunity. With Best Wishes I am Sir

Yours Respectfully
Jn McLoughlin

Mess Pettygrove & Co have handed me a Bag of Money about I Believe Eight hundred Dollars to send it to the Cowlitz Capt Winter for you. All I can do is to Keep it to be sent by Next Opportunity. In the Mean time if you have funds of mine you can place that Amount to their Credit.

Jn McLoughlin

The relations of Fenton and McLoughlin at this time are not completely clear. McLoughlin was evidently helping the miller to establish a rather large mill of his own, perhaps in anticipation of Fenton's coming retirement from the Company. The mill for Fenton was delivered about 1849, and that year the Company charged McLoughlin's account with £ 1,000 paid to Messrs. Albert Pelly & Co. McLoughlin, *Financial Papers*, p. 78.

149. John G. Campbell, who was Archibald McKinlay's assistant at the Hudson's Bay Co. store in Oregon City (see Letter 11, to David McLoughlin, n. 39). Campbell had left Oregon for St. Louis and Washington, D.C., with the Company's brigade on 5 May 1847; and, after an interview with President Polk concerning the defense of Oregon, he returned to the Columbia on the *Janet*, which entered the river on 16 March 1848. *Oregon Spectator*, 13 May, 10 June 1847, 23 March, 4 May 1848.

[95]

85. To Charles L. Ross[150]

Mr C L Ross

Oregon City 3rd April 1848

Sir

I Beg to Acknowledge the Receipt of yours of 5th Janry last by the Henry Capt Kilborn and to Apologise to you for having Omitted to do so by same Channel on its Return to San Francisco to Thank you for the trouble you took to communicate Valuable information to me and which I duly appreciate.

By the Eveline[151] Capt Goodwin I Received a letter from Capt Gelston informing me that he Expects to Remit me the proceeds of my flour which he has for sale through you. If he has done so you will oblige me if there is an Opportunity to Remit it to George Pelly Esqr Oahu. But if there is no Opportunity for Oahu But for this place please to Remit it to me And oblige

Yours Respectfully

Jn McLoughlin

[A postscript to this letter of five lines has been clipped from the manuscript.]

86. To Charles L. Ross
[probably an enclosure with Letter 85]

Oregon City 3 April [1848]

Mr A E Wilson [L C Ross (*sic*) is written above Mr A E Wilson]

Dear Sir

Capt Gelston has 93 Barrels of flour of Mine for sale and he Writes me By the Eveline Capt Goodman [Goodwin] that he will have to pay me through Mr Ross of San Francisco and I wrote the last "If Mr A E Wilson of the firm of Pettygrove & Co is at San Francisco you can hand

150. For biographical information on Ross, see Appendix C.

151. The *Eveline*, an American brig of 196 tons commanded by S. T. Goodwin, first arrived in the Columbia in April 1848. Her cargo of general merchandise was used to stock "The New Store" in Oregon City which was operated by Hiram Clark, who entered into partnership with George Abernethy in 1849. *Oregon Spectator*, 4 May 1848; Bancroft, *History of Oregon*, 2:17.

any Money You have of Mine to him." I have done this as I presume you would be Willing to Oblige me By Bringing this money to me. I am

Dear Sir
Yours Respectfully
Jn McLoughlin

87. To Albert E. Wilson

Oregon City 3rd April 1848

Mr A E Wilson

Dear Sir

Capt Gelston has 93 Barrels of flour of mine for Sale and he writes me by the Eveline Capt Goodwin that he will have to pay me through Mr Ross of San Francisco and I wrote the last "If Mr A E Wilson of the firm of Pettygrove & Co is at San Francisco you can hand any Money you have of Mine to him." I have done this as I persume [*sic*] you would be Willing to oblige me [A five-line section of the manuscript containing the last line (see preceding letter), the closing, and the signature as well as a small portion of the first line of the postscript has been clipped from the letter book.]

[PS If] you find an opportunity of purchasing Goods to advantage for the trade of your Concern you are at liberty to do so provided you consider you can Return me the Money in the Course of the Summer.

Jn McL

88. To George Pelly

Oregon City 20th April 1848

George Pelly

Dear Sir

Since I last addressed you on the 28th March Copy of which is on this sheet and Inclosed is a Copy of the Memorandum which I sent Capt Dring has been here and placed his Goods for sale on Commission with Mess Pettygrove & Co and purchased 180 M feet Lumber from Mr Pomeroy at $15 pr M delivered alongside which he is to take to California and Return here for a Cargo which he will purchase from Mr Pomeroy or Mr Pomeroy will ship According to Circumstances and

[97]

you may depend there will be a good deal of Lumber shipped from the Columbia this year. I am sorry to hear from Capt Dring that you were too Unwell to Write But I hope that long before this your health has been Restored. No Accounts yet of the Vancouver[152] Capt Mott.

Yours Respectfully
John McLoughlin

PS I had written this far When yours of 13th March was handed me with my Account In which I see ten Barrels flour pr Toulon — Cash for his Note $410 for 41 Barrels Salmon — I sent you no Salmon. Cash on Account Sales Lumber $896.75. My Son is not here and I do not know what you have written to him But his account is open and I see Nothing in it to his Credit. When I Understood from him and Pettygrove that they had shipped on the Brutus Capt Adams Lumber and Salmon to you and which by mistake you have carried to my Credit as all I sent you is 10 Barrels flour Shipped on the 17th April on the Henry the Lumber p Janet Capt Dring — 952 Dollars Cash p the same and Capt Adams of the Brutus wrote me he paid $18.80 to you on my Account, But which I do not find put to my Credit. I am much disappointed at Capt. Leidesdorff not Remitting to you as I Instructed. Instead of which he Sold Goods to Capt Kilborn to pay me here the Charge of Interest on my Draft in favour of Capt Couch as It was Cash I expected But on Goods I expected as Usual 12 Months Credit.

Jn McLoughlin

152. The *Vancouver* never reached the Columbia, for on 8 May 1848 she struck "Shark's Spit" while attempting to enter the river. Only a small part of her valuable cargo, which included a threshing machine and a large number of much-needed scythes, was saved, and the ship itself was a total loss. *Oregon Spectator*, 18 May 1848.

The *Vancouver*, a teak-built vessel of about 400 tons, was built for the Hudson's Bay Co. in 1838. In 1844 Andrew Cook Mott was given command of the *Vancouver*, and after her loss he returned to England and left the Company's service. The wreck of the Vancouver probably was not the fault of Mott, for the ship was being piloted by Selah C. Reeves at the time of the disaster. Indeed, Reeves was censured and removed from his post as Columbia River pilot on the charge of "conniving at the wreck of the *Vancouver* for the sake of plunder. . . ." The charge of secreting goods from the wreck was probably ill-founded, but his incompetency rendered the benefits of his services somewhat dubious. McLoughlin, *Letters, Second Series*, pp. 5n, 141n; Wright, ed., *Lewis & Dryden's Marine History of the Pacific Northwest*, p. 24; Bancroft, *History of Oregon*, 2:24–25; *Oregon Spectator*, 27 July, 24 August 1848.

Excuse haste the Messenger is Waiting please Bear in mind that the Shipment p the Janet is to be sold for Pomeroy, that the Net proceeds only come to my Credit. Therefore it is necessary I have a seperate account of the shipment & Sale of Lumber pr Janet for him.

Jn McLoughlin

89. To Captain David Dring

Oregon City 24th April 1848

Capt Dring

Dear Sir

I owe you a Thousand Apologies for not Answering your Letter by David, when he handed it to me, I was Busily Engaged in Business with two persons and I put your letter on my table with the address downwards where it lay to this moment. I am sorry to say it would not be convenient for me to give you a Bill of £ 300 But this I can do — I can lend you the Dollars to purchase a Bill on your paying the Oahu Interest till repaid. I gain nothing by the measure and lend it to you instead of Remitting it to him as he has property of mine in his hands out of which he can repay himself and I am paying him Interest.

Yours Respectfully
Jn McLoughlin

PS — I write down to the Eveline on Wednesday. It will therefore be necessary for me to know your Decision in time. My Respects to the Ladies.

Jn McLoughlin

90. To F. W. Pettygrove and Company

Oregon City 26th April 1848

Messr Pettygrove & Co

I do myself the pleasure to send you with this by J C Campbell[153]

153. McLoughlin probably means John G. Campbell, who was Archibald McKinlay's assistant at the Oregon City Store of the Hudson's Bay Co. (See Letter 11, to David McLoughlin, n. 39, and Letter 84, to George Pelly, n. 149.)

Esqr all the cash I have and Mr Pettygroves note to Mr McKindlay which I paid one hundred and three Dollars say

In Cash Bag no 1		$ 700
		[$1495]
2		446 12
3		355.50
		1496..62
Mr Pettygroves note to McK		103. 34
		1599 96

from which please take
amt handed me by A E Wilson Esq

17 January 1848 –	$460	
My Note paid at Portland	460	
handed me by Mr P.	355.50	1275.50
		$323.46

Which please Remit to George Pelly Esqr on my Account and oblige yours

Jn McLoughlin

I had calculated instead of sending this Money to Oahu to hand out of it a sufficiency to Capt Dring to purchase a Bill on London on his paying the Oahu rate of Interest, till he replaced it there as there is nothing lost by the transaction — Pelly cannot be long out of his Money as we have property there which must soon sell and bring him more Money than we owe him. I owe him for Pomeroy and Myself $4344 — But of this Pomeroy owes $3180 — to meet this Collective Debt he has $180 ft [sic] Lumber Capt Dring has not Answered my letter and I infer he is gone to Vancouver to purchase a Bill — If he has been able to purchase a Bill I would Recommend Lending them the Dollars on the Oahu Rate of Interest, By which nothing can be lost and he will be Accomodated But if he cannot purchase a Bill at Vancouver rather than he should be Incommoded and Run the Risk of sufferring an Injury — I Enclose a draft on the Hudson Bay Co Which he can have on Condition of paying it with Interest in England at the Expiration of one Year as I will Require it to pay for a purchase I have Instructed to be made. I would have let Capt Dring have the Draft at once But I know the great difficulty there is in sending money to

[100]

England from this Country, and I do this as a favour and not as a Matter of Business. I trust you will do the Needful.

J McLoughlin

NB send all the money to Pelly on your account and send no money on mine as I do not owe him much and he has a great deal of mine in his hands and the freight is Enormous to send money from this to the Islands. For this Reason rather than pay this freight it would be Better for you if Captain Dring can purchase a Bill to Lend him the money on his paying Interest on it till returned in Oahu.

91. To the Governor and Committee, Hudson's Bay Company
[not sent]

Oregon City 26th April 1848

£ 300 stg

To the Governor Deputy Governor
and Committee H H B Co London

Honbl Sirs
    Please pay to Captain David Dring on order sixty Days after Sight the sum of three hundred pounds Sterling which please Charge to

Jn McLoughlin

To The Governor Deputy Governor and Committee London

[This letter has been crossed out and the notation "Not Sent" written vertically across the body.]

92. To the Governor and Committee, Hudson's Bay Company
[not sent]

Oregon City 26 April 1848

To
The Governor Depty Governor and Committee HHCo [sic]154 London

154. McLoughlin no doubt meant to write "H H B Co" for "Honourable Hudson's Bay Company."

Honble Sirs

I Beg to inform you that I have this day drawn on You for three hundred pounds Stg in favour of Capt D Dring which please pay and Charge to

Your Obedient
Humble Serv
Jn McLoughlin

[This letter has been crossed out and the notation "Not Sent" written vertically across the body.]

93. To F. W. Pettygrove and Company

Oregon City 27th April 1848

Mess Pettygrove & Co

Gentlemen

If Capt Dring can purchase a Bill I would advise you to lend him the Money on the terms I mentioned in mine of yesterday. If he cannot purchase a Bill Will you please hand him the Enclosed and take a promissory Note from him payable this fall By a Note of hand with Interest Sept 1850 By a Bill of Exchange on London.

Yours Respectfully
Jn McLoughlin

NB — all I Intend is to Accomodate Capt Dring as this is not in my Line of Business.

94. To George Pelly

Oregon City 26th April 1848

To
George Pelly Esqr

Dear Sir

In case of Accident I Beg to Enclose a Copy of mine 20th April and its post script to which I Beg to refer you and I hope that Before long you will be able to sell off Lumber to pay up what I owe you as the Interest is a heavy Drawback as you know. I have also written to Captain Leidesdorff who has yet about two thousand Dollars of mine to Remit to you and Capt Gelston who took 93 Barrels of my flour

to Mazatlan last fall for sale is instructed to Remit to you the proceeds
— this with the sale of Lumber ought to put me Very soon out of
Debt And as I mentioned already the Cargo by the Janet is for Mr
Pomeroy he only transfers to me the net proceeds of the sale in part
payment of the Debt he owes me. It will be necessary you be so good
as to furnish me a seperate Account of the transaction to hand him.

Mess Albert Pelly & Co if they can will consign to you some Goods
for me which I hope you will Receive by first safe oppotunity [*sic*].
I notice in your Accounts the omission of the Charge of Commission
to me, which is not the thing as you ought not to give your services
Gratuitously to any One, and it is the same thing for me to pay you
as I would another, But I prefer you to do it — Because from my knowledge I know you will do what is Right. With Best Wishes Believe me to Be

> Yours Respectfully
> Jn McLoughlin

95. To Charles L. Ross

Oregon City 15th May 1848

Mr C L Ross

Sir

In one of my letters 3rd April last I Requested you to Remit any
Money Capt Gelston might have remitted you of mine to George Pelly
Esqr Oahu and in An other I wrote you to hand it to A E Wilson
Esqr. In case you have been Unable to do Either if you have any money
of mine I Request you would be so good as to deliver it to Capt Dring
and if after he leaves you have any money of mine I would Thank you
to send it by first opportunity to George Pelly Esqr Oahu.

> Yours Respectfully
> Jn McLoughlin

96. To William A. Leidesdorff

Oregon City 17 May 1848

William Leidesdorff Esqr

Dear Sir

I wrote in mine of 1st March Requesting you to hand any Balance

[103]

you had of mine in your hands to A E Wilson Esqr. In case you have not done so or Remitted it to George Pelly Esqr will you please to hand it to Captain Dring and oblige

> Yours Respectfully
> Jn McLoughlin

97. TO CAPTAIN DAVID DRING

> Oregon City 17 May 1848

Captain Dring

Dear Sir

The Enclosed letters speak for themselves and show that I Request Mess Leidesdorff and Ross to pay you any money they may have of mine in their hands. Attending to which will oblige

> Yours Respectfully
> Jn McLoughlin

My Respects to Mrs and Miss Dring.

98. TO MESSRS. STARKEY, JANION AND COMPANY

[not in McLoughlin's handwriting]

> Oregon City 21st May 1848

Messrs Starky Janeon & Co

Gentlemen

I beg to inform you that the crops of Wheat are very promising and I would thank you to let me know by return of Capt Dring if there is any prospect of a demand for flour in Calefornia this fall and the price — you would give for it p Barrel. I will have some flour to send to Market the produce of my grist — but if there was a demand in the Market I would [*purchase Wheat and some*] enter into the business more largely. Expecting to have an answer from you to mine of 12th March last

> I am Gentlemen
> Yours respectfully
> Sd John McLoughlin

[104]

99. To George Pelly [not in McLoughlin's handwriting]

[*Oregon City 26th April 1848*]

[To

George Pelly Esquire

Dear Sir

(See letter dated 20th April to George Pelly Esquire)
The above is a C]

Oregon City 26th April 1848

To George Pelly Esquire

Dear Sir

In case of accident I beg to enclose a copy of mine 20th April and its postscript to which I beg to refer you and I hope that before long you will be able to sell off Lumber to pay up what I owe you as the Interest is a heavy drawback as you know — I have also written to Captain Leidesdorff who has yet about two thousand Dollars of mine to remit to you and Captain Gelston who took 93 barrels of my Flour to Mazatland [*sic*] for sale is instructed to remit you the proceeds — this with the sale of Lumber ought to put me very soon out of debt and as I mentioned already the cargo by the Janet is for Mr Pomeroy he only transfers to me the net proceeds of the sale in part payment of the debt he owes me, it will be necessary you furnish me a seperate account of the transaction to hand him. Messr Albert Pelly & Co if they can will consign you some goods for me which I hope you will receive by first safe opportunity. I notice in your Accounts the omission of the charge of commission to me which is not the thing as you ought not to give your services gratuitously to any one and it is the same thing for me to pay you as I would another but I prefer you to do it because from my knowledge of you I know you will do what is right. With best wishes believe me to be

Yours respectfully
(Sd) John McLoughlin
Oregon City
22nd May 1848

George Pelly Esquire

Dear Sir

The above is a copy of my last and I also enclose a copy of the 20th April with its postscript which I wrote you in mine of 20th April that

[105]

I enclosed but did not send. You will learn with this of the unfortunate loss of the Vancouver, Captain Mott[155] at the Mouth of the River, there is not above a thousand Dollars in Value of her Cargo saved and that will not pay the expense of saving it all that you sent me by her was lost. The syrup as I understand, was to be delivered me by the H B Co at Vancouver. If so they will recover it from the underwriters. I wish you therefore to send by first opportunity the same quantity of the same articles you shipped for me by the Vancouver. Mr Pomeroy's lease of my saw Mills expires in June and he does not wish to renew it. If you have not sold all his Lumber I wish you to inform me what it is worth so as I may if necessary purchase it of him — so as to close my affairs with [him] and I wish you would send me a statement account of the Sales &c &c you have made the expenses &c &c of the Cargo per Janet to present to him as the Cargo is his and to be sold on his account but he transfers the net proceeds to me as part payment of my claims on him. As I informed you in my last Messrs Albert Pelly & Co are to ship some Goods to you for me if they can they write by a Vessel to sail to Oahoo from Liverpool. If you receive them I hope you will send them by the first safe opportunity.

Yours respectfully
Sd John McLoughlin

100. To Messrs. Albert Pelly and Company

[not in McLoughlin's handwriting, not sent]

Oregon City 27th May 1848

Messrs Albert Pelly and Co
   London

Gentlemen

I duly received yours of 18th Sept 1847 which Capt Mott forwarded to me from Woahoo p Barque Janet Capt Dring with Invoices Bills Lading and Samples and I am much obliged to Sir J H Pelly and you for the prompt manner in which you attended to my request as the Goods as appear from the Pattern Samples to be well selected but I am sorry to inform you that all you shipped for me by the Hudsons

155. See Letter 88, to George Pelly, n. 152.

Bay Companys Vessel Vancouver Capt Mott has been lost. The Vessel was lost at the entrance of the Columbia and as I understand not above 200£ worth of the Cargo saved which will not cover the expense of saving them this misfortune is a serious injury to all concerned as our population is about twenty thousand who are dependent on the H B Co for all the articles of British Manufacture and this year the Americans expect an immigration of twenty thousand to the Country and there never was such appearance of Good Crop of wheat in the Country as this year.

But there not being a regular Government is a great draw back as we do not know how we will be situated that is what duties will be put on English Manufacture.[156] The people say they will not submit to custom house duties as they say the Government has done nothing for them — and therefore they must give them some years of Grace before they can make them pay custom house duties but of course this is all talk. But if I knew there was an unrestricted trade between this country and British that English Goods were admitted free of duty I would request you to send me if this get to you in time this fall the quantity of the different articles you sent me by the Vancouver but which were unfortunately lost on board the Vancouver; except the following.

$ 23 a case 6 doz M frame lookg Glasses
   62   ditto   Indigo &c &c
   63   Cask   Pearl ash
  1 to 6 Boxes   yellow soap
 73 a Barrel   white chalk
  1 to 12 –   12 Boxes Glass 9x7
  1 to 10 –   10 ———   7 1/2 x 8 1/2

156. McLoughlin's well-founded concern about customs duties was not realized until 1849, when the customs district of Oregon was created with Astoria as the port of entry. By 1 January 1850 duties in the amount of $23,000 had been levied on goods imported from London, of which $6,800 was paid under protest by the Hudson's Bay Co., since such duties were considered to be in contravention of the second article of the Oregon Treaty of 1846 which guaranteed the free navigation of the Columbia River to the British. Without the duties, however, it has been estimated that the Company would have enjoyed a 35 percent advantage over other importers. Ralph R. Martig, "Hudson's Bay Company Claims, 1846–69," p. 64; Throckmorton, *Oregon Argonauts*, pp. 76–77.

$ 5 a Case 3 dz Hay scythes
      1 " double rein Bridles
      5 " single   ditto
    12   shaving Cases
    6 pair Carvers
In Case 90 – 10 x Cut saw 6 feet

and which are to be omitted — but as I said if you can you will please send me the same quantity of the Goods sent me p Vancouver to replace those Lost. I have only heard of the *Mary Dare* sailing to Oahoo about an hour ago — which will not allow me time to draw up a requisition and I hope will serve as an apology for my making it in this way and it is only the want of the articles and the want of time to make out a regular requisition that obliged me to send it in this way. I will write you again by the first opportunity.

I am
Yours respectfully
Sd John McLoughlin

Mrs Rae request[s] you would send the same kind and quantity of the Goods &c &c to replace those lost in the Vancouver.
["Not Sent" has been written vertically across the three manuscript sheets of this letter.]

101. To Messrs. Albert Pelly and Company

[not in McLoughlin's handwriting]

Oregon City 27th April [May] 1848

Messrs Albert Pelly & Co
    London

Gentlemen

I duly received yours of 18th Sept 1847 which Captain Mott forwarded me from Oahoo per Barque Janet Captain Dring with Invoices Bills Lading and Samples and I am much obliged to Sir J H Pelly and you for the prompt manner in which you attended to my request as the Goods as appear from the Pattern Samples to be well selected but I am sorry to inform you that all you shipped for me by the Hudsons Bay Company's Vessel Vancouver Capt Mott has been lost. The Vessel was

[108]

lost at the entrance of the Columbia and I understood not above £ 200 worth of the Cargo saved — which will not cover the expense of saving it. If this reaches you in time before the H B Coys Vessel leaves London this fall I would thank you to get the enclosed list completed and forward to me; to be delivered at Vancouver and if that cannot be done if you can send it to Oahoo to G Pelly Esquire with instructions to forward to me by first safe opportunity. You will please to insure to F Vancouver or Portland in this River as the case May be.

I am
Yours respectfully
Sd John McLoughlin

Mrs Rae requests [that] you would send the same kind and quantity of [the] Goods &c &c to replace those lost in the Vancouver.

[The following postscript is written vertically along the left-hand side of the sheet:]

P S The Cotton Shirts Melbourn, rail road and drab Cord Trousers ought to be packed in Bales wrapped in three point Blankets covered with paper in the Same manner as the Hudson Bay Company's are Shipped — the Moleskin ought to be in cases tinned and well soldered.

```
❖◆❖◆❖◆❖◆❖◆❖◆❖◆❖◆❖◆❖◆❖◆❖◆❖◆❖◆❖◆❖◆❖◆❖◆❖◆❖◆❖◆❖◆❖◆❖◆❖
```

Appendix A
Supplementary Letters: Hawaii, 1844–48

```
❖◆❖◆❖◆❖◆❖◆❖◆❖◆❖◆❖◆❖◆❖◆❖◆❖◆❖◆❖◆❖◆❖◆❖◆❖◆❖◆❖◆❖◆❖◆❖◆❖
```

1. JOHN MCLOUGHLIN'S BOND FOR DR. IRA LEONARD BABCOCK[1]

This is to Certify that Dr Babcock has left Mikker Barkis [?] a sandwich Islander[2] with me who at the End of his Enagement [*sic*] with Dr Babcock in 1848 I promise to send Back to Oahu — Desertion and Death Excepted

Jn McLoughlin

11th Nov 1844

    1. For biographical information on Babcock, see Appendix C.

    2. Hawaiians, or Kanakas as they were generally called, were employed on vessels sailing between Hawaii and the west coast in the late eighteenth century. At least by 1811, contracts were made for the employment of Kanakas on trading vessels. That year Captain Jonathan Thorn, commanding Astor's ship *Tonquin*, engaged twelve Islanders for the intended commercial establishment on the Columbia. The term of engagement was for three years, during which the Americans were to feed and clothe them; and at the expiration of their service, each was to receive $100 in merchandise. At the same time Thorn shipped another dozen islanders as crew members. The North West Co. also utilized Hawaiian laborers, and by 1821 there were about thirty-five Kanakas on the Columbia. The North West Co. gave them only food and clothing, but by 1823 they were receiving subsistence plus £ 17 per annum from the Hudson's Bay Co., successor to the North West Co. in that area. The relatively high wages paid to the Hawaiians caused dissatisfaction among the European engagees, who also earned £ 17, and the wage was reduced to £ 10 by Governor Simpson in 1824. By 1841, however, Kanakas were being paid £ 17 per annum at the Company sawmills seven miles east of Vancouver, where they constituted a majority of the labor force.

    Governor Simpson, writing in 1824, noted that Sandwich Islanders could

[111]

2. To [Robert Crichton Wyllie][3]

Oregon City 15th July 1847

My Dear Sir

I have the pleasure to Acknowledge the Receipt pr the Janet of the Duplicate of yours pr the Toulon[4] of 24th May.

I am sorry to Learn that the Consul General Miller[5] gives you so much trouble — But it is not surprising as from his former habits and prepossession

---

be usefully employed as guards and for common drudgery, but that they were not suitable for the hard labor of sea duty. He found them especially valuable in opening new territories, for they were dependable in the face of danger from the natives. Simpson, *Fur Trade and Empire*, p. 91.

In 1841 Lieutenant Charles Wilkes hired fifty Islanders to augment his crews, and in 1843 McLoughlin found it necessary to have fifty men sent from "Woahoo" (Oahu) to replace the servants who were about to retire in 1844. By 1850, when the first census was taken in Oregon Territory, there were fifty Sandwich Islanders resident in the Pacific Northwest. However, few of the Owyhees became permanent residents, for the contracts for their labor stipulated that they were to be returned to the Islands at the end of a specified number of years. The following is a copy of a Hudson's Bay Co. contract for Hawaiian labor.

Honolulu, Feb. 11, 1840

An agreement between M. Kekuanaoa [Governor of Oahu] and G. Pelly [Hudson's Bay Company agent in Honolulu].

Kekuanaoa allows Mr. Pelly to take sixty men to the Columbia River, to dwell there three years and at the end of the said term of three years Mr. Pelly agrees to return them to the island of Oahu.

And if it shall appear that any of the men have died it is well; but if they have deserted by reason of ill-treatment, or remain for any other cause, then Mr. Pelly will pay twenty dollars for each man [who may be deficient].

George Verne Blue, "A Hudson's Bay Company Contract for Hawaiian Labor," p. 72. See also Robert Carlton Clark, "Hawaiians in Early Oregon," pp. 21–31; Gabriel Franchère, *Narrative of a Voyage to the Northwest Coast of America*, trans. and ed. J. V. Huntington, pp. 84–85; Simpson, *Fur Trade and Empire*, p. 91; McLoughlin, *Letters, Second Series*, p. 182; Wilkes, *Narrative of the United States Exploring Expedition*, 3:386.

3. For biographical information on Wyllie, see Appendix C.

4. The *Janet* arrived in Oregon on 6 July 1847, twenty-four days out from Oahu; and the *Toulon* arrived on 16 June 1847, after a sixteen-day passage from Honolulu. *Oregon Spectator*, 22 July, 24 June 1847.

5. William Miller. See Appendix C.

he cannot be qualified for the Duties of his office — It is only astonishing that he should have been selected for it.

In Reply to your query if there is a Post running between this and St Louis — We expect to have one But this you will see by the papers — as soon as we will.

In Regard to Establishing a Bank the Country is not yet sufficiently advanced for that purpose and will not be so in my opinion before two or three years if Indeed so soon.[6] Our Crops this year are rather Better than last — and we hope to have enough to feed the large Immigration Expected this year and to have some to spare for our friends.

I am happy to say Business is Increasing in the Country — We have been Visited by five Ships Exclusive of those belonging to the Hudson Bay Company[7]— those who have left have had Cargo and I hope we will be able to Load the Remainder — as to our news and public affairs I must Beg to refer you to our public papers[8]— which I requested our printer to forward to you and Believe me to Be with the Greatest Respect

Yours faithfully

Jn McLoughlin

[The following appears on the cover of the letter:]
    1847
Dr McLoughlin
Oregon City   15 July
  Received —   23 Sept
  Ansd —   11th December
          1847 by the
          Mary Dare

6. McLoughlin's view was realistic, for not until 1859, when the banking firm of Ladd & Tilton opened with a capitalization of $50,000, was there a locally owned bank in Oregon. Previously, all banking transactions were made through the Portland agencies of Adams & Co. and Wells, Fargo & Co., which were established in 1851 and 1852, respectively. Both of these firms were based in San Francisco. Charles H. Carey, *A General History of Oregon prior to 1861*, 2:753–54.

7. The five ships to which McLoughlin referred were: *Brutus* (arrived 14 June 1847), *Toulon* (arrived 16 June 1847), *Mount Vernon* (arrived 27 June 1847), *Henry* (arrived 4 July 1847), and *Janet* (arrived 6 July 1847). See Appendix B.

8. Oregon's "public papers" of the day consisted of the *Oregon Spectator*, edited by George L. Curry. The first issue of the *Spectator* was published on 5 February 1846.

No Overland Post
yet established

—

Not time, as yet
for a Bank

—

Opinion of Consul
General Miller

3. To Robert Crichton Wyllie

Oregon City 15th March 1848

To
The Right Honble R C Wyllie

My Dear Sir

I have the pleasure to Acknowledge the Receipt of your favour 11th Dec 1847 and 3rd Janry 1848 with the Accompanying Polynesians[9] for which please Accept my thanks.

I am Extremely sorry to learn that our friend Pelly[10] is so Unwell and I am afraid from what you write that his constitution is Breaking Up — his difference with Sir George Seymour[11]— must have hurt his feelings Great-

9. The *Polynesian*, published in Honolulu, was the official journal of the Hawaiian government in the 1840s. James Jackson Jarves began publishing the weekly *Polynesian* on 6 June 1840, but the paper was discontinued after a year and a half for lack of support, a not uncommon malady of papers of the period. In May 1844 Jarves resumed publication, and in July the *Polynesian* was purchased by the government, which used the paper as its official organ until publication was discontinued in 1864. Riley H. Allen, "Hawaii's Pioneers in Journalism," pp. 76–83; Kuykendall, *The Hawaiian Kingdom*, p. 249.

10. George Pelly. See Appendix C.

11. Rear Admiral Sir George Francis Seymour was commander in chief of Her Majesty's Pacific Squadron, 1844–48. Pelly's troubles with Sir George began with the visit of the latter to Honolulu in 1845. The differences between the two men are perhaps best indicated in Seymour's own words: ". . . it is my duty to inform you (in order that the Hudson's Bay Company should be apprised) that their Agents at this Island offered me no information or assistance on arrival, although the present state of affairs would appear to render it necessary that those who conduct their business should communicate with Officers of H.M. Navy whose duty brings them to the Island, & connects them with the defence of the Country in which the interests of the Hudson's Bay Company

ly — and I cannot see how Sir George Seymour can reconcile it to his conscience — to have Aspersed Mess Pelly and in the Way he did when it was so Easy for him to ascertain if he really was the Drunkard reported to him. But really a number of these men do not care what they say — and certainly Pelly Acted as he ought and Exposed Sir George Seymour as he deserved.

I am surprised and Astonished to see by the Polynesian that Charlton[12] has

---

are principally involved, every information thereon which such Agents may possess.

"At the end of 3 days I sent for Mr. Allen [George T. Allan], one of the Agents, to inform me what the state of the Oregon was by the last accounts who gave as reasons for holding aloof, that the Consul General had not replied to some note, and Mr. Pelly had not been civilly treated by the Captain of the Carysfort in 1843. The Agents sent me, however, afterwards, such Papers, as I wanted to see, but with a Note . . . which though couched in the most respectful terms, desires to communicate with me only in writing. I understand that neither of these Agents associates with the English & that Mr. Pelly, after following about a Band playing American Tunes — in a state of intoxication, which — I am told — is habitual to him, at a dinner to celebrate the independence of the United States, insulted Admiral Thomas & the British Navy. . . .

"The Printed Records of the Foreign Office, also furnish proof of the bias Mr. Pelly possesses towards the United States; a change in the Agency therefore appears to me to deserve the consideration of the Directors." Sir George Seymour to the Right Honourable H. T. L. Corry, Oct. 4, 1845, in Knuth, ed., "HMS Modeste," pp. 423–24.

Sir George Simpson, never one to dissemble in evaluating his employees, makes no mention of either drunkenness or irascibility in his characterization of Pelly in 1842. Simpson did say, however, that Pelly's management of the Company's affairs in Hawaii lacked "a business like finish or neatness," and he further stated that although Pelly's business transactions were stamped with integrity, he had not "on all occassions followed his orders implicitly." Simpson to McLoughlin, 3 March 1842, McLoughlin, Letters, Second Series, p. 280. See also ibid., Third Series, p. 74.

12. Richard Charlton was British consul for the Sandwich, Society, and Friendly islands from 1824 to 1843, when he was succeeded by William Miller. As early as 1829 he was acting as agent for the Hudson's Bay Co. in the Sandwich Islands, and he continued to represent their interests there until the Company felt that his personal interest in the coastal trade interfered with his management of their affairs. The Company, accordingly, sent George Pelly to succeed Charlton as their agent in Honolulu in August 1834.

The incident to which McLoughlin refers concerns Charlton's land claim in Honolulu and the related question of where power and authority lay in the absolutist kingdom. In 1823–24, King Kamehameha II (1819–24) was in Eng-

been supported in his pretensions to Pulu laoha — I say pretensions for even allowing the Signature of Karaimoku to be Genuine — how can the British Government support Karaimoku in giving away Another mans property and

land, and learning of Charlton's appointment to represent British interests in the Sandwich Islands, he made known his wish that Charlton should have land in Honolulu on which to reside and establish an office. The king died in London on 14 July 1824, and was succeeded by his younger brother Kamehameha III (1824–54), who was a minor. Until 1833, when Kamehameha came of age, Hawaii was governed by a regency, about which there is more than a little confusion.

In brief, the story is this. Kamehameha I (1795–1819) had appointed as his principal executive officer a younger chief named Kalanimoku (known to contemporaries as "Karaimoku," as spelled by McLoughlin). Kalanimoku's duties were analogous to those of a prime minister and treasurer, and he took for himself the name of his contemporary British equivalent, William Pitt. Kalanimoku continued to hold this office upon the accession of Kamehameha II in 1819, but the new king appointed his father's chief wife, Kaahumanu, as kuhina-nui, an officer who fulfilled the chief functions of routine government administration.

Upon the departure of Kamehameha II for England in November 1823, Kaahumanu and Kalanimoku became the chief officers of state. Charlton, who had personal interests at stake, later claimed that they functioned as joint regents until Kalanimoku's death in February 1827; but there is contemporary evidence which indicates that Kaahumanu was in reality sole regent and that Kalanimoku's authority as chief agent was derived from the dowager queen regent. The matter of Kalanimoku's power and authority later assumed great importance, for in December 1826 Charlton obtained from Kalanimoku a 299-year lease to a valuable piece of property in Honolulu which he occupied. In April 1840 Charlton brought forth this lease which also included a piece of land adjoining that which he occupied. The adjoining land had been occupied by the native retainers of Kaahumanu and her heirs (she died in June 1832) during the entire period since 1826. One of these heirs was no doubt the female orphan (Pula laoha?) to whom McLoughlin refers, though this editor was unable to locate any documentation of this.

King Kamehameha III rejected Charlton's claim, his decision being principally based on the statement that Kalanimoku had not had the authority to make the grant without the assent of Kaahumanu. In 1843 Charlton returned to England with charges and complaints against the Hawaiian kingdom, among which was the matter of the denial of the validity of his lease in Honolulu. Early in February 1843 the H.M.S. *Carysfort*, commanded by Lord George Paulet, arrived in Honolulu. Alexander Simpson, the acknowledged proconsul during Charlton's absence, used the presence of British gun power to force the king to surrender the land claimed by Charlton and to sign a ratification of the 299-year lease. The claims of British subjects in Hawaii were submitted to

yet you see the British ministers talk of the Invasion of Crackow[13] while the Decision they sanction Indeed make in Charltons case — is a more Outrageous infringement of Right. The Inhabitants of Crakow [sic] were deprived of their Government. But this Young female orphan is deprived of her property by means of the British Government — and it is given to Charlton. It seems to me the case admits of no other construction — and wherever the case is known must have its Effect. Our Winter has been fine — and our people have three times as much Wheat in the Ground as they ever had and it looks very [sic] if the season is any way fine — this Country will have this fall a large Quantity of flour for Sale —

I am Sir
Yours Respectfully
Jn McLoughlin

---

the British Foreign Office for review, and on 12 September 1843 Lord Aberdeen wrote to the Hawaiian representatives in London that the issue of Charlton's lease rested on the genuineness of the document of conveyance and the power of the person by whom it was executed.

As the document was in Honolulu, it was left to Charlton's newly appointed successor, General William Miller, to determine if the lease was in part or wholly a forgery. Concerning the authority of Kalanimoku to make the grant, Aberdeen, relying on Charlton's statements, decided that Kalanimoku was indeed regent in December 1826 and therefore had the right to make the grant. Consul General Miller determined that only a test of the genuineness of the signatures was necessary, and satisfying himself that they were genuine, he decided in favor of Charlton. The Hawaiian kingdom, in spite of its agreement to Aberdeen's terms in February 1844, attempted to bring into review the whole question of the grant. Miller queried his government on the matter and received instructions "to insist upon the land in question being immediately delivered up to Mr. Charlton." Miller presented this demand to the Hawaiian government, now represented in its foreign relations by Robert C. Wyllie, in August 1845, and the government yielded. That is where matters stood at the time of McLoughlin's letter to Wyllie quoted above.

One final maneuver was yet to be made in the dispute, however. A fresh attempt was made to get the British government to review the case on its own merits, and the final answer, presented in Honolulu in August 1847, simply confirmed the previous decision. Kuykendall, *The Hawaiian Kingdom*, pp. 53–434 *passim*, particularly pp. 215, 245–46, 431–34; McLoughlin, *Letters, First Series*, pp. xciii, 76.

13. McLoughlin was referring to the revolt of Polish patriots in Galicia (Austrian Poland) in 1846. This revolt, led by landowners and intellectuals, was suppressed by Austrian authorities who called on the peasants to rise against their masters. The revolt presaged the eruptions of April 1848 in Cracow, a month after this letter was written.

I send you with this a small quantity of [*Clover*] Timothy seed — it is sown in the fall in General with Oats sowed thin — so as to protect it when Young from the scorching Effect of the Sun — I can get no clover seed.

Jn McLoughlin

[Address on cover:] The Right Honble R C Wyllie Oahu
[In another hand on the cover:]
   1848
Dr McLoughlin
Oregon City   15 March
  Red —   6 May
  And   23 -"
Remarking upon the
award of *Pulaluloha*
to Mr Charlton
     and sending
some Timothy
Seed

Commercial Shipping Other Than Hudson's Bay Company Vessels, Columbia River, 1846–48 [a]

Ship	Commander	Tons	Registry	Arrival
Admiral Morsom, bark	McKnight	---	England	29 July 1846
Brutus, ship	James Adams	470	U.S. (Boston)	14 June 1847
Commodore Stockton, schooner[c]	P. Young	100	U.S. (Newburyport, Mass.)	25 Mar. 1847
Eveline, brig	S. T. Goodwin	196	U.S. (Newburyport, Mass.)	Apr. 1848
	Nathaniel Crosby, Jr.			July 1848
				13 Oct. 1848
Henry, brig	William K. Kilborne[e]	153	U.S. (Newburyport, Mass.)	1 Mar. 1847
	Bray			4 July 1847
	Bray[g]			1 Oct. 1847
	William K. Kilborne			7 Feb. 1848
	William K. Kilborne[i]			9 Aug. 1848
Janet, bark	David Dring	333	England	6 July 1847
				Nov. 1847
				16 Mar. 1848
L'Etoile du Matin, bark	François Marie Menes	235	France	14 Aug. 1847[l]
				10 July 1849
Mariposa, bark	Parsons	---	U.S.	26 June 1846
Mount Vernon, ship	J. O. Given	446	U.S.	27 June 1847
Toulon, bark	Nathaniel Crosby, Jr.	272	U.S. (New York)	14 Oct. 1845[m]
				24 June 1846
				25 Oct. (?) 1846[n]
				18 Mar. 1847
				16 June 1847
				9 Sept. 1847
Whiton, bark	Roland Gelston	---	U.S. (New York)	22 June 1847
				11 Sept. 1847

[a] The information for this table was obtained from: *Oregon Spectator*, 5 February 1846 to 4 January 1849, *passim*; Bancroft, *History of Oregon*, 2:15–19; State of Hawaii, Public Archives, to W. R. Sampson, Honolulu, 23 January 1964, MS; Bernice P. Bishop Museum to W. R. Sampson, Honolulu, 24 December 1963, MS; and Lowe, "Private Journal Kept at Fort Vancouver," pp. 47, 51.

The *Spectator's* coverage of marine news was erratic, particularly during 1848. Following are the names of ships and their captains which came into the Columbia for provisions or cargoes of lumber and flour for the San Francisco and Hawaii markets, but which are not mentioned above: Hawaiian schooner *Mary Ann*, Belcham; American schooner *Honolulu*, Newell; Hawaiian schooner *Starling*, Menzies; whaler *Maine*, Netcher; American schooner *Maria*, De Witt; brig *Sabine*, Crosby; schooner *Ann*, Melton; and *Harpooner*, Morice. All of these were in Oregon during the spring and summer of 1848, and so far as is known, each made only one visit.

The Hudson's Bay Co. ships and their captains were: *Cadboro*, schooner, Scarborough, 70 tons; *Columbia*, bark, Duncan, 289 tons; *Cowlitz*, bark, Wynton, 289 tons; *Mary Dare*, brig, Cooper; *Vancouver*, bark (lost on Columbia bar, May 1848), Mott, 289 tons.

[b] Sailed 3 Nov. 1847, Oahu to New York.

[c] Former *Pallas*, Capt. Avery Sylvester, arrived at the Columbia River in Sept. 1843. It was wrecked on 20 Jan. 1848 in Marguerite Bay, Lower California, en route to Mazatlán and South America from San Francisco.

From	Cargo	Cleared	For	Cargo
		July 1846		
Boston, San Francisco (17 days)		15 July 1847	Oahu (arr. 16 Aug.)[b]	
San Francisco (20 Feb.)		12 Apr. 1847 (Portland), 21 Apr. 1847 (Columbia River)	California	450 bbls. flour, 7,000 ft. lumber
	General merchandise	7 May 1848	Honolulu (arr. 27 May)	Lumber
Honolulu (8 June)		31 July 1848	Honolulu (arr. 14 Aug.)	
Honolulu (14 Sept.)		Dec. 1848[d]	San Francisco	Lumber, provisions
Newburyport, Oahu	General merchandise	1 May 1847	Honolulu (arr. 22 May)	70,000 ft. lumber[f]
Oahu (29 days)				
San Francisco (13 days)		23 Oct. 1847	San Francisco, Oahu	Lumber, flour, beef[h]
San Francisco (22 days)	Merchandise	Mar. 1848	California	
California[j]		6 Nov. 1848	San Francisco	
Oahu (24 days)[k]				
California		Jan. 1848	Oahu	Lumber
Honolulu (17 days)		8 June 1848	California	
Brest, France (5½ months)		Sept. (?) 1847	Tahiti, France	
France				
Honolulu (24 days)		July 1846		
Oahu (24 days)		15 July 1847	San Francisco, Oahu, Manila	
New York	General merchandise, sugar, coffee, molasses, cotton	1 Mar. (?) 1846	Oahu	
Oahu (22 days)		23 Aug. 1846 (Fort Vancouver), 5 Sept. 1846 (Columbia River)	Oahu (18 days)	
Oahu (21 days)		18 Jan. 1847	California	600 bbls. flour
San Francisco (20 Feb.)		14 Apr. 1847	California, Oahu	386 bbls. flour
Honolulu (16 days)		15 July 1847	Oahu (14 days)	94,000 ft. lumber
Oahu (29 days)		27 Nov. 1847	Oahu (20 days), Hong Kong[o]	
New York (162 days)		15 July 1847	San Francisco[p]	
San Francisco (21 days)		19 Oct. 1847	San Francisco, Panama[q]	

[d] Ran aground on Peacock Spit at the mouth of the Columbia, 5 Dec. 1848.

[e] Bray was the captain outbound.

[f] Also carried 96,000 shingles.

[g] Kilborne was the captain outbound.

[h] Also carried salmon and produce.

[i] Bray was the captain outbound.

[j] Brought news of the California gold rush (the schooner *Honolulu* had brought verbal intelligence of the discovery of gold on 31 July 1848).

[k] Had arrived in Oahu from Tahiti on 3 June 1847.

[l] Arrived with Blanchet and 20 Roman Catholic clerics and nuns. Wrecked on the Columbia bar in the summer of 1849.

[m] Arrived with goods for F. W. Pettygrove; Benjamin Stark, supercargo

[n] Arrived with news of the provisions of the Oregon Treaty.

[o] From Oahu, the *Toulon* sailed to Hong Kong.

[p] Artist John Mix Stanley was an incoming passenger.

[q] Gelston was carrying the Yamhill Petition on this voyage.

ABERNETHY, GEORGE

George Abernethy (1807–77), hired as mission steward for Jason Lee's Methodist Mission in Oregon, left his native New York on the *Lausanne* with the "Great Reinforcement" in 1839. The *Lausanne* arrived at Fort Vancouver on 1 June 1840 with the fifty-one members of the mission and a cargo of supplies which included the machinery for a gristmill. As steward, or business manager, for the Methodist Mission, Abernethy persuaded Jason Lee to establish a retail store at Willamette Falls in 1841, whereupon a group of settlers, mostly members of the mission, formed the Island Milling Company. The following autumn, the new company erected a gristmill and a sawmill on the small island (two and one-half acres) adjacent to the mainland at the Falls.

John McLoughlin had claimed the land at the Falls, including the island, as early as 1829; but in spite of his protests, the Methodists asserted that no foreign corporation would be allowed to occupy the land once American law prevailed. To compete with the Methodists, McLoughlin built a gristmill and a sawmill on the mainland opposite Abernethy Island (as it came to be called) in 1843, and the same year the newly organized Provisional Government, dominated by the Methodists, passed a land law prohibiting all persons from holding claims on "City or Town sites, extensive water privileges or other situations necessary for the transaction of Mercantile or Manufacturing operations . . . provided that nothing in these laws shall be so construed, as to affect any claim of any Mission of a Religious character made previous to this time of an extent not more than six miles square." [1] Although this provision was re-

1. Duniway and Riggs, eds., "Oregon Archives," p. 279.

pealed in the land law of 1845, the Methodists continued to occupy the island, and in 1846 Abernethy acquired complete control of the Island Milling Company. In 1849 he sold the mill and logs on hand to Judge William P. Bryant in a questionable move to have McLoughlin deprived of his claim to Abernethy Island by the pending Donation Land Law. Abernethy evidently repossessed the mills soon after Congress enacted the law in 1850.[2]

In 1843 Abernethy purchased Walter Pomeroy's land claim at Green Point, which adjoined McLoughlin's claim. Abernethy requested a new survey of the land, and the result was Jesse Applegate's survey of Oregon City which was recorded on 16 December 1843.[3] Abernethy disliked McLoughlin and in a private letter he referred to his rival as "a Catholic and one of the most bigoted kind." [4] Yet, he usually managed to avoid open clashes which would embarrass him or the mission. From notes furnished by Robert Shortess, Abernethy framed the Shortess Petition to Congress of 1843, which charged McLoughlin and the Hudson's Bay Company with obstructing the "improvement and enterprize of American Citizens" and requested that Congress extend the jurisdiction of the United States to Oregon. Abernethy feared the consequences of this petition to the secular business of the mission, however, and he therefore had Albert E. Wilson make the final copy — which Abernethy did not sign.[5]

Late in 1845, Abernethy helped to organize the Oregon Printing Association of which he became treasurer. In February 1846 the association began the publication of the fortnightly *Oregon Spectator*, a paper which strongly supported the Methodist cause and often denounced the Hudson's Bay Company.[6] Such was his influence among the early settlers, that when the Provisional Government was reorganized in 1845 with a single executive instead of an executive committee, Abernethy, who was in Hawaii at the time, was elected governor with a plurality of ninety-eight of the 504 votes cast for the four candidates. He was re-elected by a small majority in 1847 and reached the height of his political power during the Cayuse War.[7]

Abernethy, engaged in the retail trade as well as the milling business, was one of the leading merchants in Oregon during the 1840s. He was the first of Oregon's merchants to establish credit in New York, and he became Oregon's

2. Throckmorton, *Oregon Argonauts*, p. 96; *Oregon Spectator*, 12 November 1846.

3. *Oregon Spectator*, 6 January 1848.

4. Throckmorton, *Oregon Argonauts*, p. 96n.

5. Bancroft, *History of Oregon*, 1:207; Duniway and Riggs, eds., "Oregon Archives," p. 228.

6. *Oregon Spectator*, 5 February 1846.

7. Bancroft, *History of Oregon*, 1:471–72; *Dictionary of American Biography*, 1:29–30.

first wholesale merchant. But competition in the carrying trade, indebtedness, and depressed conditions from 1859 to 1861 ruined him; in February 1861 the firm of Abernethy and Clark failed with deficits of $120,000. The final blow came in 1861 when the disastrous Willamette flood washed away Abernethy's mill and the brick warehouse, the first in Oregon, which he had built in the early 1840s. Thereafter Abernethy operated as a commission merchant in Portland until his death.[8]

Babcock, Ira Leonard

Dr. Ira Leonard Babcock (ca. 1808–88) was born in New York. Upon completion of his medical training, he joined Jason Lee's group of reinforcements for the Methodist missions in the Oregon country and sailed from New York with his wife and child on the *Lausanne*, which arrived at Fort Vancouver on 1 June 1840. On 17 February 1841 the settlers of the Willamette Valley met to appoint officers for the government of the community, and particularly to settle the estate of Ewing Young, who had died intestate earlier in the month. At this meeting Dr. Babcock was elected to fill the office of supreme judge with probate powers. In 1842, he served as chairman of a committee which organized the Oregon Institute, since grown to Willamette University, at Salem. On 2 May 1843, Dr. Babcock was chosen chairman of the famous Champoeg Meeting which voted to organize a provisional government for Oregon. Shortly thereafter, he and his family went to Hawaii. On his return in 1844, Babcock was again elected supreme judge; but his tenure of office was short, for in November he moved from Oregon and entered military service, becoming examining surgeon in the United States Army. At the time of his departure in November 1844, McLoughlin assumed the unexpired portion of the contract for the services of the Sandwich Islander, Mikker Barkis, whom Babcock had evidently brought from Hawaii in 1844 (see Appendix A).[9]

Beaver, Herbert

The Reverend Herbert Beaver (1800–1858) received a B.A. degree from Oxford in 1821 and was ordained a priest of the Anglican church in 1823. Following an appointment as army chaplain at St. Lucia, British West Indies, he was chosen to become the first chaplain at Fort Vancouver. He arrived at Fort Vancouver on 6 September 1836 aboard the *Nereide*. Although his appointment at £ 200 per annum was for a five-year period, he was unable to adjust either his style of living or his narrowly doctrinaire viewpoints to life in the

8. Throckmorton, *Oregon Argonauts*, pp. 217–19.
9. Corning, ed., *Dictionary of Oregon History*, p. 16; Duniway and Riggs, eds., "Oregon Archives," pp. 220, 236.

Oregon Country, and early in November 1838 he returned to England aboard the *Columbia* to prefer charges against John McLoughlin. The Company paid him £110 as full settlement and dropped him from its service.

From 1839 to 1843 he held the chaplaincy at Leavenheath, England. From Leavenheath, he went to Fort Beaufort, South Africa, where he had both civil and military duties. He died at Fort Beaufort on 21 May 1858.[10]

During his brief stay on the Columbia, Beaver showed his intransigence and general unsuitability for the position he occupied by constant complaints about his living conditions and the inadequacy of his wine ration, and his general opposition to McLoughlin and all that he did. In spite of the fact that many of the Company employees were Roman Catholics without a priest, Beaver protested McLoughlin's actions as a lay leader at Catholic services. A second source of friction was the responsibility for the school which McLoughlin had started at Fort Vancouver in 1832. Beaver felt that his duties as chaplain included control of the school; but when he began to catechize the Roman Catholic children in the forms of the Church of England, McLoughlin insisted that the school was his and released Beaver from responsibility for it.

The most serious cause of trouble between the two strong-minded men was the tradition of informal "fur-trade" marriages among Company employees who had taken Indian or part-Indian wives. McLoughlin himself had married in this fashion, and he resented Beaver's attempts to have him submit to a religious ceremony. Although he did become sufficiently concerned about the status of his marriage to have James Douglas, a justice of the peace, perform a civil ceremony, this act was indeed kept from Mr. Beaver. Matters came to a head when Beaver, in his third report to the governor and committee dated Fort Vancouver, 10 October 1837, alluded to Mrs. McLoughlin as "a female of notoriously loose character" and asked that "no woman, living in a state of concubinage, be permitted to dwell therein" (within the fort).[11] Beaver, realizing that his reports had to be delivered unsealed to McLoughlin, delayed submitting these remarks until 19 March 1838, the the eve of McLoughlin's departure for England. Unfortunately for Beaver, McLoughlin did take the time to read the report and what happened next is best told in the words of Beaver himself:

> I was walking quietly by myself across the Fort Yard towards my house, at the door of which my wife was standing, and at the same instant Chief Factor McLoughlin was advancing from his own house, about twenty yards distant from mine, in an oblique direction to meet me. We met a few

10. Herbert Beaver, *Reports and Letters of Herbert Beaver, 1836–1838*, ed. Thomas E. Jessett, pp. xiii, 79; G. Hollis Slater, "New Light on Herbert Beaver," pp. 17–18, 25–26.

11. Beaver, *Reports and Letters*, pp. 56–57.

yards from my door, when I turned aside to make way for him; upon which he said, "Mr. Beaver, you refused to come to me when I sent for you." I replied, still walking away from him, for he appeared to be very angry, "I did not, Sir." He then, immediately and without my offering any further cause of irritation, came behind me, I still trying to avoid him, and inflicted upon me several kicks and blows. I raised a stout walking stick, which I generally carry, to repel the cowardly and brutal attack, but which he, being an exceedingly powerful man, quickly wrenched from my hand, and struck me severely with it on the shoulders. He then seized me around the waist, and attempted to throw me on the ground in such a determined manner, that I fear more serious consequences would have ensued, but for the interposition of my wife and several other persons, who had by this time come up.[12]

James Douglas, who was in charge of Fort Vancouver during McLoughlin's absence, tried to cooperate with Beaver, and the chaplain was given more freedom than he had enjoyed under McLoughlin. However, Beaver continued his libelous ways, and Douglas found it necessary to complain of Beaver's failure to discharge his duties for the benefit of the Company's employees. In November 1838 Beaver left the Columbia for London to prefer charges against McLoughlin; but by the time he reached London, McLoughlin had left England, and the Company discharged Beaver from its service.[13] However, the matter evidently was not dropped by Beaver, for McLoughlin's allusion to him in his letter to James Douglas, dated 6 April 1847 (see Letter 3), seems to indicate that Beaver was still seeking balm for his injured ego.

COUCH, JOHN H.

John H. Couch (1811–70) was born in Newburyport, Massachusetts. In 1839 John Cushing, a prominent Newburyport merchant, acting on the advice of Jason Lee, outfitted the ship *Maryland* to trade in the Sandwich Islands and on the Columbia. Couch was made captain of the *Maryland*, and in June 1840 he crossed the bar of the Columbia, the first American trader to do so since Nathaniel Wyeth's *May Dacre* had arrived in 1834. Couch was unable to obtain a cargo of salmon for the return voyage, and the virtually empty *Maryland* sailed to the Sandwich Islands, where she was sold. The Cushing firm, undaunted by Couch's initial failure, then built the brig *Chenamus* for the Columbia River trade. When Couch returned to Oregon with her in April 1842, he took a land claim adjacent to the future site of Portland. The *Chenamus'* cargo of trading goods was taken to Oregon City, where Couch established a store — the second

12. Ibid., pp. 94–95.
13. Ibid., pp. xiii, 104–5, 148.

to be located there — and traded his merchandise for wheat and lumber which he sold in the Sandwich Islands.

Couch was one of the original directors of the *Oregon Spectator*, which began publication on 5 February 1846, and in March of that year he was appointed to succeed Francis Ermatinger as treasurer of the Oregon Provisional Government. In September 1847 Couch sailed to Newburyport, but returned to Oregon in August 1849 and settled on his claim at Portland, a site he had early recognized as the head of navigation on the Willamette River. In 1850 Couch opened Portland's direct trade with the Orient by sending the *Emma Preston* to China. In succeeding years he was county commissioner and the federal inspector of hulls at Portland.[14]

CROSBY, NATHANIEL, JR.

Captain Nathaniel Crosby, Jr. (ca. 1812–56) was born in Massachusetts. As master of the New York based bark *Toulon*, he arrived in Oregon on 14 October 1845 with a cargo of goods consigned to Francis W. Pettygrove. A portion of his cargo consisted of dressed lumber from Maine that was used to construct the first frame house in Portland. During 1846 and 1847 he made six trading voyages from the Columbia River to Honolulu and San Francisco with cargoes of wheat and lumber from both McLoughlin and Pettygrove. Late in October 1846 he returned to Oregon from Honolulu with the first reports of the ratification of the Oregon Treaty, which had been published in the *Polynesian*. Crosby evidently remained in Oregon when the *Toulon* sailed for the United States late in 1847, for during the summer of the following year he was acting as a pilot on the bar of the Columbia River, and in 1850 he became a member of the board of commissioners to examine and appoint pilots (a position that he had also held in the spring of 1847 when the commission was first formed by Crosby, John H. Couch, George L. Curry, and Francis W. Pettygrove). Crosby became a merchant and, probably early in 1850, he formed a partnership with T. H. Smith which operated in Portland and Milton, Oregon, as commission merchants, real estate dealers, and express and mail agents. During 1850 the firm also sought to raise money for the construction of a railroad from St. Helens on the Columbia River to Milton and Lafayette. Crosby died on a voyage to the Orient and was buried at Hong Kong.[15]

14. Bancroft, *History of Oregon*, 2:717; Corning, ed., *Dictionary of Oregon History*, p. 64; George H. Himes, "John H. Couch," pp. 59–65; *Oregon Spectator*, 4 March 1846, 30 September 1847.

15. Corning, ed., *Dictionary of Oregon History*, p. 67; *Oregon Spectator*, 5 February, 12 November 1846, 18 March 1847, 27 July 1848, 8 February 1849, 7 February, 18 April, 2, 16 May (advertisements), 28 November (advertisement) 1850, 12 June, 22 August 1851 (advertisements).

DOUGLAS, JAMES

James Douglas (1803–77) was born probably in Demerara, British Guiana, but possibly in Lanarkshire, Scotland. In 1819 he left England to enter the service of the North West Company as a clerk. During the next two years he served at Fort William and Ile-à-la-Crosse, and at the coalition of the Hudson's Bay and North West companies in 1821, he was kept on as a clerk at Ile-à-la-Crosse. Late in the summer of 1825, he was transferred to Fort St. James at Stuart Lake in New Caledonia, where he was stationed for five years. In 1830 he was transferred to Fort Vancouver because his determined attempts to avoid being intimidated by the Carrier Indians of New Caledonia had placed him in danger of assassination. At Fort Vancouver he held the post of accountant, and in 1832 and 1833 he accompanied the annual express to York Factory with the books of the Columbia Department.

In his "Character Book" of 1832, Governor Simpson described Douglas as "a stout powerful active man of good conduct and respectable abilities; — tolerably well Educated, expresses himself clearly on paper, understands our Counting House business and is an excellent Trader. Well qualified for any Service requiring bodily exertion, firmness of mind and the exercise of sound judgement, but furiously violent when roused. Has every reason to look forward to early promotion and is a likely man to fill a place at our Council board in course of time. . . ."[16] Simpson's evaluation proved accurate, for in December 1834 Douglas was promoted to the rank of chief trader, and in June 1835 he was invited to attend the meeting of the council of the Northern Department of Rupert's Land held at Red River.[17]

When McLoughlin was called to England in 1838, Douglas was appointed to manage the Columbia Department during his absence. Douglas was made a chief factor in November 1839, and upon McLoughlin's return he resumed his position as accountant. In 1840 he was sent to the Alaskan coast to carry out the agreement of 1839 between the Hudson's Bay Company and the Russian-American Company. He took over the Russian fort at Stikine and also established Fort Taku about twenty-five miles below present-day Juneau. As the company had determined to open a post at San Francisco, Douglas was sent to California late in 1840 with goods to trade for produce and cattle. He also obtained an agreement with Governor Alvarado which granted the Company a trading license and permitted it to purchase a building lot in San Francisco.

Douglas accompanied Simpson to Sitka in the autumn of 1841. In the rough draft of a private letter to Andrew Colvile, a member of the Company's committee, written from Fort Vancouver in November, Simpson remarked that "Douglas

16. McLoughlin, *Letters, Third Series*, p. 312.
17. Oliver, ed., *The Canadian North-West*, 2:709.

. . . has long been under the Doctor [McLoughlin] & has acquired much of his mode of management, with perhaps a little more system; & being less over bearing in his disposition, will I think be very fit for the charge of this Depot whenever the Doctor may withdraw. . . ."[18] In the summer of 1842, Douglas examined the southern end of Vancouver Island for the site of a new post, and under his direction Fort Victoria was begun in the spring of 1843.

McLoughlin's personal troubles, his distress at the murder of his son, and his treatment by both the American settlers and the Company over his land claim at Willamette Falls so preoccupied the aging chief factor that his management of the affairs of the Company was called into question by the governor and committee in London. In June 1845 the council of the Northern Department removed him from sole responsibility for the Columbia Department and established a three-man board of management consisting of McLoughlin, Peter Skene Ogden, and James Douglas. Douglas' private comments to Simpson on the appointment of the board reveal that for some time he had been carrying the weight of administration at Fort Vancouver. "I have no objections whatever to the arrangements made for the future management of this District," he wrote on 20 March 1846; "the difference to me will not be great, for I presume I shall still have the fag and wear and tear of the work, as has fallen to my share for the last five years. In fact I am harassed beyond reason, and see no prospect of relief."[19] Following McLoughlin's retirement to Oregon City in January 1846, Douglas assumed the routine management of Fort Vancouver, for Ogden was often absent and John Work, who had been added to the board of management, was somewhat unfamiliar with the fort since he had spent most of his time at Fort Simpson.

In 1849 the British government ceded Vancouver Island to the Hudson's Bay Company. Richard Blanshard was appointed governor, and Douglas was appointed to be the Company's agent on the island. On 17 May 1849 Douglas left Fort Vancouver and carried with him the records and papers of the Columbia Department, for Fort Vancouver had ceased to be the headquarters of the department. Governor Blanshard arrived at Vancouver Island in March 1850, but in November he tendered his resignation. Before his departure in September 1851, he appointed a council with Douglas as senior member to manage the affairs of the island until his successor should be chosen. Douglas had already been appointed to succeed Blanshard, and in November 1851 his commission as the second governor of Vancouver Island arrived from England. For seven years Douglas continued to represent both the British crown and the Hudson's Bay Company at Victoria. In 1858 he was offered the governorship of the newly created Crown Colony of British Columbia on the condition that he should

18. McLoughlin, *Letters, Third Series*, p. 313.
19. Ibid., p. lviiin.

dispose of his interests in both the Hudson's Bay and the Puget's Sound Agricultural companies. Douglas agreed and resigned from the Company. His five-year commission as governor of Vancouver Island expired in 1863, and in that year he was created a Knight Commander of the Bath. On 13 April 1864 he retired from the government of the Crown Colony of British Columbia and spent his remaining years in Victoria.[20]

ERMATINGER, FRANCIS

Francis Ermatinger (1798–1858), born in Portugal and educated in England, entered the service of the Hudson's Bay Company in 1818. Following several years of service at York Factory on Hudson Bay, Ermatinger was transferred to McLoughlin's Columbia Department in the summer of 1825. He was stationed at both Kamloops and Fort Colvile until 1832. In that year Governor Simpson reported him as being "a stout active boisterous fellow who is a tolerable Clerk & Trader and qualified to be useful where bustle and activity without any great exercise of judgement are necessary."[21]

From 1832 to 1838 Ermatinger was in charge of the trade with the Flathead Indians near the borders of the Snake country and along the headwaters of the Missouri. In 1838 he was placed in charge of the Snake country trade at Forts Hall and Boise, and he remained in charge of Fort Hall until 1842 when he was promoted to the rank of chief trader. George T. Allen, who frequently saw Ermatinger at Fort Vancouver during these years, described him as a "regular jolly jovial Cockney whom we sometimes styled Bardolf from the size and colour of his nose."[22]

John H. Couch and Francis W. Pettygrove established mercantile houses in Oregon City in 1842 and 1843, respectively. As the American settlements were largely concentrated in the vicinity of Willamette Falls, these stores received the business of the settlers who had formerly been dependent on the supplies at Fort Vancouver. The Columbia Department could ill afford to lose this profitable trade, and in 1844 McLoughlin established a branch store at the Falls with Ermatinger in charge. Ermatinger was a popular figure in Oregon City, and when the Provisional Government was reorganized in the summer of 1845 to include the British residents of the Willamette Valley as well as the Hudson's Bay Company, Ermatinger was appointed treasurer of the territory, a position

20. Hussey, *History of Fort Vancouver*, pp. 93–94; McLoughlin, *Letters, Third Series*, pp. 309–14; Walter N. Sage, *Sir James Douglas and British Columbia*; Walter N. Sage, "James Douglas on the Columbia, 1830–1849"; Margaret A. Ormsby, "Sir James Douglas," pp. 238–49.

21. Robertson, *Correspondence Book*, p. 212.

22. Allan, "Reminiscences of Fort Vancouver."

which he held until he resigned to return to Canada. He was succeeded by John Couch.

In June 1845 Governor Simpson instructed the board of management of the Columbia Department (McLoughlin, Ogden, and Douglas) to close the store at the Falls and send Ermatinger either to Fort Colvile or by sea to England. Although the Company's property at the Falls was sold to McLoughlin, the Company continued to maintain a store there; but Ermatinger was transferred to York Factory and departed with Warre and Vavasour in March 1846, leaving his wife and daughter behind with the McLoughlins. In 1847–48 he had charge of the Athabasca district at Fort Chipewyan at the west end of Lake Athabasca, a position he retained until 1850 when he spent a year in Canada on furlough. As seen in McLoughlin's letter to Ermatinger of 15 March 1848 (Letter 78), his family did not rejoin him until the late spring of that year. He was in charge of Fort William on Lake Superior in 1852–53 and then retired from the Company on June first. He moved to St. Thomas, Ontario, where he died in 1858.[23]

ERMATINGER, CATHERINE SINCLAIR

Catherine Sinclair Ermatinger (ca. 1824–76), a granddaughter of Mrs. John McLoughlin, was the daughter of Mary Wadin McKay, Mrs. McLoughlin's daughter by her first marriage to Alexander McKay. In 1839 McLoughlin brought Catherine to Fort Vancouver on his return from Europe via Canada, and on 12 August 1841 she married Francis Ermatinger. From 1844 to 1846 the Ermatingers lived in Oregon City, where Francis was in charge of the Company's store. Following his transfer to Canada in 1846, Catherine and her daughter Fanny stayed with the McLoughlins. In March 1848 Catherine and her daughter left Oregon to rejoin Ermatinger who was by then stationed at Fort Chipewyan on Lake Athabasca.[24]

GELSTON, ROLAND

Roland Gelston, the master of the bark *Whiton*, arrived in the Columbia River on 22 June 1847 after a passage of 162 days from New York via San Francisco. Among Gelston's passengers were two Methodist missionaries and John Mix Stanley, a noted artist. Before leaving San Francisco in June, Gelston

23. McLoughlin, *Letters, Third Series*, pp. 137–38, 290; Robertson, *Correspondence Book*, pp. 212–13; Throckmorton, *Oregon Argonauts*, p. 38; *Oregon Spectator*, 4 March 1846.

24. T. C. Elliott, "Marguerite Wadin McKay McLoughlin," pp. 338–39; Robertson, *Correspondence Book*, pp. 212–13; Throckmorton, *Oregon Argonauts*, p. 38. See also Letter 78, to Francis Ermatinger.

[131]

had established the trading house of Gelston and Company, which occupied quarters in William A. Leidesdorff's store, and he had placed Charles L. Ross in charge of the *Whiton's* cargo. During the two years that the firm was active, George Abernethy tried without success to form a partnership with Gelston. Abernethy had no vessel of his own, and the high freight rates charged him on his competitor's ships injured his prospects for the profitable export of flour and lumber to the improving California market. A partnership with Gelston would have solved that problem and would have given Abernethy the means to import goods directly from New York.

Gelston sailed from Oregon for San Francisco on 15 July 1847, but was back in the Columbia on 11 September; and on his departure for San Francisco and Panama on 19 October he carried the Yamhill Petition which had been signed on 2 October by twenty-four delegates. The petition, to be forwarded to Washington from Panama, requested the immediate extension of American laws to Oregon and the donation of lands to the settlers. Jessy Quinn Thornton sailed with Gelston bearing credentials from Governor Abernethy to Congress authorizing him to present his own memorial, which he prepared upon his arrival in Washington.

Little is known of Gelston's subsequent career, but he was still in the San Francisco area in 1853 when he was a claimant for lands in San Francisco and the Sacramento Valley.[25]

GRIMES, ELIAB

Eliab Grimes (1780–1848) was a native of Fitchburg, Massachusetts, and served in the War of 1812. About 1828 he established the firm of E. and H. Grimes in Honolulu with his nephew. Having visited San Francisco in 1838, he returned there in 1842 to select a ranch in the Sacramento Valley, which was granted to him in 1844 following his return from another trip to Honolulu. About 1847 Hiram Grimes also moved to California, and the firm operated until 1848 in San Francisco. Eliab Grimes served as a member of the California legislative council in 1847 and died the following year. Hiram Grimes was still in California in 1854, but seems not to have continued the export business after his uncle's death. While still in Honolulu, the firm of E. and H. Grimes had served as an agency for both John H. Couch and George Abernethy.[26]

25. Bancroft, *History of California*, 3:754, 5:678; *Oregon Spectator*, 8, 22 July, 30 September, 14, 28 October 1847; Jessy Quinn Thornton, *Oregon and California in 1848*, 2:48–49; C. J. Pike, "Petitions of Oregon Settlers, 1838–48," pp. 232–35; Throckmorton, *Oregon Argonauts*, p. 90.

26. Bancroft, *History of California*, 3:767–68; *Oregon Spectator*, 23 July 1846, 8 February 1849.

HASTINGS, LANSFORD W.

Lansford W. Hastings (1819–70) was born in Knox County, Ohio, and following his admission to the bar, he practiced law at Mount Vernon in his native state. In 1842 he went to Independence, Missouri, where he joined Dr. Elijah White's party of 160 emigrants bound for Oregon. Hastings, with knowledge of western travel, was elected to the "first office" of the emigrant train. The party left Independence on 16 May 1842, and soon after leaving Fort Laramie, Dr. White hired Thomas Fitzpatrick to guide the group to the Green River, where Stephen Meek was engaged to serve as guide to Fort Hall. The party arrived at the Willamette River in the fall, and in December McLoughlin had his land claim at the Falls surveyed and subdivided under the direction of Hastings. At the newly laid out site of Oregon City, McLoughlin embarked on an extensive building program which thereby gave immediate employment at the highest wages to those who wished to work.[27]

In 1841 McLoughlin had permitted Jason Lee of the Methodist Mission to erect a mission house at the Falls. McLoughlin permitted the house to be located on his land claim, and it was constructed from squared timber which Lee found lying there. Lee assigned Rev. Alvin F. Waller to the Willamette Falls Mission, and the good missionary seems to have spent much of his time in trying to whittle away McLoughlin's claim. To protect the joint interests of himself and the Company, McLoughlin hired Hastings, who managed only to extract a small sum from Waller in consideration of the fact that the mission site had already been cleared at the time Jason Lee took title. Hastings was able to do nothing about the problem of McLoughlin's contested land title. For his legal advice, McLoughlin paid Hastings £ 150.[28]

Having remained in Oregon as long as he had originally planned, Hastings, with fifty-three of the 1842 immigrants, left Oregon City on 30 May 1843 to journey overland to California. Many of the destitute travelers were advanced funds at the expense of the Hudson's Bay Company with the expectation that they would repay their debt to the Company's officer in San Francisco. Few did so, and those remaining in Oregon accused McLoughlin of making the advances to those going to California to reduce the American influence in Oregon.[29]

Hastings proceeded to Sutter's New Helvetia on the Sacramento River, and, according to McLoughlin, was granted ten square leagues by the California government. In 1844 he returned to the East to raise money for the publication of *The Emigrant's Guide to Oregon and California*, which promoted California

27. Hastings, *A New History of Oregon and California*, pp. 6–19, 56.
28. McLoughlin, *Letters, Third Series*, pp. xli–xliii, xlvii.
29. Ibid., p. 290.

at the expense of Oregon and proposed a short cut on the long overland route to the Pacific Coast, a short cut which Hastings had never seen. In 1845 Hastings returned to California to lay out the town of Suttersville on his land claim and then, in April 1846, he went east once more to persuade prospective emigrants to head for California rather than Oregon. Rumor had it that he was acting as the agent for a large contingent of Mormons bound for New Helvetia. The Mormon immigration went elsewhere, but several parties were persuaded by Hastings to use his cut-off which routed the unsuspecting immigrants from Fort Bridger to the southeast end of the Great Salt Lake and thence directly to the Humboldt River in Nevada. Unfortunately for Hastings' reputation, the last group to attempt the route in 1846 was the ill-fated Donner Party, which did not leave Fort Bridger until late July. The delays and hardships of the desolate route recommended by Hastings forced the group to spend the winter of 1846/47 in the snowbound Sierras, and of the eighty-two who reached Truckee Meadows on 25 October 1846, only forty-seven remained alive when rescue parties reached them in February 1847.[30]

Upon his return to California, Hastings seems to have planned the overthrow of the existing government and the establishment of a republic with himself as head. In 1849 he represented Sacramento at the California constitutional convention in Monterey, but his political role was short-lived. During the Civil War, he sought authority from the Confederate government to organize an expedition to wrest Arizona and New Mexico from federal control, but nothing came of this scheme to unite the Pacific Coast with the Confederacy. At the end of the war he turned his attention to aiding emigration from the American South to Brazil, and in 1866 he surveyed the Amazon River for a site on which to locate a colony. He chose Santarém, five hundred miles from the mouth of the river, and received a grant of 960 sections (614,000 acres) from the president of the province of Para. He agreed to bring a minimum of one hundred immigrants and pay twenty-two cents per acre in three annual installments beginning at the end of the third year. The government promised to supply temporary housing for the immigrants and agreed to exempt the colony from military duty and from import duties on implements, machinery, and supplies brought by the colonists. Hastings returned to Mobile, Alabama, to recruit settlers and publish his *Emigrant's Guide to Brazil*. By 1870 the colony numbered some two hundred persons, but that year Hastings died while taking out a second shipload of emigrants.[31]

30. Bernard DeVoto, *The Year of Decision: 1846*, pp. 44–45, 86, 113, 115, 166, 342, 430.

31. Lawrence F. Hill, "The Confederate Exodus to Latin America," pp. 127–32, 189–91.

HEDGES, ABSALOM F.

Absalom F. Hedges (1818–90) was born in Ohio and moved to Oregon from Iowa in 1844. In 1846 he was operating a tannery with Walter Pomeroy and a man named Kirbey at Oregon City, and from June 1846 until 1847 he was a partner with Pomeroy in the lease of McLoughlin's sawmills at the falls of the Willamette River. Following his withdrawal from that partnership, he seems to have operated a store and perhaps a sawmill with his brother-in-law, William Barlow. He was a member of the provisional legislature of 1849, and from 1850 to 1854 he pioneered in the construction of steamboats, of which the *Canemah*, named for the town he had laid out in 1845, and the *Wallamet* were the most famous. In 1849 he was appointed U.S. Indian agent for Oregon. He represented Clackamas County (Oregon City) at the state constitutional convention in 1857, and served as a member of the last territorial legislature in 1858/59. In 1866 he was an incorporator of the unsuccessful Oregon Central Railroad, and in the 1870s he moved to eastern Oregon, where he held a minor position on the Malheur Indian Reservation. He died on 10 January 1890 at North Yakima, Washington.[32]

KILBORNE, WILLIAM K.

William K. Kilborne (frequently spelled "Kilborn" in contemporary accounts), captain of the American brig *Henry*, arrived in the Columbia River from Newburyport, Massachusetts, about 1 March 1847. His cargo, worth $6,000, was largely composed of second-hand articles which were repaired and sold to the settlers. He formed the firm of Kilborne, Lawton and Company in Oregon City, which he managed while the *Henry*, now commanded by Captain Bray, took cargoes of lumber, flour, beef, salmon, and produce to San Francisco. On 6 October 1847, Governor George Abernethy appointed Kilborne to the office of territorial treasurer succeeding John H. Couch, who had resigned to return to Newburyport.

In 1848 Kilborne made two trips to California in command of the *Henry*, and on his return from the second trip on 9 August he carried the official news of the discovery of gold in California. Kilborne, with seven others, organized the Oregon Exchange Company in February 1849 to mint five- and ten-dollar gold pieces for use in the territory. With the arrival of Governor Joseph Lane in March, the company's activities became illegal, but in its brief existence some $58,500 in gold "beaver money" was produced. On 19 September

32. Corning, ed., *Dictionary of Oregon History*, p. 111. For additional information on Hedges' business relations with McLoughlin, see the biographical sketch of Walter Pomeroy in this appendix.

1850, fifty-six men, of whom Kilborne was one, signed a petition memorializing Congress against the passage of Samuel R. Thurston's Donation Land Bill. Kilborne had been dismissed as master of the *Henry* during the spring of 1850, and he served as mayor of Oregon City from August 1850 to April 1851 when he was succeeded by John McLoughlin.[33]

LEIDESDORFF, WILLIAM A.

William Alexander Leidesdorff (1810–48) was born in the Danish West Indies (probably on the island of St. Croix), the son of a Danish father and a Creole mother. He moved to the United States while still a youth, and later became the master of various ships sailing from New York and New Orleans. He sailed to California in 1841 as master of the *Julia Ann*, in which he made frequent trading trips between San Francisco and the Sandwich Islands until 1845.

In 1843 Leidesdorff acquired the fifty-vara (about 150 feet) lot at the northwest corner of Clay and Kearney streets in San Francisco where, in June 1846, he completed the lower story of a large adobe building which became the City Hotel housing the alcalde's offices as well as the offices of Shelly and Norris (see Letter 2, to Peter Skene Ogden and James Douglas, no. 7) and Messrs. Starkey, Janion and Company of Honolulu. In 1844 he built a warehouse on what was then beach-front property at California and Leidesdorff streets and began a general export business. The same year he became a naturalized citizen of Mexico and received a grant of some 35,000 acres (eight Spanish leagues) on the left bank of the American River. The Leidesdorff grant, known as "Rancho Rio de los Americanos," was located some two or three leagues (about ten miles) from Sutter's New Helvetia. In October 1845, Thomas Oliver Larkin, a prominent Monterey merchant and United States consul in California, appointed Leidesdorff as vice-consul.[34]

In 1841 the Hudson's Bay Company established a store in San Francisco, and McLoughlin's son-in-law, William Glen Rae, was placed in charge. In January 1842, while Sir George Simpson was on a tour of inspection, McLoughlin visited San Francisco, and it appears that he met Leidesdorff at that time. Rae committed suicide in January 1845, and in December Dugald Mactavish was sent to San Francisco to close out the Company's business and sell its property.

33. James Athey, "Workshops at Oregon City"; Bancroft, *History of Oregon*, 2:126–27; Throckmorton, *Oregon Argonauts*, pp. 64, 99; *Oregon Spectator*, 15 April, 14 October 1847, 7 September 1848, 7–21 March 1850 (advertisement); *Oregon City Enterprise*, 12 August 1948, quoting the first Book of City Council Records, Oregon City.

34. Bancroft, *History of California*, 4:711; Robert Ernest Cowan, "The Leidesdorff-Folsom Estate," pp. 105–6.

When Mactavish left San Francisco in May, the property had been sold to the firm of Mellus and Howard, and Leidesdorff was appointed the Company's agent to collect the outstanding debts of approximately $10,000.[35]

By 1846, Leidesdorff was well on his way to becoming one of the most prosperous merchants in California. According to McLoughlin, Leidesdorff had begun business in 1842 with a capital of only £500, but by 1846 he had $37,000 in goods and property free and clear.[36] That same year, the *Oregon Spectator* announced that Leidesdorff had erected buildings in San Francisco worth $15,000 and had a valuable contract for supplying the Russian-American Company with beef, flour, and provisions.[37] With Leidesdorff's widely spread contacts and growing influence, McLoughlin could hardly have chosen a more suitable agent for his business in San Francisco. The two were evidently on very cordial terms, and McLoughlin, perhaps in the depths of despair about his affairs in Oregon, at least once openly considered joining Leidesdorff in San Francisco. However, by the spring of 1848, as these letters indicate, McLoughlin felt that Leidesdorff was not adequately discharging his obligations, and in his last letter to Leidesdorff on 17 May 1848 (Letter 96), McLoughlin requested that Leidesdorff give any balance due him to Captain David Dring of the bark *Janet*. This letter never reached Leidesdorff, for he died the day after it was written.

In 1847, soon after securing his contract with the Russian-American Company, Leidesdorff bought a small, thirty-seven-foot steamboat from the company and launched it in San Francisco Bay. He had hoped to use it for his trade in hides and tallow, but with a top speed of eight miles per hour it took her six days and seven hours to paddle upstream to Sacramento. Leidesdorff's *Sitka* was the first steamboat on San Francisco Bay, but her career was short, for on 12 February 1848 she was swamped at her moorings. Shortly thereafter she was raised and converted to a schooner. The engine was reported to have seen eventual service as a coffee grinder.[38]

Leidesdorff was a prominent member of the town council and school board of San Francisco and also served as treasurer of the city. In April 1848 he learned that gold had been discovered on his American River ranch, but he did not live to profit from it. At his death he left the largest estate in California, which, when the last piece of property was sold, had produced $1,442,232.[39]

35. Larkin, *Larkin Papers*, 4:363; McLoughlin, *Letters, Third Series*, p. xxix.

36. McLoughlin, *Letters, Second Series* (McLoughlin to Sir J. H. Pelly, 12 July 1846), p. 167.

37. *Oregon Spectator*, 26 November 1846.

38. John Haskell Kemble, "The First Steam Vessel to Navigate San Francisco Bay," pp. 143–46.

39. Cowan, "The Leidesdorff-Folsom Estate," pp. 106, 110; John A. Hawgood, ed., *First and Last Consul*, pp. 95–96.

LOVEJOY, ASA L.

Asa Lawrence Lovejoy (1808–82) was born in Groton, Massachusetts, and studied law in Cambridge and at Amherst College. In 1840, following his admission to the bar, he moved to Sparta, Missouri, and in 1842 joined Dr. Elijah White's Oregon-bound emigrant party. The party arrived at the Whitman Mission in October, and Marcus Whitman persuaded Lovejoy to accompany him on his now-famous ride to the States. The two left Waiilatpu in November, but Lovejoy was stopped at Bent's Fort on the Arkansas River for want of a fresh horse. In July 1843 Lovejoy left Bent's Fort to rejoin Whitman who was leading the 1843 emigrant train over the Oregon Trail.

Arriving in Oregon City in November, Lovejoy established a law practice and became active in public affairs. In 1844 he was elected as one of eight members of the legislative committee of the Provisional Government and was appointed attorney general as well. The executive committee of the Provisional Government was abandoned in 1845 in favor of a single executive, and Lovejoy ran for governor as a representative of the American party. However, he was defeated by George Abernethy of the Mission party, who also had the support of the independent Canadians. At its December 1845 session, the legislature formally incorporated Oregon City, and Lovejoy was elected mayor. In 1847 he again opposed Abernethy for the office of governor, and was again defeated, but only by the small margin of sixteen votes.

Following the Whitman Massacre in November 1847, Lovejoy, with George L. Curry and Jesse Applegate, pledged his personal credit to the Hudson's Bay Company for supplies to support the Oregon Volunteers, and during the Cayuse War which followed, he served as adjutant general. In 1846 he was re-elected to the legislature, and in 1848 he began yet another term, this time holding the office of supreme judge as well. With the organization of Oregon Territory in 1849, Lovejoy was elected speaker of the house. He later served on the council (1851–52), but returned to the lower house in 1854 and 1856, and was a member of the constitutional convention of 1857.

Although prominent in public affairs, Lovejoy is best remembered as a cofounder of Portland. Lovejoy occupied a land claim on the west side of the Willamette, and in 1845 he and his neighbor, Francis W. Pettygrove, laid out the townsite of Portland and began the construction of a plank road across the hills to tap the commerce of the Tualatin Valley.

An early exponent of the need for transportation facilities in Oregon, Lovejoy chaired a meeting which memorialized Congress for a transcontinental railroad in 1847. He later served as director of the east-side Oregon Central Railway Company, which built the first road through the Willamette Valley.[40]

40. *Dictionary of American Biography*, 11:433–34; Bancroft, *History of Oregon*, 1:415, 471–72, 699; "A. L. Lovejoy," p. 48.

McKinlay, Archibald

Archibald McKinlay (1811–91) was born in Perthshire, Scotland, and entered the service of the Hudson's Bay Company as a clerk at York Factory in 1831. Following service at Fort Garry, he was transferred in 1835 to Fort St. James, the administrative headquarters of New Caledonia, where Peter Skene Ogden was chief factor. From Fort St. James he went to Fort George on the upper Fraser and was later posted to Fort Alexandria on the Fraser. From Fort Alexandria he was transferred to Fort Hall until his appointment as clerk in charge at Fort Walla Walla in 1841.[41] In February 1846 McKinlay was obliged to leave Fort Walla Walla because of failing eyesight; and in March he was appointed to succeed Francis Ermatinger at Oregon City, where the Company, following the release of its property to McLoughlin in 1845, had rented a dwelling, a store, and a granary from McLoughlin for two years.[42] That same year, McKinlay was promoted to the rank of chief trader.

He remained at Oregon City until 1849, when he left for England to procure medical attention; but because of the disruption of shipping caused by the gold rush, he was able to proceed only as far as San Francisco. He returned to the Columbia, and his leave of absence evidently continued until his retirement in June 1851, when he entered into partnership as a commission merchant with George Traill Allan and Thomas Lowe at Oregon City in quarters leased from John McLoughlin and formerly occupied by the Hudson's Bay Company. Allan, McKinlay and Company sold lumber in San Francisco during the gold rush, and when disillusioned miners began settling on the Umpqua River in southern Oregon, the company established a branch there.[43]

During the 1850s, McKinlay occupied a Donation Land Claim known as "The Cliffs" just south of Oregon City, and there his father-in-law Peter Skene Ogden died in 1854, leaving his daughter an inheritance of more than £2300. McKinlay began investing in sheep and cattle, and in 1855 he offered to buy 5,000 to 6,000 ewes from the Puget's Sound Agricultural Company. In 1858 he sold "The Cliffs" to David McLoughlin (reserving two lots and a house for Peter Skene Ogden's widow) and bought a farm of 320 acres on the Willamette in Yamhill County.[44]

41. Archibald McKinlay, "Narrative of a Chief Factor of the Hudson's Bay Company," 1878, typed transcription of an interview, in the Archives of British Columbia, Victoria, from an original in the Bancroft Library, University of California, Berkeley.

42. McKinlay to William Fraser Tolmie, 28 April 1884, in the papers of Archibald McKinlay in the Archives of British Columbia, Victoria.

43. McKinlay to William Fraser Tolmie, 3 April 1850 and 25 May 1853, ibid.

44. Cash Account of Archibald McKinlay, Lachine, 1856; McKinlay to William Fraser Tolmie, 20 April 1855; Indenture, 2 March 1858, between McKin-

The firm of Allan, McKinlay and Company was dissolved in 1863 following McKinlay's financial ruin in the floods of 1861. McKinlay provided for the care of Mrs. Ogden and her dependent children and left Oregon for British Columbia, where he became a merchant and farmer at Lac la Hache about 1865.[45] In 1871 McKinlay requested an appointment to the office of commissioner of Indian affairs in British Columbia, and in 1876 he was appointed by the crown to be one of the three commissioners charged with the settlement of the Indian reserve question in the province.[46] Sometime between December 1880 and March 1881 McKinlay apparently resigned from his office as commissioner, possibly because of failing health. However, there was some dispute over a voucher that McKinlay claimed had been forged, and he was increasingly frustrated by the failure of the government to make adequate provision for the distribution of lands to the Indians.[47]

Sometime after the death of his wife's mother at Lac la Hache in January 1886, McKinlay and his wife, Sarah Julia, whom he had married at Fort Vancouver in June 1840, moved to Savona Ferry on Lake Kamloops, where they lived at the home of their daughter, Sarah Ellen, and her husband, A. B. Ferguson, who owned the Lakeview Hotel. McKinlay died there in 1891.[48]

McLoughlin, David

David McLoughlin (1821–1903) was the second son and youngest child of Dr. John McLoughlin and his wife Marguerite Wadin McKay. In 1824 David and his sister Eloisa accompanied their parents to the Columbia District, while the two older children, John, Jr., and Marie Elizabeth, remained in Montreal where they were attending school. In 1833 or 1834, young David was sent to Paris to live with his uncle, Dr. David McLoughlin, who proposed "to Educate him for the Engineer Department and send him out to India."[49]

---

lay and John S. and Rachel Smith; and Indenture, 4 March 1862, between McKinlay and Julia Ogden, all ibid.

45. McKinlay to Capt. A. C. Ainsworth, 12 January 1865, ibid.

46. McKinlay to Joseph Wood Trutch, 12 September 1871; and Commission to Archibald McKinlay to act in reference to certain inquiries with Indian Affairs in British Columbia, 28 September 1876, both ibid.

47. McKinlay to Lt. Col. J. W. Powell, 28 March 1881; and McKinlay to William Saul, 7 January 1881, letter book copies, ibid.

48. Affidavit of Marriage, Archibald McKinlay and Sarah Julia Ogden, ibid., Archibald McKinlay, Record of Death. See also A. Barclay to Archibald McKinlay, 3 April 1846, in miscellaneous papers of Archibald McKinlay, Oregon Historical Society, Portland; and McLoughlin, *Letters, Second Series*, pp. 394–95.

49. McLoughlin to John Fraser, 14 February 1836, in Barker, *The McLoughlin Empire*, p. 221.

Preparatory to his intended East Indian service, David McLoughlin entered the East India Company's Military Seminary at Addiscombe in April 1837 and passed his public examination in December 1838.

However, he resigned in 1839 and returned to North America with his father, who had been in Europe on furlough. David entered the service of the Hudson's Bay Company and joined his older brother, John, Jr., as a clerk at Fort Vancouver. John was murdered in 1842, and the elder McLoughlin came to rely heavily on David for assistance in managing his affairs at Oregon City. On 5 March 1845, David notified the Company of his intention to retire in the following year, and accepting the resignation, Governor Simpson waived the usual Company stipulation that retiring servants of the Company return to Canada.[50]

Following his resignation from the Hudson's Bay Company, young McLoughlin visited Hawaii, perhaps on business for his father, arriving there on the *Toulon* on 23 September 1846, after an eighteen-day passage from the Columbia. The *Toulon* returned to the Columbia late in October, and David hastened on to Fort Vancouver by canoe with the news, published in the *Polynesian*, that the Oregon boundary dispute had finally been settled.[51]

Later that year, David McLoughlin joined F. W. Pettygrove and Company, a partnership formed on 14 July 1846 by Francis W. Pettygrove and Albert E. Wilson for the transaction of a general commission business in Oregon City and Portland.[52] According to Pettygrove's own reminiscences, John McLoughlin had asked Pettygrove to take David into the partnership so that young McLoughlin might learn the American method of doing business. Pettygrove protested that David was unacquainted with business methods and that he already had all the capital he needed. The elder McLoughlin prevailed, however, and David was made a partner of the firm on 10 November 1846 upon the payment of $20,000 furnished by his father. David remained with F. W. Pettygrove and Company until the fall of 1848, when Pettygrove closed the business and went to San Francisco.[53]

David's duties with F. W. Pettygrove and Company are not known, but he seems to have had the freedom to pursue his father's affairs. During December 1846 he collected a cargo of about six hundred barrels of flour, which he took to

50. McLoughlin, *Letters, Second Series*, pp. 395–96.
51. Thomas G. Thrum, "History of the Hudson's Bay Company's Agency in Honolulu," p. 46; Thomas Lowe, "Private Journal Kept at Fort Vancouver Columbia River 1843–1850," pp. 51–52; *Oregon Spectator*, 12 November 1846.
52. *Oregon Spectator*, 23 July 1846.
53. Pettygrove, "Oregon in 1843," pp. 21–23. The formal notice of the formation of the partnership with David McLoughlin as a member is printed in the *Oregon Spectator*, 10 December 1846.

San Francisco aboard the *Toulon* when she sailed from the Columbia in mid-January 1847. He returned to Oregon aboard the *Toulon* in mid-March, and in April the elder McLoughlin sent him to California and Oahu to deliver goods, collect debts, and obtain orders for lumber and wheat.[54] Young McLoughlin returned to Oregon City from San Francisco on 14 June 1847 aboard the *Brutus* and he seems to have remained in Oregon until the spring of 1849. On 18 March of that year David wrote to his cousin, John Fraser, saying that he was "on the eve of starting for the gold region with large numbers of Indians hired to me for a year." He added that "Money is flying about here in large quantities especially Gold dust I have made for my share these last five months about twenty thousand dollars in Gold dust. . . ."[55]

Just when David McLoughlin returned from California is not known. According to one of his eight daughters, he went from Fort Vancouver to Wyndel, British Columbia, where he operated a Hudson's Bay Company store. About 1865 he married Annie Grizzly, the daughter of Chief Grizzly, a full-blooded Kutenai Indian, and later moved to Idaho where he settled on a farm of one hundred sixty acres and laid out the townsite of Porthill, where he lived until his death in 1903.[56]

MILLER, WILLIAM

William Miller (1795–1861) served in the British Army during the Peninsular Campaigns of 1811–14. He later became a close friend of Simón Bolívar and earned the rank of general while fighting for South American independence in Chile and Peru, but was banished from Peru in 1829 on account of a changing political climate. In 1843, following the restoration of Hawaiian independence after its five months under the British rule of Lord George Paulet (February-July 1843), Miller was appointed as Her Majesty's consul general for the Sandwich, Society, Friendly, and other islands of the Pacific with headquarters in Honolulu. On 12 February 1844, Miller secured ratification by King Kamehameha III of the so-called Lahaina Treaty which guaranteed the rights of Britons in the islands, but pointedly ignored the question of the payment of an indemnity to Hawaii for the five months of British usurpation of sovereignty. Miller was high-handed in his treatment of the weak kingdom, and the controversies concerning the rights of Britons and their land claims were dealt with in a manner that was far from being conciliatory and cool-headed. His difficulties were complicated by a "most unseemly personal quarrel between Miller and R. C. Wyllie,

54. Lowe, "Private Journal Kept at Fort Vancouver," pp. 56, 58–60; Letter 4, McLoughlin to David McLoughlin.
55. *Oregon Spectator*, 24 June 1847; Barker, *The McLoughlin Empire*, p. 253.
56. Ibid., pp. 136, 139–40, 317.

who became Hawaiian minister of foreign relations in March, 1845. The two dignitaries snarled at each other like two ill-mannered dogs and nearly came to blows on more than one occasion."[57]

As early as 1843, Miller was transmitting mail between the London committee of the Hudson's Bay Company and McLoughlin. In February 1845, Henry Williamson attempted to squat on land at Fort Vancouver and on 24 March McLoughlin reported the incident in detail to Miller, who was the nearest official British representative. McLoughlin added an urgent request that a British warship be stationed in the Columbia, but Miller did little or nothing about the matter and did not bother to reply to McLoughlin until 22 August. Thus, McLoughlin's opinion of Miller was based on some personal experience which was not altogether conducive to admiration.[58]

MOFFATT, GEORGE

George Moffatt (1787–1865) was born at Sidehead, Durham, England. He immigrated to Canada in 1801 and entered Sir Alexander Mackenzie's XY Company. On 5 November 1804, the XY Company was absorbed by the North West Company, and Moffatt served in the west with the Nor'Westers until about 1810. In 1811 he appeared in Montreal in a mercantile partnership, and shortly thereafter he entered the firm of Parker, Gerrard, and Ogilvy, which had been the supply house of the XY Company and had an interest in the North West Company. In time he acquired a contolling interest in this firm, which came to be known as Gillespie, Moffatt, and Company.

In September 1819 he put John McLoughlin in touch with Samuel Gale and through Gale with Andrew Colvile of the Hudson's Bay Company. Although McLoughlin was unsuccessful in his attempt to lead the disaffected partners of the North West Company into the Hudson's Bay Company on their own terms, his association with Moffatt continued until his death. As early as 1835, Moffatt was acting as McLoughlin's agent in eastern Canada, for that year he was evidently handling the funds for the medical schooling of John McLoughlin, Jr., and in 1845 the senior McLoughlin sent Moffatt copies of all the documents relating to the murder of John, Jr., with instructions that Moffatt was to prosecute the murderers if neither the Hudson's Bay Company nor the crown took action. Even as late as 1848, as these letters show, McLoughlin found it necessary to call on Moffatt for funds to meet his business expenses.

In 1830 Moffatt was called to the legislative council of Lower Canada, and in 1839 he became a member of the executive council. At the time of the

57. Kuykendall, *The Hawaiian Kingdom*, pp. 221–98 *passim* (quotation from p. 247); McLoughlin, *Letters, Second Series*, p. 193n.
58. McLoughlin, *Letters, Third Series*, pp. liv, 259–82, 284–85.

union of the two Canadas in 1841, Moffatt was elected to represent Montreal in the legislative assembly, a seat he held until 1847 when he retired from active politics. Moffatt was a strong supporter of the Hudson's Bay Company, and in 1833 George Simpson said: "He is without exception the most influential man in Canada at this hour, and the most active useful and noisy man in the House of Assembly."[59] Moffatt died in Montreal on 25 February 1865.[60]

OGDEN, PETER SKENE

Peter Skene Ogden (1794–1854) was born in Quebec, Lower Canada, where his father, the Honorable Isaac Ogden, was a judge of the admiralty court. Shortly after his son Peter was born, Judge Ogden moved his family to Montreal, the center of Canada's fur trade, and Peter found himself attracted more to the life of a trader than to that of a lawyer. While still a youth, he became a clerk in John Jacob Astor's Montreal office, but in 1809 or 1810 he joined the North West Company as a clerk and spent his early years in the Ile-à-la-Crosse Department, which was an important supply area for the Athabasca brigades. In 1818 he was transferred to the company's Columbia District on the Pacific slope, and in 1820 he was made a partner.

When the North West Company combined with the Hudson's Bay Company in 1821, Ogden was one of the three Nor'West partisans not given employment in the new firm. He went to England in 1822 to appeal his case, and after reconsideration by the Company he was made a chief clerk in the Hudson's Bay Company in March 1823. He returned to the Columbia District via Canada and was promoted to the rank of chief trader in 1824. From 1824 to 1830 he was in charge of the important Snake country brigades which were in direct competition with the highly successful Missouri fur traders in Idaho, Montana, Utah, and Wyoming. While trapping the country into a fur desert, Ogden and his men made several important discoveries, the most important of which was the Humboldt (originally called Ogden's) River. In 1834 he was made a chief factor, and in 1835 he went to northern British Columbia to manage the New Caledonia District of the Columbia Department where he remained until his return to Fort Vancouver in 1844.

In June 1845, the council of the Northern Department of Rupert's Land appointed Ogden and James Douglas to act with McLoughlin as a joint board of management for the Columbia Department. Following the resignation of McLoughlin in March 1846, Ogden and Douglas were joined in the management of the department by John Work.[61] During the late 1840s, Ogden and Douglas

59. Robertson, *Correspondence Book*, p. 236.
60. McLoughlin, *Letters, Second Series*, pp. xxv, xlvi; William Stewart Wallace, *The Dictionary of Canadian Biography*, 2:458.
61. Hussey, *History of Fort Vancouver*, pp. 85–86, 93n.

were confronted with the difficult task of maintaining the operations of the Hudson's Bay Company on foreign soil. Americans south of the Columbia River deeply resented the economic power of the Company which controlled most of the region's markets. Yet, in spite of their antipathy, Americans looked to the Company in time of need.

Such a time came in late 1847. On 7 December a Company courier arrived at Fort Vancouver from Fort Walla Walla with news that the Cayuse Indians to the east of the Cascades had murdered Dr. and Mrs. Whitman and twelve others who were at Waiilatpu ("Place of the Rye Grass") near modern Walla Walla, Washington. The following day Ogden left Fort Vancouver with sixteen men to aid those who had been captured. From the stock of trade goods at Fort Walla Walla, at the junction of the Columbia and Walla Walla rivers, Ogden obtained enough blankets, shirts, guns, ammunition, flints, flour, and tobacco to ransom the fifty-three prisoners. By 8 January 1848 he was back at Fort Vancouver with the ill and frightened survivors, who were taken to new homes at Oregon City the following week. The Company never sought repayment for the $500 worth of goods used as ransom for the survivors.[62]

Ogden was left in charge of Fort Vancouver when Douglas moved the Columbia Department headquarters to Fort Victoria on Vancouver Island in 1849. In December 1851, Ogden went on furlough and traveled to Canada and upon his return in March 1853, he resumed the management of Fort Vancouver, which he retained until his death at Oregon City in 1854.

Ogden, who was known as a writer of considerable ability, may have been the anonymous author of *Traits of American Indian Life and Character* (London, 1853). Although his authorship has not been definitely established, it is known that sometime between 1843 and 1849 Jesse Applegate was allowed to read "as a winter's amusement" a manuscript which Ogden had written on the Indians. Applegate revised the work and Ogden later gave it to Washington Irving for editing; but Irving died before completing it, and the fate of the work is unknown.[63]

62. *Oregon Spectator*, 10 December 1847, 29 January 1848; Hussey, *History of Fort Vancouver*, p. 96.

63. Jesse Applegate, "Views of Oregon History." For further details of Ogden's long and varied career with the Hudson's Bay Company see: Peter Skene Ogden, *Peter Skene Ogden's Snake Country Journals, 1824–25 and 1825–26*, ed. E. E. Rich, esp. pp. xiii–xxv, lxii–lxv, lxxv–lxxix; Peter Skene Ogden, *Peter Skene Ogden's Snake Country Journal, 1826–27*, ed. K. G. Davies, pp. xiii–lxxii; Peter Skene Ogden, *Peter Skene Ogden's Snake Country Journals, 1827–28 and 1828–29*, ed. Glyndwr Williams; Robertson, *Correspondence Book*, p. 238; Wallace, ed., *Documents Relating to the North West Company*, pp. 489–90; T. C. Elliott, "Peter Skene Ogden, Fur Trader," pp. 229–78.

PELLY, GEORGE

George Pelly (1791–1866) was born in Gloucestershire, England. He was a first cousin of John Henry Pelly (created a baronet in 1840), who was governor of the Hudson's Bay Company from 1822 to 1852. Following a tour of duty in the East Indian Civil Service, Pelly was appointed Hudson's Bay Company agent in the Sandwich Islands (23 October 1833) to replace Richard Charlton, whose private fur trading interests on the Northwest Coast were in opposition to those of the Company. Pelly was to sell the salmon and timber sent from the Columbia River and was instructed to provide freight ·for the Company's ships returning to England. His operations were under the supervision of the chief factor of the Columbia Department, John McLoughlin. The mercantile business begun by Pelly for the Company continued for twenty-five years, and there is evidence that in the early years of the establishment, the Company proposed to control the Sandwich Island market.[64]

Pelly ended his career with the Hudson's Bay Company deeply in debt, and it is of interest that after only six years of employment by the Company, the governor and committee found it necessary to issue instructions that Pelly's drafts on England were not to exceed his salary of £300.[65] In 1842 the Company's overseas governor, Sir George Simpson, scrutinized Pelly's business conduct in Honolulu. "With regard to Mr. Pelly's management," he wrote to McLoughlin on 3 March, "it has not been characterized by a business like finish or neatness, and I am aware he has not on all occasions followed his orders implicitly; but I consider it due to that Gentleman to say, that great zeal has been manifested throughout his Agency, and if each transaction he ever entered into for the Company were scanned, I am quite sure it would bear the stamp of integrity, upright and honorable conduct and devotion to the interests of his employers."[66] In spite of Simpson's expression of confidence in Pelly, the northern council, meeting at the Red River Settlement in June 1844, resolved that the Sandwich Islands should be detached from the Columbia Department and that Pelly and his assistant, George T. Allan, were thereafter to be subject only to the instructions of the governor and committee in London.[67]

As a result of their unhappy experience with Charlton, the Company, during Pelly's first years in Hawaii, required him to do business only on their behalf. But, during his trip to the islands in 1842, Sir George Simpson retained Pelly at his old salary of £300 per annum and gave permission for Pelly to do business

64. James Douglas to the Governor and Committee, 14 October 1839, in McLoughlin, *Letters, Second Series*, p. 227.

65. Ibid., p. 227.

66. Ibid., p. 280.

67. McLoughlin, *Letters, Third Series*, p. 91n.

on his private account.[68] On the basis of this arrangement, Pelly was allowed to act as McLoughlin's agent in the islands following the retirement of the latter from the Hudson's Bay Company in January 1846. Pelly sold the wheat and lumber which McLoughlin consigned to him and purchased retail goods for McLoughlin's Oregon City mercantile business. The details of his relationship are not completely known, for the editor has not been able to locate any of Pelly's correspondence. However, from the letters which McLoughlin addressed to Pelly during 1847 and 1848, the reader gets the strong impression that the association was not a formal one, but was based on respect and trust. Two examples will suffice to indicate the nature of their business relations. On 2 July 1847 (see Letter 22) McLoughlin thanked Pelly for honoring the former's draft for $2,000 even though Pelly did not have that amount in McLoughlin's account. And, on 26 April 1848 (see Letter 94), McLoughlin reproved Pelly for omitting a commission charge "which is not the thing as you ought not to give your services Gratuitously to any One, and it is the same thing for me to pay you as I would another, But I prefer you to do it — Because from my knowledge I know you will do what is Right."

Pelly's speculations were not entirely to his profit, however, for on the eve of his departure for England in October 1850, he had to assign all of his real and personal property except his wardrobe and small stores to a trustee, Asher B. Bates, as security for a promissory note for $36,514.38, the amount of his debt to the Hudson's Bay Company. The property was to be sold with reasonable speed, and at the end of ten months, if the note was unpaid, all the remaining property was to be sold at auction and the creditors paid in proportion to the amounts due them. Pelly retired from the Company's service at this time and returned to England.[69]

PETTYGROVE, FRANCIS W.

Francis W. Pettygrove (1812–87) was born in Calais, Maine. For a time he worked as a merchant's clerk in New York, and in 1842 he was employed by A. G. and A. W. Benson of that city to take about $15,000 worth of general merchandise to Oregon. Pettygrove left New York in March 1842 aboard the ship *Victoria* which was loaded with merchandise for Valparaiso and the Sandwich Islands. The *Victoria* arrived in Honolulu on 7 October, and Pettygrove remained in the islands until April 1843, when he boarded the bark *Fama* sailing for the Columbia River. He arrived at Fort Vancouver about May first and spent two weeks there before going on to Oregon City with his family and goods. Pettygrove had come to Oregon strongly prejudiced against the

68. Simpson to McLoughlin, 1 March 1842, in ibid., *Second Series*, p. 269.
69. Ibid., *Third Series*, p. 353; Thrum, "History of the Hudson's Bay Company's Agency in Honolulu," pp. 47–48.

Hudson's Bay Company, but the generosity and kindness of McLoughlin, who would accept no money for Pettygrove's expenses while at Fort Vancouver, so impressed the American that the two became closely associated in spite of their different commercial interests.

Once established in Oregon City, Pettygrove, in partnership with Philip Foster, his brother-in-law, established a trading firm. He began trading in furs, and when McLoughlin sent Francis Ermatinger to notify him that the Hudson's Bay Company had exclusive rights to the fur trade of the Oregon Country, Pettygrove insisted on his right to trade in anything that did not conflict with the claims of the United States. It is a mark of the esteem in which McLoughlin held his American competitor that he offered to buy all of Pettygrove's furs at the same price the latter could expect to receive for them in New York.[70]

Pettygrove's was the third American store at Oregon City, following those established by the Methodist Mission in 1841 and by John H. Couch in 1842. Although McLoughlin may have opened a branch store at the Falls as early as 1841 or 1842, it seems likely that the Hudson's Bay Store at Oregon City was not opened until 1843 or 1844 as a result of the American stores' drawing trade away from Fort Vancouver.[71]

On Pettygrove's arrival in Oregon City, Alvin F. Waller, the representative of the Methodist Mission at the Falls, exerted pressure on the new merchant to purchase lots for his mercantile business from the Methodists. Pettygrove, however, respected McLoughlin's prior claim to the land and "preferred to obtain a piece of ground with permission to build upon it, using it in this way until the time arrived when I could ascertain the legal owner and obtain the right thereto, which I subsequently obtained from John McLoughlin, who was my lasting friend, for as an Englishman he appreciated the fact that I would not accept from an American land which would have swindled him out of his rights."[72] In 1844 Pettygrove built the first granary and warehouse at Champoeg, twenty-five miles south of Oregon City. There he obtained most of the business of the Catholic Mission, amounting to some $1,200 or $1,500 per annum. To prevent him from getting an undue advantage, the Hudson's Bay Company was forced to erect a granary there shortly afterward. Pettygrove continued his operations at Champoeg until his departure from Oregon in 1848.[73]

In 1843 Pettygrove paid fifty dollars to William Overton for the latter's claim to 320 acres on the present site of Portland at the head of navigation on the Willamette River. The following year, Pettygrove and Asa L. Lovejoy,

70. Pettygrove, "Oregon in 1843," pp. 1–3.

71. McLoughlin, *Letters, Third Series*, p. li; Bancroft, *History of Oregon*, 1:422–23; Throckmorton, *Oregon Argonauts*, p. 35.

72. Pettygrove, "Oregon in 1843," pp. 18–19.

73. Ibid., pp. 20–21.

who owned the adjoining site, cleared the land and laid out the town of Portland, which was named by Pettygrove for the city in his home state of Maine after Lovejoy, who favored the name Boston, had lost the toss of a coin. During the summer of 1846, Pettygrove built a home and large store at the new townsite and then moved to Portland, leaving only a branch store in Oregon City. That same summer he seems to have relinquished his formal ties with Benson and Brother of New York, for in July he formed a partnership with Albert E. Wilson under the name F. W. Pettygrove and Company. In November 1846, McLoughlin was able to persuade Pettygrove to take in McLoughlin's son David as a third partner.[74]

In the fall of 1848, Pettygrove closed out his business in Oregon and left for San Francisco the following spring. He was back in Portland in 1850, and that year he served as foreman of the grand jury which heard the trial of the Indians accused of murdering the Whitmans in 1847. Together with Thomas Brown, he continued to work on a road from Portland to the rich Tualatin plains, fourteen miles west, which he and A. L. Lovejoy had begun in 1844. In 1851 Pettygrove left Portland for Puget Sound, where he founded the town of Port Townsend.[75]

POMEROY, WALTER

Walter Pomeroy, a lawyer, was about forty years old when he left his native Massachusetts to join the Oregon-bound party led by Dr. Elijah White and Lansford W. Hastings in 1842. Pomeroy settled in Oregon City, where in March 1843 he bought a lot from John McLoughlin (presumably the one at Green Point which he sold to George Abernethy later in the year). That summer he and Philip Foster contracted with McLoughlin for the construction of a flour mill, and by fall the two men were building a house in Oregon City for Pomeroy.

Sometime during 1843, Pomeroy acquired a land claim at Champoeg, possibly the one on which McLoughlin's stepson Tom McKay had built his mill that was severely damaged in the flood of February 1843. A year later, however, Pomeroy had 180 acres under cultivation on the Tualatin plains and was said to be the largest wheatgrower in the valley. At the same time, Robert Newell occupied Pomeroy's former claim at Champoeg, and there is some justification for believing that the two men had merely exchanged their respective claims.[76]

Pomeroy, never without new projects, soon returned to Oregon City where

74. Ibid., pp. 21–23; *Oregon Spectator*, 23 July, 10 December 1846.

75. Pettygrove, "Oregon in 1843," pp. 9, 24; Corning, ed., *Dictionary of Oregon History*, p. 195.

76. Hussey, *Champoeg*, pp. 106–8; Corning, ed., *Dictionary of Oregon History*, p. 199; letter from "Philo" in the *Oregon Spectator*, 6 January 1848.

he operated a tanning business until May 1846, when his partnership with Absalom F. Hedges and a man named Kirbey was dissolved.[77] On 12 June 1846, Pomeroy and Hedges leased McLoughlin's sawmills at Oregon City for two years at a thousand dollars a year. The Catholic Mission provided the necessary security. Hedges withdrew from the partnership in April 1847; and at the expiration of the lease in June 1848, McLoughlin did not renew the contract with Pomeroy, for he felt that he could do better by running the mills himself.[78]

Little is known of Pomeroy's subsequent career, but on 19 September 1850 he was one of fifty-six signers of the Oregon City petition memorializing Congress against the passage of Samuel R. Thurston's Donation Land Bill, which jeopardized the validity of claims purchased from McLoughlin at the Falls. In 1855 Pomeroy was one of the incorporators of the Pacific Telegraph Company, and he was also a member of the Portland and Tualatin Plains Plank Road Company.[79]

RAE, ELOISA MCLOUGHLIN

Mrs. Eloisa McLoughlin Rae (1817–84) was McLoughlin's younger daughter. She married William Glen Rae, an employee of the Hudson's Bay Company, in 1838, and accompanied him to San Francisco in 1841 when he took charge of the Company's trading interests there. Following his suicide in 1845, Eloisa returned to Fort Vancouver and lived with her parents until her marriage to Daniel Harvey in 1850. Eloisa died in Portland in 1884.[80]

ROBERTS, EDWARD

Edward Roberts (ca. 1787–1874) joined the Hudson's Bay Company as an accountant in 1803, at the age of sixteen. He was McLoughlin's agent in London, and continued to serve in that capacity following McLoughlin's retirement from the Company. He retired from the Hudson's Bay Company in 1870 at the age of eighty-four and died in 1874.[81]

ROSS, CHARLES L.

Charles L. Ross arrived in San Francisco aboard the *Whiton* in 1847, and for a time he seems to have been a member of the merchandising firm of Gelston

77. *Oregon Spectator*, 28 May 1846.
78. Ibid., 29 April 1847. See also Letter 76, to Messrs. Starkey, Janion & Co.
79. *Oregon Spectator*, 26 September 1850; Corning, ed., *Dictionary of Oregon History*, p. 199.
80. Barker, *The McLoughlin Empire*, p. 127; McLoughlin, *Letters, First Series*, p. 355.
81. McLoughlin, *Letters, Second Series*, pp. 401–2. See also Letter 46, to Edward Roberts, and Letter 81, to Sir William Drummond Stewart.

and Company. In 1847 he built the "New York Store" which he occupied until 1849 as a member of the firm of Ross, Benton and Company. In 1866 he was keeping a hotel in Calistoga, California, but he returned to San Francisco and shortly before 1885 went to the Hawaiian Islands.[82]

STARK, BENJAMIN

Benjamin Stark (1822–98) was born in New Orleans. He attended Union School in New London, Connecticut, graduating in 1845, and that same year he embarked for Oregon on the *Toulon* as a supercargo for Benson and Brother of New York. Following the delivery of the *Toulon*'s cargo of general merchandise to Francis W. Pettygrove, Stark remained in Oregon in association with Pettygrove. In 1845 he purchased Asa L. Lovejoy's land claim at Portland; but the call of gold was stronger than that of commerce, and in 1848 he went to California. On his return to Oregon in 1850, Stark was admitted to the bar, and served in the territorial legislature in 1853. In the 1850s, before the formation of the Oregon Steam Navigation Company, he managed the Columbia River Navigation Company which provided triweekly service to the portages at the Cascades. Stark, a strong proslavery advocate, was appointed to serve the unexpired term (October 1861 to December 1862) of U.S. Senator E. D. Baker, who was killed at the Battle of Ball's Bluff.[83]

STEWART, SIR WILLIAM DRUMMOND

Sir William Drummond Stewart (1795–1871), a Scottish nobleman and adventurer, was born on his family's estate at Murthly Castle. During the Napoleonic Wars he fought in Spain and at Waterloo with Wellington's troops, and in 1821 he retired from the army with a captaincy. In 1832 he came to the United States, and the following year he went to the trappers' rendezvous on the Green River. In 1834, armed with a letter of introduction from Edward Ellice, he accompanied Nathaniel Wyeth to Fort Vancouver, where he remained from October until the following February, when he went up the Columbia with Francis Ermatinger and the Company's brigade. In 1835 and 1836 he met Marcus Whitman at the rendezvous, and in the latter year he probably suggested Waiilatpu as the appropriate site for the mission the Whitmans planned to establish. In 1837 he was accompanied to the rendezvous by Alfred Jacob Miller, whom he had commissioned to portray the West for murals at Murthly Castle. At that same rendezvous, Stewart presented a suit of English armor to Jim Bridger.

82. Bancroft, *History of California*, 5:683, 704; William F. Swasey, *The Early Days and Men of California*, p. 274.
83. Corning, ed., *Dictionary of Oregon History*, p. 231; *Oregon Spectator*, 23 July 1846; Throckmorton, *Oregon Argonauts*, pp. 57, 206.

During the years 1839–42, Stewart was in Scotland, for he had inherited the Stewart estates on the death of his older brother in 1838. But the West had captured the imagination of Stewart, and in 1842 he once more returned to the United States, where he completed *Altowan*, a novel based on his western adventures. In 1843 he was once more in the familiar haunts of the beaver country, but the day of the trapper was over, the last rendezvous had been held in 1840. Stewart was accompanied on this, his last, western trip by Matthew C. Field, editor of the New Orleans *Picayune*, Karl A. Geyer, the German botanist, and three other naturalists. After visits to Texas and New Orleans, Stewart returned to Murthly Castle in the summer of 1844, where he lived until his death.[84]

WILSON, ALBERT E.

Albert E. Wilson (ca. 1813–61), a native of Massachusetts, arrived in Oregon in 1842 with John H. Couch aboard the brig *Chenamus*. During Couch's absences with the *Chenamus*, Wilson managed the J. P. Cushing and Company's store at Oregon City. By March 1845, Wilson had left the Cushings and had established himself as a commission merchant about a mile above Fort George. At the same time he became a partner in the nearby lumber milling firm begun by Henry H. Hunt and Tallmadge B. Wood. On 23 July 1843, Wilson and Francis W. Pettygrove formed a partnership for the transaction of a general commission business at Oregon City and Portland under the name of F. W. Pettygrove and Company. Through Wilson's connection with Hunt's mill, Pettygrove and Company secured cargoes of lumber for the Honolulu and San Francisco markets. In March 1847, Wilson sold his interest in the mills to Hunt.[85]

Wilson was also active in the early moves to establish a civil government in Oregon. In March 1843, he copied into its final form the famous Shortess Petition to Congress which complained of the treatment of Americans by McLoughlin and the Hudson's Bay Company and requested the immediate extension of the authority of the United States over Oregon. At the Champoeg meeting of 2 May 1843, Wilson helped to organize the Provisional Government of Oregon and was elected supreme judge with probate powers.[86]

WYETH, NATHANIEL J.

Nathaniel Wyeth (1802–56) was born in Cambridge, Massachusetts. In 1824, the year of his marriage to his cousin, he became the manager of an ice company

84. Porter and Davenport, *Scotsman in Buckskin*; McLoughlin, *Letters, First Series*, p. 126.
85. Sylvester, "Voyages of the *Pallas* and *Chenamus*," p. 263; McLoughlin, *Letters, Third Series*, p. 182; *Oregon Spectator*, 23 July 1846, 29 April 1847.
86. Duniway and Riggs, eds., "Oregon Archives," pp. 228–32, 239.

owned by Frederic Tudor, and with Tudor he established an important ice trade with the West Indies. Wyeth, influenced by the schemes of Hall Jackson Kelley for the colonization of Oregon, left Boston in 1832 to collect furs and cure salmon on the Columbia. Wyeth and eleven men arrived at Fort Vancouver late in October to find that the ship *Sultana*, which was carrying their supplies, had been wrecked in the South Pacific. All but two of his men took their discharge, and Wyeth was forced to abandon his enterprise temporarily. He left Fort Vancouver early in February 1833 with Francis Ermatinger and the Company's brigade. From Fort Colvile, Wyeth wrote to Governor Simpson proposing that the Company furnish him with supplies at an advance of 50 percent on their original cost, and buy all of his furs at the rate of five dollars for "full Beavers." In return, Wyeth would limit his activities to the area south of the Columbia.[87]

In the meantime, during the winter of 1833/34, Wyeth organized the Columbia River Fishing and Trading Company and outfitted the *May Dacre*, which was scheduled to reach the Columbia early in the summer of 1834, to catch and pack salmon. In addition, Wyeth contracted to supply the Rocky Mountain Fur Company at their annual summer rendezvous and set out overland in company with Jason Lee and the first contingent of Methodist missionaries. The fur company failed to honor their contract, and Wyeth determined to establish a trading post of his own. He built Fort Hall, named for the senior partner of the firm which supported his venture, and moved on to the Columbia, arriving at Fort Vancouver on 14 September 1834. The *May Dacre*, delayed for repairs at Valparaiso, arrived the following day, too late for the season's salmon run. McLoughlin and Wyeth concluded a trading agreement on 23 September, and Wyeth spent the winter building Fort William on Wappato (now Sauvie) Island, establishing farms, and trading in the Snake country.

In October, the Company's ship *Eagle* brought dispatches informing McLoughlin that Governor Simpson had rejected Wyeth's proposal of the previous year. McLoughlin felt that Wyeth's enterprise was unsound and would collapse of its own weight, but he feared that should the Company refuse to aid him, Wyeth would establish a connection to bring reasonably priced goods to the Columbia from independent sources, thus competing more strenuously with the Hudson's Bay Company. So long as Wyeth was dependent on the Company, he could be controlled and his activities would not greatly threaten the profits and monopoly of the British. This difference of opinion was to disturb McLoughlin's relations with the governor and committee for some years.

In May 1836 Wyeth made a new proposal for an agreement with the Company. McLoughlin was to furnish supplies at a 75 percent advance, and Wyeth was to be allowed to hire men and horses from the Company. The Company was

87. Wyeth, *Correspondence and Journals*, p. 58.

to purchase Wyeth's furs at the rate of one pound sterling for each merchantable beaver of one pound. In return, Wyeth agreed to give up Fort Hall and to limit his activities to the areas of the Colorado River, Great Salt Lake, and the rivers on the east side of the Rockies.[88] With slight alterations, McLoughlin accepted this proposal; but the Company, remaining adamant against American competition, rejected it and ordered vigorous opposition to Wyeth. However, Wyeth's hopes were evaporating, for by September 1835 he had collected only half a cargo of salmon, his men were ill, and seventeen had been killed by accident or massacre. Disillusioned, Wyeth spent the winter of 1835/36 at Fort Hall and returned to Boston in the fall of 1836.[89] In the fall of 1837, McLoughlin purchased Fort Hall for five hundred dollars, and Wyeth abandoned the whole enterprise.[90]

In 1832 Wyeth had written that "Doct McGlaucland the Gov. of the place [Fort Vancouver] is a man distinguished as much for his kindness and humanity as his good sense and information and to whom I am so much indebted as that he will never be forgotten by me." [91] The two men remained friends to the end of their lives, and as these letters show, McLoughlin attempted to protect Wyeth's claim at Fort William during the 1840s when squatters and the Provisional Government were threatening it. When in 1850 Samuel R. Thurston, Oregon's territorial delegate to Congress, was attempting to defend his role in securing the passage of the Donation Land Bill which dispossessed McLoughlin of his Oregon City claim, he wrote to Wyeth seeking support for his claims that McLoughlin had "rendered his name odious among the people of Oregon, by his endeavors to prevent the settlement of the country, and to cripple its growth." Wyeth replied that McLoughlin had treated him generously, and he praised McLoughlin's honor. On 11 January 1851, Wyeth sent copies of his correspondence with Thurston to McLoughlin with an offer of aid.[92]

WYLLIE, ROBERT CRICHTON

Robert Crichton Wyllie (1798–1865) was born in Ayrshire, Scotland, and educated for the medical profession. He served as a surgeon in Spanish America,

88. McLoughlin, *Letters, First Series*, pp. 340–42.
89. Wyeth, *Correspondence and Journals*, p. 153.
90. McLoughlin, *Letters, First Series*, pp. cxiii, 208, 279.
91. Wyeth, *Correspondence and Journals*, p. 181.
92. "Correspondence of John McLoughlin, Nathaniel J. Wyeth, S. R. Thurston, and R. C. Winthrop," pp. 105–9 (quoting from the *Milwaukee* [Oregon] *Star*, 10 April 1851); *Oregon Spectator*, 3, 17 April 1851. For further details on Wyeth's activities and his association with the Hudson's Bay Company, see McLoughlin, *Letters, First Series*, pp. xcvi, cvii–cix, cxi, cxiii; Sampson, "Nathaniel Jarvis Wyeth," 5:381–401.

and became a merchant in Mazatlán, Mexico, where he lived from 1825 to 1830. He returned to London in 1830, where he worked as a shipping merchant and became one of the original directors of the Pacific Steam Navigation Company. In 1843 he was visiting in Mexico when the newly appointed British consul general for the Sandwich Islands, General William Miller, crossed that country on his way to assume his new post. Wyllie accompanied Miller to Honolulu, expecting to return to England via China. He served as honorary secretary to Miller at the signing of the convention between Great Britain and the Kingdom of Hawaii on 12 February 1844, and later in the year, when Miller sailed from Honolulu (21 July) to visit the islands of the South Pacific, Wyllie was appointed proconsul to represent the British government during Miller's absence. Miller returned to Honolulu on 15 March 1845, and eleven days later Wyllie was appointed Hawaiian minister for foreign relations, a position he held until his death in 1865.[93]

McLoughlin and Wyllie met in London in 1839 and appear to have corresponded subsequently on matters of mutual interest. In 1844 Wyllie requested McLoughlin to supply information relative to the state of economic and political affairs in Oregon and California, so his interest in the Pacific Northwest was not a new one.[94]

93. Alfons L. Korn, *The Victorian Visitors*, pp. 292–94; Kuykendall, *The Hawaiian Kingdom*, p. 249.

94. McLoughlin, *Letters, Third Series*, pp. 68, 257–58.

Bibliography

1. CONTEMPORARY ACCOUNTS

A. MANUSCRIPT SOURCES

Allan, George Traill. "Reminiscences of Fort Vancouver on Columbia River, Oregon, as it stood in 1832 and some account of the Hudson Bay Company's farm there at that period, their mode of trade with the Indians and personal recollections of Doctor John McLoughlin and others, by a then resident of that place." Typescript copy at Fort Vancouver National Historic Site, Vancouver, Wash., from the originals in the possession of the Corporation of the Township of Langley, Murrayville, British Columbia.

Applegate, Jesse. "Views of Oregon History." Yoncalla, Ore., 1878. Oregon Manuscripts, Microfilm #4470. Bancroft Library, University of California, Berkeley.

Athey, James. "Workshops at Oregon City: James Athey's Narrative." Oregon City, Ore., 1878. Oregon Manuscripts, microfilm. Bancroft Library, University of California, Berkeley.

Bacon, John M. "Mercantile Life at Oregon City." Oregon City, Ore., 1878. Oregon Manuscripts, microfilm. Bancroft Library, University of California, Berkeley.

Brown, James H. "Settlement of the Willammette [sic] Valley." Salem, Ore., 1878, microfilm. Bancroft Library, University of California, Berkeley.

Lowe, Thomas. "Private Journal Kept at Fort Vancouver Columbia River, 1843–1850." Typescript. Archives of British Columbia, Victoria, B.C.

McKinlay, Archibald. Miscellaneous papers. Oregon Historical Society, Portland, Ore.

[157]

————. Papers. Archives of British Columbia, Victoria, B.C.

————. Record of Death. Division of Vital Statistics, Province of British Columbia, Victoria, B.C.

Parrish, J. L. "Anecdotes of Intercourse with the Indians." Salem, Ore., 1878. Oregon Manuscripts, microfilm. Bancroft Library, University of California, Berkeley.

Pettygrove, Francis W. "Oregon in 1843." Port Townsend, Wash., 1878. Oregon Manuscripts, Microfilm #4774. Bancroft Library, University of California, Berkeley.

Shaw, William. "Mississippi and Columbia River Valley Pioneer Life Compared." Salem, Ore., 1878. Oregon Manuscripts, microfilm. Bancroft Library, University of California, Berkeley.

Strong, William. "History of Oregon." Portland, Ore., 1878. Oregon Manuscripts, Microfilm #4972. Bancroft Library, University of California, Berkeley.

Wilson, Elizabeth. "Oregon Sketches Gathered in 1878." The Dalles, Ore., 1878. Oregon Manuscripts, microfilm. Bancroft Library, University of California, Berkeley.

B. PUBLISHED PRIMARY SOURCES

[Allan, George Traill.] "Reminiscences of Fort Vancouver . . . as it stood in 1832. . . ." *Transactions of the . . . Oregon Pioneer Association for 1881*, pp. 75–80.

Beaver, Herbert. *Reports and Letters of Herbert Beaver, 1836–1838*. Edited by Thomas E. Jessett. Portland, Ore.: Champoeg Press, 1959.

Clyman, James. *James Clyman, Frontiersman, 1792–1881: The Adventures of a Trapper and Covered-Wagon Emigrant as Told in His Own Reminiscences and Diaries*. Edited by Charles L. Camp. Portland, Ore.: Champoeg Press, 1960.

"Correspondence of John McLoughlin, Nathaniel J. Wyeth, S. R. Thurston, and R. C. Winthrop, Pertaining to Claim of Doctor McLoughlin at the Falls of the Willamette — the Site of Oregon City." *The Quarterly of the Oregon Historical Society* 1, no. 1 (March 1900):105–9.

"Cost of Improvements Made by Dr. John McLoughlin at Willamette Falls to Jan. 1, 1851." *The Quarterly of the Oregon Historical Society* 14, no. 1 (March 1913):68–70.

Douglas, James. "James Douglas and the Russian American Company, 1840." Edited by Willard Ernest Ireland. *The British Columbia Historical Quarterly* 5, no. 1 (January 1941):53–66.

Drury, Clifford Merrill, ed. *First White Women over the Rockies: Diaries, Letters, and Biographical Sketches of the Six Women of the Oregon Mission who made the*

Overland Journey in 1836 and 1838. 2 vols. Glendale, Calif.: Arthur H. Clark Co., 1963.

Duniway, David C., and Riggs, Neil R., eds. "The Oregon Archives, 1841–1843." *Oregon Historical Quarterly* 60, no. 2 (June 1959):211–80.

Dunn, John. *History of the Oregon Territory and British North American Fur Trade; with an Account of the Habits and Customs of the Principal Native Tribes on the Northern Continent.* 2nd ed. London: Edwards and Hughes, 1846.

Evans, Oliver. *The Young Mill-Wright and Miller's Guide.* 4th ed. Philadelphia, Pa.: M. Carey & Son, 1821.

Farnham, Thomas J. *Travels in the Great Western Prairies, the Anahuac and Rocky Mountains, and in the Oregon Territory.* New York, 1843.

Fleming, R. Harvey, ed. *Minutes of Council Northern Department of Rupert Land, 1821–31.* Publications of the Champlain Society, Hudson's Bay Company Series, vol. 3. Toronto: The Champlain Society, 1940.

Franchère, Gabriel. *Narrative of a Voyage to the Northwest Coast of America in the Years 1811, 1812, 1813, and 1814 or the First American Settlement on the Pacific.* Translated and edited by J. V. Huntington. New York: Redfield, 1854.

Frémont, John Charles. *Narratives of Exploration and Adventure.* Edited by Allan Nevins. New York: Longmans, Green & Co., 1956.

Hastings, Lansford W. *A New History of Oregon and California; containing Complete Descriptions of those Countries, together with . . . a Vast Amount of Information Relating to the Soil, Climate, Productions, Rivers, Lakes, and the Various Routs [sic] over the Rocky Mountains.* Cincinnati, Ohio: George Conclin, 1847.

Hawgood, John A., ed. *First and Last Consul: Thomas Oliver Larkin and the Americanization of California.* San Marino, Calif.: The Huntington Library, 1962.

Howison, Neil M. "Report of Lieutenant Neil M. Howison on Oregon, 1846." *The Quarterly of the Oregon Historical Society* 14, no. 1 (March 1913):1–60.

Hudson's Bay Company. *Charters, Statutes, Orders in Council, &c. Relating to the Hudson's Bay Company.* London: Hudson's Bay Company, 1960.

Ireland, Willard E., ed. "James Douglas and the Russian American Company, 1840." *British Columbia Historical Quarterly* 5, no. 1 (January 1941):53–66.

Johnson, Overton, and Winter, William H. *Route across the Rocky Mountains.* Reprinted with preface and notes by Carl L. Cannon from the edition of 1846. Princeton, N.J.: Princeton University Press, 1932.

Knuth, Priscilla, ed. "HMS *Modeste* on the Pacific Coast, 1843–47: Log and Letters." *Oregon Historical Quarterly* 61, no. 4 (December 1960):408–36.

Larkin, Thomas Oliver. *The Larkin Papers: Personal, Business, and Official Correspondence of Thomas Oliver Larkin, Merchant and United States Consul in California.* Edited by George P. Hammond. 10 vols. Berkeley: University of California Press for the Bancroft Library, 1951–64.

Lattie, Alexander. "Alexander Lattie's Fort George Journal, 1846." Edited by Thomas Vaughan and Priscilla Knuth. *Oregon Historical Quarterly* 64, no. 3 (September 1963):197–245.

McLoughlin, John. "Copy of a Document Found among the Private Papers of the Late Dr. John McLoughlin." *Transactions of the . . . Oregon Pioneer Association for 1880*, pp. 46–55.

————. "Documentary: Letter, Doctor John McLoughlin to Sir George Simpson, March 20, 1844." Edited by Katharine B. Judson. *The Quarterly of the Oregon Historical Society* 17, no. 3 (September 1916):215–39.

————. "Dr. John McLoughlin's Last Letter to the Hudson's Bay Company, as Chief Factor in charge at Fort Vancouver, 1845." Edited by Katharine B. Judson. *American Historical Review* 21, no. 1 (October 1915):104–34.

————. *The Financial Papers of Dr. John McLoughlin.* Edited by Burt Brown Barker. Portland, Ore.: Oregon Historical Society, 1949.

————. "Letter of Dr. John McLoughlin to *Oregon Statesman*, June 8, 1852." *The Quarterly of the Oregon Historical Society* 8, no. 3 (September 1907):294–99.

————. *The Letters of John McLoughlin from Fort Vancouver to the Governor and Committee, First Series, 1825–38.* Edited by E. E. Rich. Publications of the Champlain Society, Hudson's Bay Company Series, vol. 4. Toronto: The Champlain Society, 1941.

————. *The Letters of John McLoughlin from Fort Vancouver to the Governor and Committee, Second Series, 1839–44.* Edited by E. E. Rich. Publications of the Champlain Society, Hudson's Bay Company Series, vol. 6. Toronto: The Champlain Society, 1943.

————. *The Letters of John McLoughlin from Fort Vancouver to the Governor and Committee, Third Series, 1844–46.* Edited by E. E. Rich. Publications of the Champlain Society, Hudson's Bay Company Series, vol. 7. Toronto: The Champlain Society, 1944.

————. "A Narrative of Events in Early Oregon Ascribed to Dr. John McLoughlin." *The Quarterly of the Oregon Historical Society* 1, no. 2 (June 1900):193–206.

Newell, Robert. *Robert Newell's Memoranda: Travles in the Territory of Missourie; Travle to the Kayuse War; together with a Report on the Indians South of the Columbia River.* Edited by Dorothy O. Johansen. Portland, Ore.: Champoeg Press, 1959.

Ogden, Peter Skene. *Peter Skene Ogden's Snake Country Journal, 1826–27.* Edited by K. G. Davies. Publications of the Hudson's Bay Record Society, vol. 23. London: The Hudson's Bay Record Society, 1961.

————. *Peter Skene Ogden's Snake Country Journals, 1824–25 and 1825–26.* Edited by E. E. Rich. Hudson's Bay Record Society, vol. 13. London: The Hudson's Bay Record Society, 1950.

————. *Peter Skene Ogden's Snake Country Journals, 1827–28 and 1828–29.* Edited by Glyndwr Williams. Hudson's Bay Record Society, vol. 28. London: The Hudson's Bay Record Society, 1971.

Oliver, Edmund H., ed. *The Canadian North-West: Its Early Development and Legislative Records: Minutes of the Councils of the Red River Colony and the Northern Department of Rupert's Land.* Publications of the Canadian Archives, no. 9. 2 vols. Ottawa: Government Printing Bureau, 1914–15.

Palmer, Joel. *Journal of Travels over the Rocky Mountains, to the Mouth of the Columbia River; Made During the Years 1845 and 1846. . . . .* Early Western Travels, edited by Reuben Gold Thwaites, vol. 30. Cleveland, Ohio: Arthur H. Clark Co., 1906.

Phillips, Paul C., ed. "Family Letters of Two Oregon Fur Traders, 1828–1856." In *Frontier Omnibus*, edited by John W. Hakola. Missoula: Montana State University Press, and Helena: Historical Society of Montana, 1962.

Roberts, George B. "The Round Hand of George B. Roberts: The Cowlitz Farm Journal, 1845–51 and Letters to Mrs. F. F. Victor, 1878–83." Edited by Thomas Vaughan and Priscilla Knuth. *Oregon Historical Quarterly* 63, nos. 2–3 (June–September 1962):101–241.

Robertson, Colin. *Colin Robertson's Correspondence Book, September 1817 to September 1822.* Edited by E. E. Rich. Publications of the Champlain Society, Hudson's Bay Company Series, vol. 2. Toronto: The Champlain Society, 1939.

Schafer, Joseph, ed. "Documents Relative to Warre and Vavasour's Military Reconnoissance in Oregon, 1845–6." *The Quarterly of the Oregon Historical Society* 10, no. 1 (March 1909):1–99.

Scott, Leslie M., ed. "Report of Lieutenant Peel on Oregon, 1845–46." *Oregon Historical Quarterly* 29, no. 1 (March 1928):51–76.

Simpson, George. *Fur Trade and Empire: George Simpson's Journal: Remarks Connected with the Fur Trade in the Course of a Voyage from York Factory to Fort George and Back to York Factory, 1824–1825; together with Accompanying Documents.* Edited by Frederick Merk. Harvard Historical Studies, vol. 31. Cambridge, Mass.: Harvard University Press, 1931.

————. "Letters of Sir George Simpson, 1841–1843." Edited by Joseph Schafer. *American Historical Review* 14, no. 1 (October 1908):70–94.

————. *Narrative of a Journey Round the World during the Years 1841 and 1842.* 2 vols. London: Henry Colburn, 1847.

————. *Part of Dispatch from George Simpson, Esqr., Governor of Ruperts Land, to the Governor & Committee of the Hudson's Bay Company, London, March 1, 1829: Continued and Completed March 24 and June 5, 1839.* Edited by E. E. Rich. Hudson's Bay Record Society, vol. 10. London: The Champlain Society for the Hudson's Bay Record Society, 1947.

Sylvester, Avery. "Voyages of the *Pallas* and the *Chenamus,* 1843–45." *Oregon*

Historical Quarterly 34, nos. 3–4 (September–December 1933):259–72, 359–71.

Thornton, Jessy Quinn. *Oregon and California in 1848.* 2 vols. New York: Harper and Brothers, 1849.

Wallace, W. Stewart, ed. *Documents Relating to the North West Company.* Publications of the Champlain Society, vol. 22. Toronto: The Champlain Society, 1934.

Wilkes, Charles. *Narrative of the United States Exploring Expedition, during the Years 1838, 1839, 1840, 1841, 1842.* 5 vols. New York: G. P. Putnam & Co., 1856.

Wilkes, George. *The History of Oregon, Geographical and Political . . . also an Account of the Characteristics and Present Condition of the Oregon Territory, by a Member of the Recently Organized Oregon Legislature.* New York: Wm. H. Colyer, 1845.

————. *An Account and History of the Oregon Territory; together with a Journal of an Emigrating Party across the Western Prairies of America, and to the Mouth of the Columbia River.* London: William Lott, 1846.

Wood, Tallmadge B. "Letter of Tallmadge B. Wood (April, 1844)." *The Quarterly of the Oregon Historical Society* 3, no. 4 (December 1902):394–98.

————. "Tallmadge B. Wood to Isaac M. Nash, February 19, 1846." *The Quarterly of the Oregon Historical Society* 4, no. 1 (March 1903):80–84.

Wyeth, Nathaniel J. *The Correspondence and Journals of Captain Nathaniel J. Wyeth, 1831–6.* Edited by F. G. Young. Sources of the History of Oregon, vol. 1, parts 3–6. Eugene, Ore.: University Press, 1899.

II. Secondary Sources

"A. L. Lovejoy." *Oregon Native Son and Historical Magazine* 1, no. 1 (May 1899):48.

Allen, Riley H. "Hawaii's Pioneers in Journalism." *Thirty-Seventh Annual Report of the Hawaiian Historical Society for the Year 1928,* pp. 69–103.

Bancroft, Hubert Howe. *History of California.* 7 vols. San Francisco, Calif.: The History Co., 1886–90.

————. *History of Oregon.* 2 vols. San Francisco, Calif.: The History Co., 1886–88.

Barker, Burt Brown. *The McLoughlin Empire and Its Rulers: Doctor John McLoughlin, Doctor David McLoughlin, Marie Louise (Sister St. Henry).* Glendale, Calif.: Arthur H. Clark Co., 1959.

Beidleman, Richard G. "Nathaniel Wyeth's Fort Hall." *Oregon Historical Quarterly* 58, no. 3 (September 1957):197–250.

Bird, Annie Laurie. "Thomas McKay." *Oregon Historical Quarterly* 40, no. 1 (March 1939):1–14.

Blue, George Verne. "A Hudson's Bay Company Contract for Hawaiian Labor." *The Quarterly of the Oregon Historical Society* 25, no. 1 (March 1924):72–75.

Brosnan, Cornelius J. *Jason Lee: Prophet of the New Oregon.* New York: Macmillan, 1932.

Campbell, Marjorie Wilkins. *The North West Company.* New York: St. Martin's Press, 1957.

Carey, Charles H. *A General History of Oregon prior to 1861.* 2 vols. Portland, Ore.: Metropolitan Press, 1936.

————. "Lee, Waller and McLoughlin." *Oregon Historical Quarterly* 33, no. 3 (September 1932):187–213.

Clark, Robert Carlton. "Hawaiians in Early Oregon." *Oregon Historical Quarterly* 35, no. 1 (March 1934):22–31.

————. "How British and American Subjects Unite in a Common Government for Oregon in 1844." *The Quarterly of the Oregon Historical Society* 13, no. 2 (June 1912):140–59.

————. "The Last Step in the Formation of a Provisional Government for Oregon in 1845." *The Quarterly of the Oregon Historical Society* 16, no. 4 (December 1915):313–29.

Colville, Frederick V. "Added Botanical Notes on Carl A. Geyer." *Oregon Historical Quarterly* 42, no. 4 (December 1941):323–24.

Corning, Howard M., ed. *Dictionary of Oregon History.* Portland, Ore.: Binfords and Mort, 1956.

Cowan, Robert Ernest. "The Leidesdorff-Folsom Estate: A Forgotten Chapter in the Romantic History of Early San Francisco." *Quarterly of the California Historical Society* 7, no. 2 (June 1928):105–11.

Crawford, Medorem. "Gov. George Abernethy." *Transactions of the . . . Oregon Pioneer Association for 1886,* pp. 37–40.

Creer, Leland Hargrave. *The Founding of an Empire: The Exploration and Colonization of Utah, 1776–1856.* Salt Lake City, Utah: Bookcraft, 1947.

Davis, William Heath. *Seventy-five Years in California.* Edited by Douglas S. Watson. San Francisco, Calif.: John Howell, 1929.

DeVoto, Bernard. *The Year of Decision: 1846.* Boston: Little, Brown and Co., 1943.

Dictionary of American Biography. 20 vols. New York: Charles Scribner's Sons, 1928–36.

Drury, Clifford M. "Botanist in Oregon in 1843–44 for Kew Gardens, London." *Oregon Historical Quarterly* 41, no. 2 (June 1940):182–88.

Elliott, T. C. "Marguerite Wadin McKay McLoughlin." *Oregon Historical Quarterly* 36, no. 4 (December 1935):338–47.

————. "Peter Skene Ogden, Fur Trader." *The Quarterly of the Oregon Historical Society* 11, no. 3 (September 1910):229–78.

Galbraith, John S. *The Hudson's Bay Company as an Imperial Factor, 1821–1869.* Berkeley and Los Angeles: University of California Press, 1957.

Ghent, William J. *The Road to Oregon: A Chronicle of the Great Emigrant Trail.* London: Longmans, Green and Co., 1929.

Gilbert, James Henry. *Trade and Currency in Early Oregon: A Study in the Commercial and Monetary History of the Pacific Northwest.* Columbia University Studies in History, Economics and Public Law, vol. 26, no. 1. New York: Columbia University Press, 1907.

Grant, Louis S. "Fort Hall under the Hudson's Bay Company, 1837–1856." *Oregon Historical Quarterly* 41, no. 1 (March 1940):34–39.

Harvey, Athelstan George. *Douglas of the Fir: A Biography of David Douglas, Botanist.* Cambridge, Mass.: Harvard University Press, 1947.

Hill, Lawrence F. "The Confederate Exodus to Latin America." *Southwestern Historical Quarterly* 39, nos. 2–4 (October 1935–April 1936):100–134, 161–99, 309–26.

Himes, George H. "Dr. John McLoughlin." *Transactions of the . . . Oregon Pioneer Association for 1886*, pp. 41–58.

————. "History of the Press of Oregon, 1839–1850." *The Quarterly of the Oregon Historical Society* 3, no. 4 (December 1902):327–70.

————. "John H. Couch." *Transactions of the . . . Oregon Pioneer Association for 1886*, pp. 59–65.

Holman, Frederick V. "A Brief History of the Oregon Provisional Government and What Caused Its Formation." *The Quarterly of the Oregon Historical Society* 13, no. 2 (June 1912):89–139.

————. *Dr. John McLoughlin: The Father of Oregon.* Cleveland, Ohio: Arthur H. Clark Co., 1907.

Hussey, John A. *Champoeg: Place of Transition: A Disputed History.* Portland, Ore.: Oregon Historical Society, 1967.

————. *The History of Fort Vancouver and Its Physical Structure.* Tacoma, Wash.: Washington State Historical Society, [1957].

Kemble, John Haskell. "The First Steam Vessel to Navigate San Francisco Bay." *California Historical Society Quarterly* 14, no. 2 (June 1935):143–46.

Korn, Alfons L. *The Victorian Visitors: An Account of the Hawaiian Kingdom, 1861–1866.* Honolulu: University of Hawaii Press, 1958.

Kuykendall, Ralph S. *The Hawaiian Kingdom, 1778–1854: Foundation and Transformation.* Honolulu: University of Hawaii, 1938.

Lamb, W. Kaye. "The Advent of the Beaver." *The British Columbia Historical Quarterly* 2, no. 3 (July 1938):163–84.

MacKay, Douglas. *The Honourable Company: A History of the Hudson's Bay Company.* Indianapolis, Ind.: The Bobbs-Merrill Co., 1936.

Martig, Ralph R. "Hudson's Bay Company Claims, 1846–69." *Oregon Historical Quarterly* 36, no. 1 (March 1935):60–70.

Martin, Chester. *Lord Selkirk's Work in Canada.* Toronto: Oxford University Press, 1916.

Minto, John. "From Youth to Age as an American." *The Quarterly of the Oregon Historical Society* 9, no. 2 (June 1908):127–72.

Montgomery, Richard G. *The White-Headed Eagle: John McLoughlin, Builder of an Empire.* New York: Macmillan, 1935.

Morton, Arthur Silver. *Sir George Simpson, Overseas Governor of the Hudson's Bay Company: A Pen Picture of a Man of Action.* Portland, Ore.: Binfords and Mort for the Oregon Historical Society, 1944.

Odgers, Charlotte H. "Philip Foster, Pioneer Entrepreneur." *Reed College Bulletin* 21, no. 4 (November 1942):29–39.

Ormsby, Margaret A. "Sir James Douglas." In *Dictionary of Canadian Biography,* vol. 10, edited by Marc La Terreur. Toronto: University of Toronto Press, 1972, pp. 238–49.

Overmeyer, Philip H. "Nathaniel Jarvis Wyeth." *Washington Historical Quarterly* 24, no. 1 (January 1933):28–48.

Pike, C. J. "Petitions of Oregon Settlers, 1838–48." *Oregon Historical Quarterly* 34, no. 3 (September 1933):216–35.

Porter, Mae Reed, and Davenport, Odessa. *Scotsman in Buckskin: Sir William Drummond Stewart and the Rocky Mountain Fur Trade.* New York: Hastings House, 1963.

Rich, E. E. *The History of the Hudson's Bay Company, 1670–1870.* Publications of the Hudson's Bay Record Society, vols. 21–22. London: The Hudson's Bay Record Society, 1958–59.

Rockwood, Eleanor Ruth. *Oregon State Documents: A Checklist, 1843 to 1925.* Portland, Ore.: Oregon Historical Society, 1947.

Russell, Carl P. "Wilderness Rendezvous Period of the American Fur Trade." *Oregon Historical Quarterly* 42, no. 1 (March 1941):1–47.

Sage, Walter N. "James Douglas on the Columbia, 1830–1849." *Oregon Historical Quarterly* 17, no. 4 (December 1926):365–80.

———. *Sir James Douglas and British Columbia.* University of Toronto Studies: History and Economics, vol. 6, no. 1. Toronto: University of Toronto Press, 1930.

Sampson, William R. "Nathaniel Jarvis Wyeth." *The Mountain Men and the Fur Trade,* vol. 5. Edited by LeRoy R. Hafen. Glendale, Calif.: Arthur H. Clark Co., 1968, pp. 381–401.

Scott, Leslie M. "Pioneer Gold Money, 1849." *Oregon Historical Quarterly* 33, no. 1 (March 1932):25–31.

Slater, G. Hollis. "New Light on Herbert Beaver." *The British Columbia Historical Quarterly* 6, no. 1 (January 1942):13–29.

Storck, John, and Teague, Walter D. *Flour for Man's Bread.* Minneapolis: University of Minnesota Press, 1952.

Swasey, William F. *The Early Days and Men of California.* Oakland, Calif.: Pacific Press Publishing Co., 1891.

Thornton, Jessy Quinn. "History of the Provisional Government of Oregon." *Transactions of the . . . Oregon Pioneer Association for 1874,* pp. 43–96.

Throckmorton, Arthur L. *Oregon Argonauts: Merchant Adventurers on the Western Frontier.* Portland, Ore.: Oregon Historical Society, 1961.

Thrum, Thomas G. "History of the Hudson's Bay Company's Agency in Honolulu." *Eighteenth Annual Report of the Hawaiian Historical Society for the Year 1910,* pp. 35–49.

Wagner, Henry R., and Camp, Charles L. *The Plains and the Rockies: A Bibliography of Original Narratives of Travel and Adventure, 1800–1865.* 3rd ed. Columbus, Ohio: Long's College Book Co., 1953.

Wallace, William Stewart. *The Dictionary of Canadian Biography.* 2nd ed. 2 vols. Toronto: The Macmillan Co., 1945.

Watt, Joseph. "Recollections of Dr. John McLoughlin." *Transactions of the . . . Oregon Pioneer Association for 1886,* pp. 24–27.

Wilson, Clifford P. "The Beaver Club." *The Beaver,* Outfit 266, no. 4 (March 1936):19–24, 64.

Wright, Carroll D. *Comparative Wages, Prices, and Cost of Living.* Reprint edition from the *Sixteenth Annual Report of the Massachusetts Bureau of Statistics of Labor, for 1885.* Boston: Wright & Potter Printing Co., 1889.

Wright E. W., ed. *Lewis and Dryden's Marine History of the Pacific Northwest.* Portland, Ore., 1895, and New York, 1961.

Yarnes, Thomas D. *A History of Oregon Methodism.* Edited by Harvey E. Tobie. Portland, Ore.: Oregon Methodist Conference Historical Society, 1961.

III. Government Publications

Oregon, Territory of. *Council Journal, Seventh Session.* Salem, 1856.

———. *House Journal, Fifth Session.* Salem, 1854.

———. *Laws of a General and Local Nature passed by the Legislative Committee and Legislative Assembly . . . from the year 1843 down to and inclusive of the session of the Territorial Legislature held in the year 1849 . . .* (1853).

Richardson, James D., ed. *A Compilation of the Messages and Papers of the Presidents, 1789–1897.* 10 vols. Washington, D.C.: U.S. Government Printing Office, 1897.

United States. 21st Congress, 2d Session. Senate. Executive Document no. 39, serial 203.

————. 29th Congress, 1st Session. Senate. Executive Document no. 1, serial 470.

————. 30th Congress, 1st Session. Senate. Miscellaneous Document no. 143, serial 511.

————. *Statutes at Large.* Vol. 9 (December 1845–March 1851). "Donation Land Act," 27 September 1850.

IV. NEWSPAPERS

The Commercial Review of the South and West (De Bow's Review), July 1848.
Niles National Register, 4 October 1845.
Oregon City Enterprise, 12 August 1948.
Oregon Spectator (Oregon City), 5 February 1846–10 April 1851.

Index of Correspondents

General Index

Note: See also Index of Correspondents, p. 169

[170]

Tahiti, 42; and Columbia River salmon, 47–48; and William Glen Rae, 49 and n97; and Oregon City trade of Hudson's Bay Co., 50; and mill reserve, 50 and n99; and Fort Vancouver accounts, 52; and William A. Leidesdorff, 53, 63, 84, 103–4, 136–37; ships wheat and flour on *Janet*, 53; purchases wheat, 54; and wheat exchange with Hudson's Bay Co., 54–55; and lumber exports, 56, 61, 78; recommendation to secretary of war, 64–68, 69–71; and Indian agent for Fort Hall, 64–68, 69; and immigration of 1847, 69; and settlement of Willamette Valley, 70; attitude toward Indians and mixed bloods, 70–71; treatment of immigrants, 74–76, 75–76n127; and George Pelly, 77, 146–47; illness of, 77, 78; and Quebec property, 80–81, 80n129, 82–83; and Francis Ermatinger's property, 88–89; and William Drummond Stewart, 90–91, 92–93; and draft for Dring, 99, 100, 101, 102; and F. W. Pettygrove & Co., 100–1; and draft on Hudson's Bay Co., 101, 102; and Albert Pelly & Co., 106–9; and customs duties, 107 and n156; comments on affairs in Hawaii, 115–17; sends seed to Hawaii, 118; relations with Herbert Beaver, 125–26; and Lansford W. Hastings, 133; and settlement of California, 133; and Absalom F. Hedges, 135, 150; and William Miller, 143; and George Moffatt, 143; and Francis W. Pettygrove, 148–49; and Edward Roberts, 150; and Robert C. Wyllie, 155

McLoughlin, John, Jr. (son), xix, xxxvi, 140, 141

McLoughlin, Joseph (son), xixn15

McLoughlin, Julienne (daughter). *See* Michaud, Julienne McLoughlin

McLoughlin, Margarite (sister). *See* Talbot, Margarite McLoughlin

McLoughlin, Marguerite Wadin McKay (wife), xix, 70n126, 125

McLoughlin, Marie Elizabeth (daughter). *See* Eppes, Marie Elizabeth McLoughlin

Mactavish, Dugald, 136–37

McTavish, McGillivrays & Co., xxii, xxiii, xxiv, xxv

McTavish, Simon, xvii

Manila, xlv, 32, 43

Marcy, William L., 63, 64–68, 69–71

Mariposa, 120–21

Mary Dare, 29n62, 30, 31, 108

Maryland, 126

May Dacre, 153

Menes, François Marie, 30–31n65, 47–48, 47n94, 120. *See also L'Etoile du Matin*

Mervine, Captain, 31

Methodist Mission: and McLoughlin's Oregon City land claim, xxxvii–xxxix, 21 and n45, 22n46, 65n122, 133; closing of, xxxviii, 28n58; George Abernethy's role in, 122; and retail business, 148. *See also* Abernethy, George; Lee, Jason

Michaud, Julienne McLoughlin, 80, 81n129

Michaud, P. C., 80n129, 80–81

Miller, Alfred Jacob, 151

Miller, William: McLoughlin's opinion of, 112–13; and Richard Charlton's Honolulu land claim, 117n12; biography of, 142–43; in Hawaii, 142–43; and John McLoughlin's Oregon City claim, 143; and Robert C. Wyllie, 155

Modeste, H.M.S., 25–26 and n54

Moffatt, George: and McLoughlin's overtures to the Hudson's Bay Co., xxii, xxiii; as McLoughlin's Montreal agent, 9, 10, 25, 82–83, 87; McLoughlin's remittances to, 14; and John McLoughlin, 143; biography of, 143–44

Mormons, 58–59

Morning Star. See L'Etoile du Matin

Mott, Andrew Clark, 98 and n152, 106, 108. *See also Vancouver*

Mount Vernon, 30, 113n7, 120–21. *See also* Given, J. O.

Nesmith, James Willis, 89 and n138

New Caledonia, District of, xxx

Newell, Robert: biography of, 67–68n125; McLoughlin recommends as Fort Hall Indian agent, 67–68; and McLoughlin's Oregon City land claim, 68n125; and

Walter Pomeroy, 149; and Oregon land claim, 149

Norris, Samuel, 5n7, 14. *See also* Shelly & Norris

North West Co.: and John McLoughlin, xvii–xxvii; and Red River Colony, xix–xxi; and Pacific Northwest, xix, xxviii; and union with the Hudson's Bay Co., xxiv–xxvii

Oahu. *See* Hawaii; Pelly, George

Ogden, Peter Skene: and Snake River brigades, xxxi; and management of Columbia Department, xli, 129, 144–45; and Warre and Vavasour reconnaissance, 6n10; concern for McLoughlin's health, 11n20; and Hudson's Bay Co. store in Oregon City, 27–28n57; and Archibald McKinlay, 139, 140; biography of, 144–45; and American settlers in Oregon, 145; as author, 145; and Whitman massacre, 145; mentioned, 15, 16

Oregon: joint occupation by U.S. and Great Britain, xxvii; American settlement of, xxxix–xl, xlix–l, 61; population of, xl, xliv, 60–61, 91, 107; economy of, xlii; shipping from U.S. to, xliii; shortage of manufactured goods in, xliii; grist or flour mills in, xliv; sawmills in, xliv; and construction boom, 16n34; and transcontinental railroad, 23–24n48, 59; transportation in, 31, 135, 138; money shortage in, 34–35n74, 36 and n76; wheat production in, 40, 40–41n86, 41–42; prices in, 43–44n90; Hudson's Bay Co. treatment of settlers in, 75–76n127; customs duties in, 107 and n156; and Kanaka laborers, 111–12n2; and banking facilities, 113 and n6

Oregon, government of. *See* Provisional Government of Oregon

Oregon City: McLoughlin's land claim at, xxxvi–xxxix, xlv–xlviii, 21n45, 21–22, 22n46, 28n58, 50 and n99, 59–60, 65n122, 81, 122, 133, 143; Methodist Mission at, xxxvii, 122; mills

at, xxxvii; survey of, xxxvii, land law concerning, xxxviii; American traders in, xl; Hudson's Bay Co. profits at, xlii; population, xliii; businesses in, xliii–xliv

Oregon Donation Land Law. *See* Donation Land Law

Oregon Exchange Co., 135

Oregon Spectator, 113n8, 123

Oregon Treaty, 17 and n36, 127

Overton, William, 148

Owhyhee, xxxii

Parsons, Captain, 120

Pelly, George: as McLoughlin's Hawaiian agent, xlv, 19, 20, 30–32, 72, 72–73, 74, 146–47; David McLoughlin's accounts with, 9; McLoughlin's instructions to, 32–33, 102–3; McLoughlin's orders from, 77; and commission charges to McLoughlin, 103–5; and Kanaka labor contract, 112n2; and Sir George F. Seymour, 114–15 and n11; biography of, 146–47; and John Henry Pelly, 146; and Hudson's Bay Co., 146–47; mentioned, 63, 78, 79, 96, 100, 103, 104, 109

Pelly, John Henry, 106, 108, 146

Pettygrove, Francis W.: and Oregon City business, xliv, 130; illness of, 54, 56; and Archibald McKinlay, 100; and Columbia trade, 127; and founding of Portland, Ore., 138, 148–49; and David McLoughlin, 141; and A. G. Benson & Co., 147, 149; biography of, 147–49; and Hudson's Bay Co., 147–48; and McLoughlin's Oregon City land claim, 148; and John McLoughlin, 148–49; establishes F. W. Pettygrove & Co., 149; and closing of Oregon business, 149; and Whitman massacre, 149; and founding of Port Townsend, Wash., 149; and road-building, 149; and Benjamin Stark, 151. *See also* F. W. Pettygrove & Co.

Pomeroy, Walter: and Absalom F. Hedges, xlii, 12 and n21, 13 and n25, 30, 135, 150; and cargo for *Janet*, 39, 55, 99,